A REBEL'S STORY

By the same author:

The Conservatives in Wales 1880–1935 (Cardiff, 1996)

Capel Penybont 1856–2006 (Cardigan, 2007)

The Conservative Party (Cardiff, 2008)

Capel Ffynnonbedr Meidrim 1808–2009 (Cardigan, 2009)

Fy Ffordd Fy Hunan (Llanrwst, 2010)

A Rebel's Story

Felix Aubel

First published in 2012

© Felix Aubel

© Gwasg Carreg Gwalch 2012

Published with the financial support
of the Welsh Books Council

ISBN: 978-1-84527-401-6

Cover design: Welsh Books Council

Published by Gwasg Carreg Gwalch,
12 Iard yr Orsaf, Llanrwst, Wales LL26 0EH
tel: 01492 642031
fax: 01492 641502
email: books@carreg-gwalch.com
website: www.carreg-gwalch.com

Dedication

This book is dedicated to Dafydd Pretty MA,
a former teacher of mine, and now retired Head of the History Department
at Rhydfelen Welsh-medium Comprehensive School,
and living in Tonteg.
Without his personal influence on my character development,
his inspirational teaching methods,
and his encouragement to his pupils to always think for themselves,
this book would simply not have been possible.

Preface

In 2008 I was invited by Myrddin ap Dafydd of Gwasg Carreg Gwalch to write my autobiography, because he believed that I had a 'story worth telling'. I welcomed this unexpected opportunity and as a consequence my life has, for the past four years, often rotated around writing 'this book'.

My autobiography is the product of a substantial collection of scrap books containing newspaper cuttings, letters, minutes of meetings, election literature, and miscellaneous anecdotes that I have accumulated over the years. All these have proved to be invaluable, together with my work diaries, when writing an account of my life.

I was also particularly fortunate that my late father kept detailed written information from his life in Slovenia, Germany and Wales. In addition, there was much preserved source material relating to my mother's family in the south Wales valleys and Pembrokeshire.

The Welsh-language version of my memoirs was published in 2010. As a consequence of it obtaining favourable book reviews and being well-received by the public, I was asked by the publishers to provide an English-language edition. This I gladly agreed to do, on condition that I would be able to produce a completely revised and updated account of my life.

This book therefore includes a great deal of hitherto unpublished material that will, I hope, be of interest not only to new readers, but also to those people who may already have read the original Welsh-language edition, but still wish to learn more about me!

Felix Aubel, September 2012

Foreword

In an age of bland, centrist politicians with interchangeable policies and with their allegiances only identifiable by tie-colour, Felix Aubel stands out. But then he always has.

I first came across Felix in the school–yard of Ysgol Rhydfelen in Pontypridd and remember being struck that a little first-former had a sonic boom of a voice that carried to all corners. He couldn't be ignored then – and nobody's succeeded since!

Felix is that rarest of things – a Tory by conviction whose Welsh coal-field credentials are impeccable. The remarkable story of Felix's father goes some way to explaining the character of the son.

The tale of Felix Aubel Snr would be reason enough to buy this book. It's a tale of an extrordinary life lived in extraordinary times and every bit as gripping and ultimately uplifting as any Hollywood war story.

Growing up enthralled by his father's exploits in war-torn Europe as a Yugoslav freedom-fighter, prisoner of war and ultimately a refugee in south Wales, Felix developed a hatred of Communism and Fascism and a love of freedom and of Wales that drove him into politics.

Felix's love and hero-worship of his father shines through his telling of his life story, although, as with his descriptions of his own life, he pulls no punches about his father's faults and makes no attempt to gloss over uncomfortable truths.

Ultimately it's that brutal honesty that makes *A Rebel's Story* such a rewarding read. This is no soon-to-be-forgotten political sound-bite of an autobiography; it's a full-throated fire-and-brimstone sermon of a book crackling with sharp story-telling and strong opinions.

Felix's Westminster ambitions were never realized either during his brief flirtation with the SDP or during his decades in the Conservative Party. It may be that he lacked the necessary guile and willingness to dissemble that are necessary in modern politics.

Always driven by ideas, the day-to day business of retail politics, which is necessary in order to get elected, may have proved beyond Felix, but that does nothing to make his career less interesting or less significant.

Felix's unalloyed Welsh patriotism and love of the Welsh language and culture were rare in the Conservative Party of the 1980s. A man more at home in chapel than in the gin-and-Jag set stood out like a sore thumb in the ranks of Wales's Tory Party.

In many ways, though, he was an early harbinger of the challenges the party would face in a post-devolution Wales, as it tried to make itself relevant in an increasingly distinctively Welsh political culture. In his assessment of how far that process has come and how much work remains to be done Felix combines an insider's knowledge with the detachment of a man who was never really a member of the 'club'.

When the Welsh language version of this book appeared I remarked at the end of an interview on Radio Wales that it was a pity that non-Welsh speakers would be unable to read Felix's remarkable stories and sharp insights.

Fortunately Gwasg Carreg Gwalch have taken the hint and produced a book that will, like its author, amuse, infuriate and impress in equal measure.

Vaughan Roderick
BBC Wales Welsh Affairs Editor

1

My father Felix Aubel (1918–1987) was born in Zuzemberk, Slovenia, in the former Yugoslavia, on 22 December 1918. He was the youngest of six children, five sons and one daughter, born to Maria and Franz Aubel. Giving birth to Felix, her last child was to have far-reaching medical complications for Maria, and she was never the same woman again. Her health steadily declined. Her death from pneumonia on 1 July 1923 was largely a long-term result of Felix Aubel's birth. Franz was now left with a young and growing family to rear. His personal loss was often expressed by blaming his son Felix for the death of his wife.

Felix had to endure a very difficult upbringing on the farm and butchery business in Zuzemberk. Times were very hard economically during the inter-war years. My father also encountered several personal humiliations during his generally unhappy childhood. He once related how he was given cinders and ashes wrapped up as a Christmas present during the late 1920s, while the other children were all given 'simple but useful' presents. His father was a strict disciplinarian, and the sound of laughter was almost never heard in the household. Obedience was the norm and any transgressions were harshly punished by the belt or by being thrown into an ice-cold pool on the farm.

My father was able to find release only by joining the Yugoslav National Army as a seventeen-year-old professional soldier in 1935. As part of his training he was sent to the Military Academy in the Serbian capital, Belgrade. It soon became apparent that Felix Aubel had an extraordinary ability for measuring distances. He was therefore drafted into the artillery and established a reputation for being able to fire shells with great precision.

My grandparents, Franz and Maria Aubel, about 1908

Promotion quickly followed and by the end of 1937 my father had become a staff sergeant. The following year he became a junior officer attaining the rank of lieutenant. At the outbreak of war in April 1941 he was Captain Felix Aubel of the Yugoslav National Army.

On 25 March 1941, Prince Paul of Yugoslavia submitted to pressure from Nazi Germany and Fascist Italy and signed the Tripartite Treaty in Vienna, hoping to keep Yugoslavia out of the war. In so doing, he had alienated popular opinion, which now regarded him as an 'appeaser', and he was overthrown in a coup d'etat. The new Yugoslav Government refused to capitulate to the German demands for Yugoslavia to allow German troops to march through the country in order to attack Greece. Hitler therefore unleashed his vengeance.

At 5.12 am on 6 April 1941, German, Italian and Hungarian forces attacked Yugoslavia. The German Air Force bombed Belgrade, with my father in the middle of the

My father's home town, Zuzemberk, as it looked in 1930

devastation in the Serbian capital city. After eleven days, the hopelessly outnumbered, outmanoeuvred and inferiorly-equipped Yugoslav National Army had been almost totally destroyed by the Axis invaders. It has been estimated that some 400,000 Yugoslavs were killed, a large proportion of these during the Nazi blitzkrieg.

With Yugoslavia under German military occupation, the remaining Yugoslav resistance now divided into two parts. The majority of military personnel who had been part of the pre-war Yugoslav National Army supported the Serbian Nationalist and Royalist General Draza Mihailovic. These Chetnics, or Monarchists, wished to restore the young King Peter as head of state in the event of the Germans being forced to withdraw from the country. There were also the Communist Partisans under the command of Josip Broz Tito, who aimed to establish a communist republic in Yugoslavia after defeating the Chetniks and the Germans. As someone who had given an oath of allegiance to defend the Yugoslav monarchy prior to the war, my father felt

My father in the Yugoslav National Army, about 1940

honour-bound to continue the armed struggle against the German occupiers and Communist insurgents under the Royalist banner of General Mihailovic. However, like many other families at the time, the Aubels were divided.

My grandfather Franz Aubel assisted the Royalist side, as did three of his sons. Nevertheless, Franz's eldest son Franc and one other son declared their allegiance for the Partisans. It has been estimated that in the bitter Yugoslav Civil War, largely between the Royalists and Partisans, over one million people were killed.

Between April 1941 and May 1943 my father was at the forefront of the two-pronged Royalist war-effort, both fighting the German occupation forces and seeking to maintain supremacy over Tito's Partisans. For more than a year my father served as a Royalist officer under the command of Colonel Karabacic. This man was a Russian Cossack who had served with the White Russian forces in their struggle against Lenin's Communist Soviets in the aftermath of the October 1917 Bolshevik Revolution. He was descended from Romany stock and had come to Serbia to help train the Yugoslav National Army. Colonel Karabacich was a fanatical soldier who waged war against the Communist Partisans in the woods of Serbia with a vengeance and fierceness that suggested he had never accepted the triumph of the Soviets over the Russian Royal Family.

Colonel Karabacich's brutality became legendary.

Captured Partisan soldiers were hung upside down with meat-hooks through their ankles after being tied to a tree branch. They were then left hanging there for hours before being slowly sawn in half alive by the Colonel himself. My father recalled that this 'ritualistic ceremony' was re-enacted hundreds of times by Colonel Karabacich to remind him of what the Red Army had done to his own wife and young children during the Russian Civil War. In the Colonel's eyes there was no Geneva Convention to protect the rights of captured POWs.

Colonel Karabacich was killed by a Partisan military unit in the mountainous terrain to the north of Belgrade in May 1942. Had my father been less than 200 yards nearer to the Colonel, he would have encountered the same fate and I would not be here to write his life story.

Having escaped the Communist Partisans by the skin of his teeth, my father fled from Serbia to Croatia. Here he witnessed even more horrendous atrocities. The pro-German Croat Nazis waged a war of terror on the Serbian minority living in Croatia and even crucified captured Partisans and Royalist soldiers. Often their families suffered the same fate as part of the Croat 'Roman Catholic Holy War' against the religiously Orthodox Royalists and Atheist Partisans. Such was the scale and horror of these Croat atrocities that German soldiers were used on several occasions to restrain them from 'excessively violent behaviour'.

While on the run from the Germans near his birthplace in Zuzemberk during the spring of 1943, my father became aware that even one's fellow-countrymen can betray you. He related how, while dressed in rags and hiding in a barn, he was 'befriended' by a local Slovenian farmer and invited for supper. My father was delighted to have been pampered, washed and given new clothes to wear by this 'friendly'

Slovenian household. They then prepared a hearty supper for him, the first proper meal he'd eaten for nearly six months. After all, it was often on a diet of rabbits, squirrels, mice and even rats that he'd survived and avoided being captured while on the run.

Whilst my father was in the middle of his main course, the farmer asked if he'd like to have two more fried eggs. My father replied in the affirmative and the farmer left the dining room to go to the kitchen. As the minutes ticked by my father became increasingly suspicious of the delay in the fried eggs being brought to him. He also heard what seemed to be a rattling sound behind the closed swing doors. At that moment my father jumped out of his chair, charged towards the closed doors and pushed them as far back against the walls as he could. Two men holding large copper frying pans had been standing behind the doors, and now fell unconscious to the floor. My father ran out of the farmhouse and hid in the undergrowth as a German military patrol drove into the drive.

My father was finally captured by the Germans outside Zuzemberk in May 1943. He was then deported to Germany as a POW, arriving in the East German city of Dresden. My father was taken to his designated POW camp just outside Dresden on 2 June 1943. He was to remain there or in the surrounding countryside for the remainder of the Second World War.

Initially, life in the Dresden POW camp was very difficult for my father. He sometimes related to me how he felt guilty for having done some very unpleasant things there in order to stay alive. One of these things was killing a fellow Yugoslav prisoner just for a loaf of bread to eat. Some of the more sadistic concentration camp guards, Ukrainian Nazis in this case, withheld food rations intended for the prisoners that had been allocated to them by the 'firm but fair'

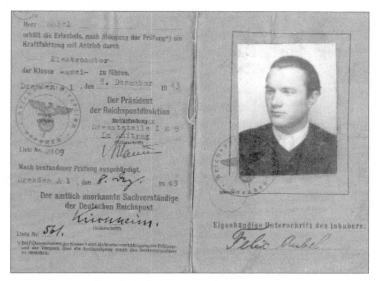

One of my father's documents from December 1943,
when he was a prisoner of war

German commandant. These Ukrainians would sometimes starve two prisoners for several days before taking them into a shed and then force them to fight to the death for a loaf of bread. Although my father had got his food for killing a compatriot, that was not the end of the story. As a result of his 'success', he had to repeat this feat on several occasions until word reached the commandant of these 'side shows' and the Ukrainian guards were severely reprimanded for their activities.

Things, however, improved for Felix Aubel in the POW camp, due to his ability to speak and write several languages. This gift for languages was brought to the attention of the commandant and my father was given several privileges for working as an interpreter. One of these was to have sexual relations with some of the female kitchen staff at the camp! There was no contraception available in these POW camps and therefore the traditional East European method of anal rather than vaginal sexual intercourse was the accepted method of avoiding unwanted pregnancies. My father recalled how this sexual practice was unacceptable to German and Anglo-Saxon women but tolerated by most women from Slavonic countries.

Whilst this brought some welcome relief from the harshness of POW life, my father contracted VD, which was often fatal prior to the advent of antibiotics. He was very fortunate that a young German doctor at the camp injected some unknown fluid into his penis, which cured him of VD. This German doctor was almost certainly using antibiotics over a decade before they were generally available to cure miscellaneous infections. My father may well have been an early 'guinea pig' in the development of these medications. Yet in his case the possible experiment worked, for he was never troubled by this disease again.

A turning point in my father's life life as a POW was being sent to work on the farm of the former World Heavyweight boxing champion Max Schmeling on the outskirts of Dresden. While Schmeling was a proud German he was no Nazi, as can be seen from the fact that he had distanced himself from the white supremacist fanatics in the build-up to his return fight against the the legendary Joe Louis in New York in June 1938. Having been KO'd by Louis inside a round, Max Schmeling was ostracised by Adolph Hitler's Nazi regime and returned to his farm. Max Schmeling recognised in my father a kindred spirit as far as interest in physical activities were concerned, and taught him various boxing techniques. While a POW on Max Schmeling's estate, my father participated in several boxing tournaments and was also allowed to keep some of the prize-money if victorious. Nevertheless, my father had to work very hard during daytime, not only undertaking general farm labouring duties, but also doing work in the nearby stone quarry. My father had the highest respect for Max Schmeling, who reminded him of his own disciplinarian father.

With the war increasingly turning against Germany, my father was taken away from Max Schmeling's custody and returned to the much harsher life in the Dresden POW camp. My father always said that the cruelest guards were not the ordinary German soldiers but their Ukrainian and Latvian assistants. These Slav Nazis were even more fanatical than the Waffen SS, and had frequently to be restrained from indulging in their excesses by their German masters.

My father recalled how he and other POWs sang 'liberation' songs during the controversial Allied bombings of Dresden between 12 and 15 February 1945. In four raids, 1,300 heavy British and American bombers dropped more than 3,900 tons of high-explosive bombs and incendiary devices on the city. The resulting firestorm destroyed 15 square miles of the city centre, and killed around 25,000 people, according to the latest independent investigation commissioned by the city itself. My father always supported the contention of Air Chief Marshal Arthur Harris, head of RAF Bomber Command, that the bombing of Dresden was a key factor in undermining the morale of the German civilian population as well as weakening the Germans militarily, thereby contributing to shortening the duration of the war. According to my father, the POWs did not care if they were killed by the Allied bombs as long as they could see the Nazis wiped out first!

The year 1945 also saw the advance of the Russian Red Army into East Germany, under the command of Marshal Zhukov, with the capture of Dresden being one of the key objectives of the Soviet forces. My father was very fortunate because the German POW Commandant released all of his prisoners before the Russians arrived in Dresden. This gave my father precious time to begin his journey westwards. When the war ended on 8 May 1945, however, my father was still in the eastern part of the country, which was now under the control of Joseph Stalin's Communist forces. Since Stalin had agreed to deport royalist Yugoslav POWs in Germany back to Yugoslavia to face the wrath of Tito's new communist regime, my father had to flee for his life to West Germany, which was under the control of the British and American forces. My father was assisted by several friendly Germans on his way westwards, but was almost dying of starvation when he was picked up by an American patrol. He now weighed less than 8 stone, just over half his normal body weight. My father never forgot the kindness of several black American soldiers who displayed a great willingness to share what little food they had themselves with him. This contrasted sharply with the patronising and even racist attitudes of some white American soldiers towards the liberated East European POWs.

Due to his ability to speak several languages, my father was recruited in late 1945 into the reconstructed German police force. This was intended to establish law and order in West Germany during the immediate post-war era. However, with the gradual reconstruction of the native German police force, those foreign officers like my father were no longer needed and he again found himself without any work. By the end of 1947, my father was one of the hundreds of thousands of displaced persons in Europe, possessing nothing of value and with nowhere safe to go.

By the end of 1947 my father was now given a stark choice: either return to his native Yugoslavia or emigrate to Great Britain or France to take part in the post-war reconstruction of these countries. As far as the first option was concerned, my father had lost everything in his home country. The family butchery business and farm in Zuzemberk had been largely destroyed during the war years. The Aubel family had been torn apart by the bloody civil war between Tito and the Royalists. Three of my father's brothers had been killed in action, and his father Franz was betrayed by his Tito-supporting eldest son, who acquired all of the family's remaining assets. Franz Aubel died on 5 May 1947 from the long-term effects of the severe beating he received at the hands of the Partisans in front of his eldest son Franc. My father realised that as a middle-ranking officer in the Royalist resistance, he faced almost certain death at the hands of Tito's Partisans if he returned to Yugoslavia.

My father was aware that many Royalist Yugoslav returnees had already encountered this fate. He often expressed his disgust at British Prime Minister Clement Attlee's 'betrayal of the Victims of Yalta', something that triggered his aversion to the Labourite collectivist mentality and centralised authority exemplified by state socialism.

2

Having decided like thousands of other displaced people to begin a new life outside the borders of their native country, my father decided to settle in Great Britain. In order to enter the country he had to gain a work permit by agreeing to undertake employment in one of the areas where there was a shortage of employees to carry out post-war reconstruction work. My father arrived at the West Wrattling Ministry of Labour Hostel in Cambridgeshire on 5 March 1948. Having made his decision to become a collier, my father was sent to EVW (European Volunteer Workers) Full Sutton, East Yorkshire, on 19 March 1948, and from there to the NCB (National Coal Board) Language Training Centre in Melbourne, Yorkshire, on 1 April. My father's first encounter with Wales was on 25 May when he was transferred to the Miners' Hostel in Oakdale, Monmouthshire, before arriving at the Pencoed Miners' Hostel, Glamorganshire, on 12 June.

Having learnt some elementary English, he was allocated accommodation in the Miners' Hostel in Hirwaun in the Cynon Valley, on 14 August. This served as a prelude to being employed as a miner at the nearby Aberaman Colliery. Life for my father and his fellow East European compatriots was 'lively' in the Hirwaun Miners' Hostel. There was much tension and even conflict between the various nationalities living under the same roof and doing the same job. The Poles hated the Ukrainians, the Czechs hated the Hungarians, while the Serbians and the Slovenians hated the Croat 'Nazi collaborators'.

There were also tensions in Aberaman Colliery between Welsh miners and the 'foreigners'. The East European workers believed in the 'work until you drop attitude' as long you were well paid for your labours. My father claimed that some East European colliers were earning more money during the late 1940s and early 1950s, due to large productivity bonuses, than miners were getting in the 1960s. He also recalled how many Yugoslavs and Poles in particular sometimes worked back-to-back shifts, thereby working more than sixteen hours a day, until this practice was outlawed in the early 1950s.

The South Wales Miners' Federation, under its communist trade union leaders, campaigned for equal pay for all workers doing the same job. They emphasised that no one should work more than an eight-hour shift and criticised those 'highly paid foreigners' for stealing Welsh jobs and making miners redundant, because the coal reserves would soon be exhausted if the 'outsiders' continued to work as they did. My father may well have echoed the sentiments of many of his East European work colleagues when he stated that 'Unions are Red Commies just like Tito and the Soviets'.

However, my father was also critical of some of the practices of his fellow East Europeans. Whilst he admired their work ethic, he just could not understand how many of them would squander their hard-earned money by consuming large quantities of alcohol and gambling a week's wages on a game of cards. Most of these people had virtually nothing to show for their labours apart from sore heads and near-empty pockets. By contrast, my father bought seven Burton made-to-measure suits from the first six months of his salary at Aberaman Colliery. This was all part of his strategy of personal advancement through hard work in order to gain respect in his new country. My father often used to use the phrase 'When in Rome do what the Romans do' in order to justify his actions. An important component of this integrationist strategy was to learn English as quickly as possible.

Dad with Ina in the Miners' Hostel, Hirwaun, in 1949

He also used to go for a drink at the Lamb Inn, Penderyn, and in order to befriend some of the locals he would often buy them drinks. However, one Friday evening my father overheard a conversation between two men who said they only came to the Lamb Inn on Friday evening because 'Felix the fool' would be there to buy them drinks. My father adopted the tactic of 'still tongue wise head' because he wanted to see if this attitude was typical of other people who came to drink in the Lamb Inn on Friday evenings. The following Friday evening my father went to the Lamb Inn and pretended to have forgotten his wallet. None of the locals offered to buy him a drink. From then onwards, my father would gain the respect of local residents by hard work and never again try to 'buy friends'.

My father used to remark how many East European men ended up marrying Welsh women of below-average intelligence. These women tended to view these hard-working and well-paid miners as good 'meal tickets'. Moreover, there were several instances where the parents of these women encouraged them to 'hook' these men by deliberately getting pregnant in order to 'pressurise' them to get married. One such person was Jigga, a university-educated Czech scientist. He hung himself because Iris the local woman he married could not rise above the level of the brush and dustpan in terms of conversation.

By contrast, my father was determined not to make the same mistake. Prior to his marriage in 1951, he is known to have had two relationships that nearly ended in him tying the knot. The first was with a German-Jewess by the name of Ina. Her father owned a jeweller's shop in Aberdare town. Four decades later, in December 1992 my mother and Ina were in the next beds to each other after having their respective hip operations in Prince Charles Hospital, Merthyr Tydfil. During one of my visits there, she said that I should have been her son and she would have called me Rudolph after her father.

Tom Beynon's shop, 72 Mill Street, Trecynon, about 1932

There were several reasons why Ina did not become Mrs Aubel. My father had become very irritated by some of the anti-Semitic comments he had to endure as a consequence of his courtship. He mentioned that many Hungarians, Ukrainians, Estonians and particularly Latvians were far more anti-Jewish than the Germans. Even my father himself insisted that Ina would have to be baptised a Christian prior to a possible marriage, something that her parents would not accept.

The second lady whom my father nearly married was Dina. She was born in Italy and had come to the Cynon Valley as a teenager with her parents who had bought a cafeteria on the outskirts of

My mother's parents, Tom and Mary Beynon, in Newport, Pembrokeshire, in 1930

Aberdare town. Apparently Dina wanted my father to leave Aberaman Colliery in order to run the business with her, but he was unwilling to exchange the macho world of the pit for serving tea and ice cream. Dina was also a devout Roman Catholic, while my father tended to associate that church with 'Croatian Nazism'.

Although the relationship did not end in marriage, Dina must still have thought a great deal of my father. She used to call me 'my little boy' if there were other customers present when I visited her shop. While on her deathbed she sent a request for my father to come and hold her hand, and for 'my now big boy' also to be present. Not long afterwards, Dina died peacefully. Both Dina and Ina went to the grave as childless spinsters. In the context of both these intelligent and hard-working ladies, it may have been the case of 'what might have been'.

Dad demonstrating his boxing skills, 1950

In October 1948, my father left the Hirwaun Miners' Hostel and moved to lodgings at 141 Brynmair Road, Godreaman, which was much nearer to Aberaman Colliery. For some unexplained reason he moved back to Hirwaun by April 1949 to live as a lodger at 41 Tramway. While resident there he enjoyed walking on Saturday afternoons around Aberdare Park on his way to town. He began calling at Tom Beynon's fruit and confectionary shop in Trecynon in order to buy cigarettes. Occasionally, he was served by Tom's daughter Kathleen, a young Welsh-speaking primary school teacher. He eventually plucked up enough courage to ask her out, thereby beginning a lasting relationship.

Tom Beynon (1880–1953) was born in 11 Bwllfa Road, Cwmdare into a mining family. He was one of sixteen children who all lived into adulthood. Whilst on holiday in Newport, Pembrokeshire Tom Beynon met Mary Thomas (1879–1950) who lived with her parents in Parrog House.

Tom Beynon and Mary Thomas were married at Dinas Church, Pembrokeshire, on 16 August 1906, and the following year Tom left the Bwllfa Colliery to establish a fruiterer and fishmonger business at 72 Mill Street, Trecynon. Mary, a devout church lady, only attended Ebeneser Welsh Congregational Chapel with her husband and children in order to keep

My mother and father on their wedding day, March 1951

the family together. She disapproved of the often prevalent practice of sending the boys to the father's place of worship and the daughters to worship with their mother. This she regarded as socially divisive, particularly in an era when the issue of disestablishing the Anglican Church in Wales was still an emotive topic. This was echoed in the Beynon household, with Tom a pro-disestablishment Lloyd George Liberal, while Mary was a Conservative who preferred to maintain an Established Anglican Church in Wales.

My mother, Miriam Kathleen Beynon, (1918–1996) was born on 13 December 1918, above the family shop. Having attended Park Junior School, Trecynon, she was a pupil at Aberdare Girls Grammar School from 1934–1937. Here Kathleen successfully completed the Central Welsh Board Certificate in Education, which enabled her to enter Swansea Training College. Kathleen resided in Swansea between 1937 and 1939, and in the latter year passed the Final Examination of the University of Wales Board for Training Colleges.

My mother began work as a schoolteacher in the Yardley district of Birmingham on 11 April 1940. As a consequence of the German bombing of the major British cities, she was evacuated with her pupils to the Children's Camp in Rhoose, Barry, on 16 July of that year. By 2 February 1942 my mother was working as a primary school teacher at Lantwit Major, remaining there until the end of 1946.

Unfortunately, there began a steady decline in the health of Kathleen's parents, particularly that of her mother Mary. My mother therefore felt obliged to seek employment nearer to Aberdare, and she was appointed as a primary school teacher in Cwmbach, some five miles from Trecynon. This now meant living at her parent's home, and she greatly missed her more carefree lifestyle in the Vale of Glamorgan. Things improved after she began dating my father during the second half of 1949.

While the relationship between Kathleen and Felix developed, with even talk of marriage, Mary Beynon died on 9 December 1950 aged 71. However, from beyond the grave, grandmother had her wish fulfilled that Felix and Kathleen would have a church wedding in her beloved St Fagan's Church, Trecynon, because the couple were married there on 26 March 1951.

My father now went to live with his wife Kathleen and father-in-law Tom Beynon at 72 Mill Street, Trecynon, on 1 April 1951. It was not until after the marriage that my mother said that she had no intention of having children. This was apparently because she did not want to interrupt her career, having been appointed to a teaching post at Glynhafod Primary School in September 1951. This issue seems to have been put on the 'back burner' for several years but would eventually nearly wreck the marriage.

My father continued to enjoy life as a miner at Aberaman Colliery, and my mother appears to have been satisfied that he kept a pre-marriage undertaking to stop prize-fighting in order to supplement his income. Whilst this promise seems to have been adhered to outside the pit confines, my father could always come home from work badly bruised and claim that he'd had an accident underground while in fact he'd been boxing for money. What changed my father's life permanently was Tom Beynon's death on 15 February 1953, aged 72. My father seems to have been 'pressurised' to leave coal-mining in order to take over the family fruit and confectionary business, since my mother had no intention of leaving teaching in order to run the shop. My uncle, David Beynon, may well have been influential here because he had emphasised to his sister on several occasions that my father's health would be ruined if he stayed working underground for very much longer.

My father left Aberaman Colliery very reluctantly, something which was only partially alleviated by his being granted British Citizenship on 28 July 1953. He was often unhappy confined behind the shop counter, and greatly missed the camaraderie of the male-dominated mining industry. Such was his frustration that my father began to buy condemned houses, to have these renovated and afterwards rented, in order to utilise what he perceived to be his 'wasted talents'.

The real 'crisis point' in the marriage occurred in early 1959. There was an East European male social gathering at the Cambrian Inn in Whitcome Street, Aberdare. During this event a gentleman by the name of Jan told my father that he was proud in having four male children. He then remarked that it was 'odd' that my father was still childless after eight years of marriage. My father 'exploded' and had

Me with my parents, October 1960

to be physically restrained by four men, or there would have been blood on the carpet.

Jan's comments nearly wrecked my father's marriage. He insisted on having a child by his wife Kathleen and if she would not agree, he would divorce her and have a child by another lady. The thought of seeing either Ina or Dina taking my father's child in a pram around Aberdare Park would have been just too painful for my mother to bear, and she therefore relented, in order to save her marriage rather than because she wanted to have children.

My mother's subsequent pregnancy was certainly a difficult time for her, apart from the fact that she was nearly forty-two years old. She insisted on continuing to teach at Glynhafod School until more than seven months pregnant. However, since there were fears there would be complications relating to the birth, my mother was taken to Glossop Hospital in Adamsdown, Cardiff. On 21 September 1960, my mother gave birth to a 6lb 12 oz boy – me. My father was elated, but an imminent falling-out was on the horizon regarding naming the child.

My father was adamant that the Slovenian tradition of giving the eldest son the father's Christian name would be maintained. Moreover, he insisted that Felix should have his second name after his Slovenian grandfather, Franz. He was, however, willing for the spelling to be changed from the original German 'Franz' to 'Franc'. By contrast, my mother wanted to name her son after her own father, Tom, and then use Felix as the second name. My mother eventually agreed to Felix as the Christian name, the more Welsh-sounding Franc as the second name, but was adamant that her son would also be given a 'proper' Welsh third name. She came up with Elfed, after the famous Welsh Congregationalist minister and hymn-writer, the Reverend Dr Elfed Lewis, who had known her father well. In order to avoid any possible confusing of father and son, both parents agreed that he would be addressed as Felix Elfed in public.

Within three weeks of giving birth to her son, my mother resumed her teaching career at Glynhafod School. In 1961 she was appointed as a teacher at Penywaun Junior School. I was brought up by Nancy Edwards, who acted as a combination of nanny and family confidante. Nancy Edwards was born in Trecynon on 30 January 1918. Her father had been a coal miner while her mother had been in domestic service. Having had little formal education, Nancy Edwards worked throughout her life in domestic service, but always seemed to gain influence over people way beyond her social standing. Indeed, my father stated on numerous occasions that if Nancy had been a British spy in Germany, the Second World War would have ended a year earlier.

Nancy had lived a very colourful life. She married Dave Williams, a bricklayer, in order to get the title 'Mrs' before reaching her fortieth birthday. After all, being 'on the shelf' and destined for a life of spinsterhood was the ultimate social stigma for a working-class woman without a profession. This was a loveless marriage, with Dave spending most of his time with his aged mother in Llwydcoed, while Nancy went out drinking. Indeed, she went on a drinking spree at Cwmdare Welfare Club on the night of her husband's funeral.

Although being unable to conceive a child herself, Nancy regarded me as her own flesh and blood. Kathleen is known to have been furious when I called Nancy 'mam' in front of her, my biological mother, on several occasions. She might well have dismissed Nancy from her work had it not been for my father's consistent support for his all-round assistant. Nancy looked after his son, cleaned the house, did the washing and ironing, served in the shop, and helped him clinch several business deals by providing invaluable information regarding the 'personal circumstances' of these property owners.

Whilst Nancy always maintained that my father was wasting his talents behind the shop counter, there is no evidence to suggest that she sought to wreck his marriage to my mother. Anyway, she had more than enough to do to bring order to the lives of several so-called 'uncles' of mine. One was a 'confirmed bachelor' (or closet homosexual) named Willie, whom Nancy promised to look after as she had begun domestic service with his late, wealthy mother. Another was Ted, a hard-working mining official who drank and gambled his money away as well as providing for Nancy. A third was Clem, a burly Territorial Army sergeant major and stone mason who was often embarrassed to be drunk under the table by this lady, who was barely five foot tall and weighed less than seven stone. There was also Pat, an Irish alcoholic, who begged my father on more than one occasion to try and stop Nancy sending him to an early grave.

Other significant early influences on me were two spinster sisters named Bronwen and Sally, who also lived in

Trecynon. These were real eccentrics who used to put sirloin steak and leg of lamb chops into cawl. They had an older bachelor brother named Davy, who used to go upstairs with Raymond, Danny and Sid to have 'Bible-reading lessons'. These men were members of the 'Trecynon daisy chain' of homosexuals. Bronwen and Sally may well have gone to the grave without knowing the true nature of these upstairs activities, especially when one considers that one of the participants was the son of a minister and another a chapel deacon.

Bronwen and Sally encouraged me to have a deep interest in history. They also lavished on me their famous cawl, which turned me into a real carnivore with an almost insatiable appetite for meat to this very day. Living not far from these were another pair of spinster sisters named Elizabeth and Adelaide. These were again real characters who encouraged me to express myself if I thought that something needed to be said. I recall nearly all of these people speaking Welsh, although they all claimed that their Welsh was not good enough to call themselves Welsh-speakers. This attitude was unfortunately typical of many working-class households in the south Wales valleys.

Someone whom I was taught never to go for a walk with up the old tram road was a man named Tommy, who lived in Trecynon. According to my parents, Tommy liked to do 'naughty things to little boys'. With the benefit of hindsight, however, one could only admire how the local community generally protected their children from Tommy without recourse to social services and the police. Tommy would, for example, come to my father's shop to buy sweets for the children whom he hoped to entice to come for a walk with him up the old tram road. As soon as Tommy had left the shop, my father would telephone Tommy's mother to say that her son, who lived with her, had just left armed with bags full of sweets to give to the children out playing in the streets. Tommy's mother would then immediately telephone her neighbours to bring their children indoors before her son could lure them with the sweets. With a couple of notable exceptions, when Tommy had his 'paedophile way' with young children, and was subsequently badly beaten-up by their fathers, this self-policing seemed to work remarkably well.

One of the most disturbing early experiences I had to encounter was the Merthyr Tydfil ironmonger's wife's testimony in 1967. This lady told my mother in front of me that my mother had only had me in order to avoid her husband divorcing her. This 'beyond the need to know' scenario was very disturbing news for a young child and surely a significant influence on my character development.

Ebeneser Welsh Congregational Church, Trecynon, was to have a great influence on me. My grandfather Tom Beynon had been a deacon there for over forty years and I attended chapel with my parents. The minister there was Reverend R. O. Thomas, who emphasised the importance of personal responsibility for one's actions. Alongside him was Margaret Morris, a Sunday School teacher and daughter of one of Aberdare's Labour MPs, David Emlyn Thomas, who taught the importance of practical Christianity. Then there was Evan Griffiths, deacon, eccentric lay preacher and socialist firebrand, who taught me the virtues of speaking my mind. The words he implanted in me as a young boy were later to stand me in good stead:

Dare to be a Daniel
Dare to stand alone
Dare to have a purpose firm
Dare to make it known.

3

I began life in the pulpit at four years of age, when I started reciting hymns and psalms during the children's service on Sunday mornings. This was after practising doing so on the shop counter on the Saturday night. I also began the first tentative steps in the field of preaching, by standing on potato sacks in order to imitate visiting ministers. These activities provided me with invaluable experience to gain confidence in public speaking.

My mother did not believe in sending children to school at a young age, preferring to teach me the '3 Rs' herself at home, before I began my formal education. As my mother had taught at Penywaun Junior School since 1961, it was agreed that I would attend Penywaun Infants School nearly a mile away. This enabled my father to take both his son and his wife to school in the car before opening the shop.

I started at Penywaun Infants School in September 1965. My headmistress Mari Davies stated on several occasions, to my embarrassment, 'Felix has the best general knowledge for his age that I have ever come across'. Another significant influence on me was Jennie Phillips, who was an excellent general subject teacher. Her father Tom had owned a draper shop next door to 72 Mill Street, and had been a close friend of the Beynon family. This did not stop me getting the cane for occasionally misbehaving in class and in the playground. Indeed, my mother had told her fellow teaching colleagues to treat her son exactly the same as every other child. Penywaun Infants School was located in the middle of quite a rough council estate and I had to learn to defend myself, with fighting seen as a toughening-up process.

In 1966 my mother had the dreadful experience of a miscarriage. She had begun to look forward to having a

*Penywaun Infants' School, July 1968
– I am fifth from the left in the back row*

second child, even if Nancy would be largely responsible for its upbringing. While doing dinner duty in Penywaun Junior School during the winter of that year my mother fell very badly on the ice while at least five months pregnant, thereby losing her unborn child. My father was very supportive of her, although he was deeply disappointed at not having the possibility of a second son. He was also informed by the family doctor that as a result of internal injuries caused by this serious fall, my mother would never be able to conceive a child again.

In the spring of 1968 my mother faced a dilemma. That September I would be old enough to enter Penywaun Junior School where she was teaching. She wanted to avoid this because she felt that it would be wrong to teach her own son. My mother was aware of similar situations where a parent had either victimised their child as an example to other pupils in their classroom or occasionally spoilt them, thereby leaving them open to the accusation of being 'teacher's pet'. In order to avoid this, she decided to send me to Ynyslwyd Welsh School, Aberaman, while she was appointed as a teacher at nearby Blaengwawr Primary School. This again enabled my father to take both his wife and son to school at the same time.

I began at Ynyslwyd Welsh School in September 1968 and remained there until July 1972. I was very fortunate because unlike many pupils there I could speak Welsh, since my father always encouraged my mother to speak Welsh with me. He also regularly attended Ebeneser Welsh Congregational Church, and the Reverend R. O. Thomas was thankfully very enlightened for the

As a pupil at Ynyslwyd School, Aberaman, 1971

times in outlining the major themes of his sermon in English.

Several members of staff were to have various influences upon me. There was Elwyn Morgan, the headmaster, who encouraged the pursuit of excellence in all his pupils. To reinforce his authority he used his 'stingy cane' on pupils in front of the whole junior school after assembly. Then there was Gordon Evans, known as the 'yardstick man'. You certainly suffered pain when that heavy wooden yardstick came crashing on your backside; nonetheless we liked this wild-looking man from the Preseli Hills. The greatest positive influence on me at Ynyslwyd School was Gwyneth William. This young lady from Penrhyndeudraeth was to a large extent responsible for nurturing my great interest in Welsh history.

Running parallel to the knowledge I gained from my excellent teachers, I developed many of my interests outside school hours from the mid 1960s to the mid 1970s. My father ensured that I could memorise the Kings and Queens of England chart on the lounge wall that included their names and dates of their reigns. I also developed a great interest in numismatics (coin-collecting). I began collecting various British coins, particularly crowns or five shilling pieces and collect these to this day. The Wongs, a Vietnamese family who had a shop in the Castle Arcade, Cardiff, were invaluable in stimulating my interest in coins. There was also P. A. Wilde in Charles Street, and particularly George Harding in the old Mill Lane Market, who told me, 'Always buy coins in the best condition that you can afford'.

I would often spend all Saturday afternoon behind the counter of George Harding's shop learning everything possible about coin-collecting, particularly grading condition and recognising rare specimens. There was, however, a most amusing incident that remains unforgettable. George Harding had the habit of throwing the left-overs from the bottom of his mug of tea out of the door without turning his back to see if anyone was coming into the shop. One Saturday afternoon a very posh-speaking lady in a lavish mink coat and expensive jewellery was about to enter the shop when she was covered by cold tea and sticky old tea leaves. When she raised her voice at him in a polite but stern manner, George Harding clearly wished he could be swallowed up by the earth beneath him. However, I just could not stop laughing. With his body shaking and lips cringing, George Harding could only blurt out the words, 'I'll pay for your coat to be cleaned' in the faint hope that he would not lose a potentially good customer.

There was also a Jew who worked in the old Jacob's Antiques Centre and who was nicknamed 'Pearls' because he seemed obsessed with these. He was wholly unscrupulous and specialised in tricking people to part with large amounts of money in order to purchase virtually worthless items. His simple but very effective motto was 'Put a poor quality ring in a classy-looking old velvet box and you're made'. He is said to have retired a millionaire.

During the same era, I was encouraged by my father to take an interest in various sports, particularly those associated with feats of strength such as wrestling and boxing. Father and son often went to the old Sophia Gardens in Cardiff to see our wrestling heroes. These included Roy 'Bull' Davies, Jackie Pallo, Bert Royal, Mike Marino, Mick McManus, Steve Logan, Les Kellet, 'Bomber' Pat Roach, Big Daddy, Giant Haystacks, and the one and only Kendo Nagasaki. Whatever its detractors may say about fixes and entertainment rather than sport, these professional wrestlers were very strong men. I saw in Sophia Gardens Giant Haystacks – 6 feet 11 inches and 46 stone – being picked up in the air by the super-strong 16-stone Kendo Nagasaki, and thrown across the ring before subsequently failing to beat the count.

There was nothing better than seeing middle-aged women coming forward to ringside in order to hit some of the 'bad guy' wrestlers with their rolled-up umbrellas and hurling verbal abuse at them. It is little wonder that becoming a professional wrestler was my first career ambition. This idea may not have been as far-fetched as one would think, especially if Orig 'El Bandito' Williams's *Restlo* had been on S4C then.

My father also encouraged me to take an interest in professional boxing, but never urged me to follow his example and do some prize fighting to supplement my income. We often went to the Plaza Cinema in Gabalfa to watch some of the greatest boxing fights during the 1970s. These included the famous 'Thrilla in Manila' and the 'Rumble in the Jungle' fights that were beamed live via satellite to the Plaza Cinema. Moreover, we had the privilege to be there during the 'Last Night of the Plaza' in September 1980. This is when over 1,200 people turned up to see the once 'I am the greatest' Muhammad Ali being beaten into retirement after ten one-sided rounds by his former sparring partner, Larry Holmes.

I left Ynyslwyd Welsh Primary School in July 1972 and in September of that year continued my education at Rhydfelen Welsh Medium Comprehensive School until the summer of 1979. At that time Rhydfelen School was run virtually as a grammar school. There were the grammar streams of 'P, O, R, T' the comprehensive streams of 'F' and 'H' followed by the remedial 'A' stream. The headmaster, Gwilym Humphreys was a stern disciplinarian and committed to establishing his school as the 'model' for Welsh-medium education throughout the country. He was supported by generally highly-motivated teachers who were committed to fulfilling the same noble ideal. I was one of a handful of children from Ynyslwyd School who entered the grammar stream – 'P' form in my case.

The head of the Lower School was Tom Vale who had been an army colonel, and was known to the pupils under him as 'King of the Size 12 Dap'. He was a stern disciplinarian but also a jovial character who was liked for his 'sorry boys but fair cop' attitude to administering punishments. 'Uncle Tom' was firm but fair. Several of the physical education teachers could be described as 'jovial sadists' who had a 'blood and guts' approach to teaching their subject. There was Gerwyn Caffrey and Arwel Owen. Even today I bear the scars on my knees from being taught to rugby tackle fellow-pupils on hard concrete. Nevertheless, I was proud to have played rugby for Rhydfelen School, usually as a tight-head prop forward but sometimes as a hooker. Gerwyn Caffrey told me after a funeral service in Aberaeron on 26 September 2008, 'You were full of enthusiasm, physically strong and courageous, but certainly not the best player as far as co-ordination was concerned'.

Two of my most influential teachers were Dafydd Pretty and Gareth Reynolds. Dafydd Pretty was probably the strictest teacher in the school, yet as the head of the History Department he was almost hero-worshipped by me and regarded as an 'icon of historical knowledge'. He would be the driving force who ensured that I would be satisfied academically only when I had earned my Doctorate in History in 1995. Gareth Reynolds, an ordained Presbyterian minister and head of the Scripture Department, also proved to be an inspiration to me. While maintaining discipline was not his strongest attribute, 'Rabbi' ensured that Scripture would always compete with History as my favourite academic subject.

Although attending Rhydfelen School was very beneficial to me, I was aware of several instances of children where the opposite was the case. Many pupils from the south Wales valleys were convinced that there was a prevalent 'Cardiff-Vale of Glamorgan social elite' at Rhydfelen. Furthermore, there were certainly cases of pupils from these areas who, because of the social standing of their parents, were given lighter punishments than children from the valleys who had committed similar offences. In other words, there were allegations of favouritism at Rhydfelen and accusations that this school was not the best one for every child from the valleys to attend.

I had been brought up in a home where current affairs were frequently discussed. My mother's background had been largely Lloyd George Liberal, since her father Tom had chaired political meetings where the 'Welsh Wizard' had spoken. Indeed, my grandfather had contemplated entering the political arena himself as a Coalition Liberal candidate during the 1918 general election. However, his Conservative wife Mary stopped this because she was pregnant with my mother at the time. With the decline of the once-dominant Liberal Party in the valleys, the Beynon family gradually drifted towards the Conservatism of Winston Churchill and Anthony Eden. My mother was almost invariably a Conservative voter in post-war general elections.

My father had right-wing political opinions, largely the result of his Slovenian background and wartime experiences. He was strongly anti-Communist and regarded Socialism as essentially 'Communism without the loaded gun'. His experiences as a coal miner had also created a dislike for left-wing militant trade unionism. Winston Churchill was his political hero, and he was an ardent royalist. I recall how the Union Flag was proudly displayed alongside the Welsh Dragon in the shop to celebrate the Investiture of Charles as Prince of Wales in Caernarfon Castle on 1 July 1969. In between the flags was a large coloured picture of the Prince alongside his mother Queen Elizabeth. Several other local shopkeepers did the same, and the Investiture was supported by the overwhelming majority of people in Aberdare. After all, it was Harold Wilson's Labour government that was behind it.

I recall that the 'Who governs Britain?' February 1974 general election was much discussed in the household. Both my parents were adamant that Prime Minister Edward Heath should not capitulate to the demands of the 'over-mighty miners' as a point of principle. My father's view was clear, 'Get back to salaries earned through productivity performance and you'll get much higher wages'.

The EEC referendum in June 1975 on whether to remain in the Common Market was a contentious issue amongst the Aubels. My parents resented the fact that Edward Heath had not held a referendum before taking Great Britain into the EEC. However, now that the United Kingdom was a member, it was felt better to vote 'Yes' in the referendum because the opponents of membership had not presented a viable case to withdraw. I delivered hundreds of 'Keep Britain in Europe' leaflets, mistakenly believing, like many other people at the time, that the Common Market was about free trade between member countries rather than a blueprint for a future European super-state.

Another issue keenly discussed in the household was the nepotism amongst some Labour Party councillors in south Wales. Fortunately much of this was exposed by the mid 1970s, with several prominent Labour councillors being imprisoned for corruption. I recall certain 'dubious' practices taking place in Trecynon Hall on polling day during the late 1960s and early 1970s. Upon entering the doors of the hall, voters would be invited by Labour Party stalwarts to sit down and have tea and biscuits before going to cast their vote in the back room. Also, some Labour Party activists used to sometimes accompany elderly voters into the actual polling booth in order to 'help' them make the 'correct' choice on the ballot paper.

There was also the topic of dubious work practices amongst some trade unionists in the Aberdare area. I remember several local bus conductors upon receiving the appropriate bus fare from passengers often saying, 'You don't want a ticket, do you?' With most people replying 'Don't bother', the conductor would place the money in a side compartment in his satchel, thereby pocketing the bus fare for himself!

Certain bus drivers would often place bets with each other in order to see who had transported the fewest passengers during the day. This 'game' entailed hiding empty buses in side streets and then ensuring that several buses arrived at the appropriate bus stop at the same time. The buses furthest away from the passenger bus queue would then just drive past the bus stop. In reality, the brilliant 1970s comedy, *On the Buses*, was sometimes a fair reflection of the 'work-shy' mentality of many public sector transport employees in the south Wales valleys.

Our summer holidays were usually spent on the Parrog in Newport, where my father used to rent a caravan from my mother's cousins on the farm and campsite for the month of August. He would bring the family down on a Sunday morning, stay there until Thursday evening and return to open the shop on the Friday and Saturday before coming back to Newport late that evening. Much of the time in Newport was spent walking on the beautiful headland, swimming, fishing and visiting places of historical interest. I would also help with the evening refuse collection on the campsite and often play cards until the early hours of the morning with friends and acquaintances who came year after year to holiday in the idyllic Newport surroundings.

I had become very friendly with a young English lady called Judy. Her father was one of the scriptwriters for *Dr Who*. Judy and I would often go walking together over the headland in the mornings before returning for breakfast. In August 1975 I had sex with Judy for the first time. Unfortunately we were seen by other campers and when word got back to our parents, they were furious.

A significant event for the Aubel family was moving to live at nearby 1 Park Lane, Trecynon, in July 1976. The prime motivation behind this was to ensure that I would be able to have enough peace to study for my forthcoming O level examinations, as living above the shop could sometimes be very noisy. My father was also motivated by the idea of buying his own home for the first time and therefore not being dependent on living in accommodations provided by other people. Moving to this large house created hostility in some quarters, both at school and in the shop.

I recall being called 'Parklanian pig' and hearing the comment 'Foreigner father buying a big house' on the school bus. Meanwhile, my parents had to endure having the words 'becoming too big for your boots' and 'thinking yourself better than others' thrust in their faces on several occasions. These derogatory remarks illustrate one of the worst aspects of life in a working-class industrial community – that of jealousy if someone is improving their lot, even if they work hard to do so. This resulted in me becoming increasingly opposed to the egalitarian Labourite culture in the valleys of south Wales.

A somewhat hypocritical characteristic of the theoretically egalitarian Labour culture of the south Wales valleys is the 'material snobbery' that is often expressed. I recall on several occasions, while shopping at the Tesco supermarket in Aberdare, hearing men boasting how their trolley was 'fuller' than someone else's. This was meant to imply that they were of a higher financial status because they were able to afford more consumer goods. I regarded this as a very pathetic state of mind. It also indicated that even amongst the mythical working-class concept of 'equality for everyone', some people were regarded as 'more equal than others'.

During August Bank Holiday Sunday in 1976 I had a 'psychic experience'. 'Seeing things' had been a trait in my maternal grandmother Mary Thomas's side of the family for several generations. For example, while a devout churchgoer, Mary's own mother still believed in the 'old ways' and is said to have 'read the tea leaves' for several people in the Newport area. Mary also inherited this 'gift' and she could 'read the chicken dung' as a young girl. Mary also had a psychic experience that is difficult to explain. Whilst on holiday in Newport with her husband Tom, the couple went walking just before midnight on the Parrog quay wall and down the steps towards the old well just above the beach. It is then that Mary saw this mysterious light hovering around the well almost like a rotating candle. Tom, although not an 'old believer' as his wife was, later claimed to have also seen this 'shadowy light'. Mary told her husband that the light was a bad omen, because it was intended to convey to her that her Uncle Dai was about to drown at sea. Three days later the news came that the Merchant Navy ship Dai was travelling had hit an iceberg just off the coast of Newfoundland, Canada, at the outbreak of the Second World War.

Mary Thomas almost certainly saw a 'corpse candle'. There is a tradition that Saint David himself prayed that the people should have some sign to prepare themselves for death, and that there should also be a sign to the living of the reality of another world. In a vision he was told that the Welsh people would have some forewarning of when and where death might be expected. This takes the form of a 'corpse candle'. This belief also included someone else occasionally receiving a sign to signify the imminent death of a person near to them, as occurred in the case of Mary Thomas.

I remember a lady in Newport during the early 1960s known as 'Martha self-raising'. This eccentric elderly lady who lived on the road leading up to Carningli Mountain used to walk down into Newport on a Friday morning to do her shopping. She dressed from head to toe in black and was given her nickname because she used to powder her face with self-raising flour. Martha was not a lady to offend because she was reputedly able to raise the souls of the dead and communicate messages from them to the living. One Friday morning Martha told my mother in front of me in August 1965, 'You will never give birth to a second child'. She could not have been more accurate.

There is another interesting story relating to 'Martha self-raising'. During the late 1940s most of the chickens in Parrog House were dying, and the remainder not laying eggs. Since no explanation could be found, Mary Beynon, who was holidaying there at the time, advised her sister Margaret Johns to send for the then young Martha to assist them. She said that whoever was responsible for placing a 'curse' on the chickens would be the last person to call at Parrog House the following evening. This person was also sticking pins in the body of a dead chicken he had taken away without the knowledge of anyone resident at Parrog House.

The following evening at approximately 10.00 pm, Margaret Johns and her husband Peter were visited by a local butcher by the name of Owen. He enquired whether the family had changed their minds regarding accepting his previously rejected financial offer for selling the chickens at his butcher's shop in Newport. As instructed by Martha, Mary Beynon took his overcoat and invited him to have a cup of tea and something to eat. She then placed a little box in the inside the top left pocket of the coat, with an effigy of the culprit and pins stuck into the heart. When confronted by Mary regarding the curse, he had the 'look of the guilty' on him and after putting on his overcoat left the house. Afterwards, no unexplained deaths occurred amongst the chickens and they began to lay eggs again. In order therefore for the curse to be 'lifted', the culprit had to handle the effigy, albeit via the box, and have it near his heart. Hence the emphasis on placing it in the top left inside pocket of his overcoat.

While this 'gift' was not passed from her mother to Kathleen Beynon, I have inherited some of its characteristics. This first became apparent in late August 1976 when I was sent by my parents to buy the Sunday papers in Collins's Newsagents in Newport. As it was a glorious summer's morning, I walked back via Feidr Brenin and Feidr Ganol.

Whilst about to turn right in order to walk down the hill towards Rock House, I saw what appeared to be a lady walking towards me. When she was within about twenty yards of me, I felt all the hairs on my body rise and was consumed with fear. My feet seem to have become cemented to the ground, making me unable to move my legs. The lady was walking beside me. I recall how her eyes appeared dead with no sparkle in them. Her skin was a deathly pale white colour as if all of the blood had been sucked from her body by a vampire. Although she was of a large frame, it appeared from her green jumper that her breasts had been removed as she looked flat-chested. Her partially open mouth also indicated that she had a plate of top false teeth.

I was certain that this lady was Mrs James whom I remembered as a child when I first came to Newport. Yet she had died from breast cancer seven years previously when I was still at Ynyslwyd Primary School. She then walked past me and when I turned my head around she had disappeared! I then ran for over half a mile towards the caravan as if my life depended on it. Running into the caravan I dropped the *News of the World* newspaper on the bed and it opened in the centre fold. My mother noticed that my sweated handprint had gone through the newspaper, visible evidence of the terrifying experience that I had had minutes before. We later went to Newport Cemetery and saw for ourselves the evidence that Mrs

James had indeed died seven years previously.

Subsequent enquiries have revealed that Mrs James used regularly to walk along the road where she was 'seen' by me just before mid-day, the very time she 'appeared' on that August Bank Holiday Sunday. Also, having had her breasts removed due to the spreading cancer and now on her deathbed, she used to say that she would give anything to go out walking on her usual route. She may have been so emotionally attached to this walk that after she died her spirit still remains there. For some unexplained reason, my earthly psyche and Mrs James's spirit psyche may have 'connected' on the same mystical wavelength, enabling her to temporarily materialise before me.

I have had other psychic experiences since the Mrs James apparition. In the autumn of 1976 I suddenly woke from a deep sleep in a very distressed state during the early hours of the morning. I informed my parents that I was upset because my coin-collecting mentor, George Harding, had just died. My mother subsequently telephoned George Harding's son at around 10.00 am to enquire about his father, who had been gravely ill with cancer, only to be told that George Harding had died just before 5.30 that morning!

During an antiques fair at Margam Park, Port Talbot, in 1997, I opened the small door of a seventeenth–century King Charles II oak cupboard and was almost unable to breathe. Moreover, I felt myself being thrown backwards and was reprimanded by the antiques dealer at the opposite side of the corridor for falling backwards towards him.

Then there was the Bancyfelin incident. While driving towards the Fox and Hounds pub in Bancyfelin, near St Clears, in 1998, I went up a side road in error because of the terrible mist and fog that evening. Here my partner Mary Davies and I felt like we were being choked due to the apparent lack of oxygen in the car. In the pub, neither of us had much appetite to eat food and we settled for a drink to calm us. Students of the paranormal have associated choking experiences with 'bad happenings'. In the Margam Park incident the cupboard may have carried the imprint of a wicked occurrence for posterity. Meanwhile, subsequent enquiries have indicated that many years ago an unsolved murder took place near the exact location of the Bancyfelin incident.

An astonishing occurrence took place at the Atlanta Hotel, Weymouth, where Mary and I were holidaying in August 2002. Whilst sleeping on my front in the double bed with Mary, I felt the blanket and sheet above me being gently moved away. When I later turned over in order to go to the toilet, I noticed that the blanket and sheet had been wrapped around Mary almost like a shroud. When she later woke up Mary was astonished when she realised that it would have been physically impossible for her to have wrapped the blanket and sheet under her body in such a way. When we came down for breakfast two builders who were staying on the top floor of the hotel looked like 'death warmed up'. They said how they had almost been scared to death by events that had occurred in their room an hour previously. The first man said that while he was shaving, he saw the head and shoulders of a person with a big moustache who looked like a policeman in the mirror. Whilst opening the shower door, the second gentleman saw someone also dressed like a policeman walking past him and disappearing through the wall in front of him.

When these events were related to Sheila, the hotel owner after breakfast, she did not appear to be at all surprised. According to her, these 'strange happenings' were quite common occurrences in the hotel. Sheila believed that these figures dressed like policemen were really guards in the former Victorian prison cells that were originally located where the Atlanta Hotel now stood. She said that paranormal activities were for some unexplained reason most prevalent on the top floor of the hotel. Indeed, in one top floor room it proved impossible for the chambermaids to keep things tidy. This was because once they had changed the beds, cleaned the room, and locked the door, the bed clothes would be scattered all over the floor by the time the occupants returned later in the day. Sheila contrasted the 'hostile' entity in this top floor room with the 'very friendly spirit' who liked to keep 'women warm' in the room Mary and I were staying in. This spirit, however, was not known to have much consideration for men if they got cold during the night. It was therefore almost certainly an earthbound spirit of a deceased lady.

4

The year 1977 was an important one for me because I sat my O levels at Rhydfelen School. This year and the one preceding it had been largely happy times for me in school. I made steady academic progress, although I tended to work very hard only in the subjects I enjoyed, such as History, Classical Studies, English Literature and Welsh Literature. However, I was falling-behind in my joint favourite subject, Scripture. Under the direction of Gareth Reynolds, I had always enjoyed studying the subject, but things took a turn for the worse when I was prepared for the O level examination by the now infamous John Owen. This was the same John Owen who in September 2001 was arrested and charged with serious criminal offences against children at Rhydfelen School. On 4 October, he was found dead at his caravan in Porthcawl having failed to turn up at court. He had committed suicide rather than face the numerous children he had sexually abused during his time as a school teacher.

In my opinion, John Owen had a very limited knowledge of Scripture and was largely responsible for an appalling set of examination results. From a class of thirty-two pupils only eight achieved passes at grade 'C' and 'B', with no one getting an 'A' grade. It was only me and two other pupils who achieved a grade 'B' pass and this was in spite of rather than because of John Owen. He was also a bully who would hit children hard with a Welsh Bible for no apparent reason, while screaming at the top of his voice 'God is love!' John Owen also had the habit of thrusting the metal tip of his umbrella between a boy's legs until the boy suffered acute pain.

John Owen was not fit to be a school teacher and should

have been dismissed from the profession several years before his 'departure' in 1991. Unfortunately, he seems to have been protected by some influential people out of a desire to protect the 'good name' of Welsh-medium education, regardless of the general well-being of schoolchildren. Yet John Owen's outrageous behaviour did not detract from my studies since I achieved eight O level passes at grade 'C' and above, which was more than enough to enter the Sixth Form, which I did in September 1977.

Life in the Sixth Form at Rhydfelen School entailed being one of a minority of pupils from the south Wales valleys in the midst of the Cardiff and Vale of Glamorgan social elite. I studied History and Scripture at A level as well as achieving a grade 'B' in Greek and Roman Literature at O level and grade 'A' in English for the Certificate in Extended Education, the latter two subjects undertaken in the Lower Sixth Form.

Although my father corresponded with members of his family in Slovenia, he never returned to visit his native Yugoslavia because he feared that it would not be safe for him to do so. However, in June 1978 an extraordinary event occurred. My father had a visit from his estranged eldest brother Franc, son Franci and daughter-in-law Lenca in his Trecynon shop. While Franc walked through the door of the empty shop, my father was in the middle of cutting a cabbage in half with a large knife. Upon seeing his eldest brother, my father came out of the door beside the counter and floored him placing the sharp blade on Franc's throat. While Franci was pushed away with one hand by my father, Lenca ran next door to fetch the local butcher, who brought in three male customers to try and restrain Felix from killing his estranged brother. Death was averted just in time, as my father is said to have had 'murder in his eyes'. My father

At Rhydfelen School, 1975

conceded later that he just wanted to kill his brother. He felt that he had to avenge the fact that his Tito-supporting brother had prospered during the post-war years at the expense of his own father and other members of the Aubel family. In my father's view, that was nothing short of treachery and the traitor needed to 'pay with his own life'.

When my father eventually calmed down, and Kathleen and I had returned from school, Franc and family accepted an invitation to stay at 1 Park Lane for the weekend. During this time the two brothers spoke for over twelve virtually uninterrupted hours. Although a 'truce' was achieved between Felix and Franc, my father could never forget the treachery of his eldest brother. Indeed, my father remarked on several occasions afterwards that he should have 'slit Franc's throat' before the four Welshmen prevented him from doing so. When my mother said that this would have led to him being imprisoned for murder, he answered, 'It would just have been a matter of family honour'.

There was another example of my father's 'extreme action' in what he perceived as a matter of family honour. I had been courting a girl called Julie in Aberdare Park. She became pregnant and her father approached my father regarding this matter in August of that year. My father is said to have bullied Julie's father to ensure that his daughter had an abortion away from Aberdare, while paying all the medical costs himself. While everything went according to plan, my mother seems to have gone to the grave without knowing anything about this. Nevertheless, I was severely reprimanded by my father. I certainly felt the coldness of metal after receiving several strokes with the belt buckle. Also, I did not receive the metaphorical 'Key to the Door' on my eighteenth birthday that year.

Another issue that diverted my attention somewhat from academic work was the Devolution referendum on 1 March 1979. I became a prominent 'No' campaigner in what was a hotbed of Welsh Nationalism at Rhydfelen School. There were several other pupils who were also vociferous opponents of a Welsh Assembly. The clear majority of these came from Labour backgrounds in the Glamorgan and Gwent valleys, although there were others whose parents had more Conservative or Liberal political allegiances. We all believed that having a Welsh Assembly would be the first step towards the slippery slope of political independence for Wales, thereby dividing the United Kingdom and removing the Queen as head of state.

British solidarity based on shared wartime experiences and support for the monarchy, were also responsible for my parents opposing a Welsh Assembly. Whatever some middle-class Welsh Nationalist academics say, these shared British values were very prevalent throughout industrial south Wales, as was demonstrated by the overwhelming public support for the Queen's Silver Jubilee in 1977. Indeed, these British loyalties were almost as strong in parts of Welsh-speaking Dyfed and Gwynedd as they were in predominantly non Welsh-speaking regions of the country.

The highlight of my participation in the 'No' campaign was listening to Enoch Powell speak in the Temple of Peace, Cardiff, during the final week of the referendum campaign. He spoke on the perils of having a Welsh Assembly. Addressing a packed audience in both English and Welsh, this great orator spoke fervently about his 'passionate love for all things Welsh, both culturally and linguistically'. He also stressed the 'vital importance of maintaining the integrity of the United Kingdom'. Nearly everyone present believed this man of principle was right on the issue of devolution, as with so much else.

Opponents of a Welsh Assembly encountered considerable opposition from some teachers at Rhydfelen School for wearing 'No' stickers. Their objection was on the premise that we were displaying political insignia, which was supposed to be contrary to school rules. This was complete hypocrisy because these same teachers ignored those pupils who were wearing 'Yes' badges. Indeed, one over-zealous Welsh Nationalist teacher gave out pro-Welsh Assembly literature, while several others had 'Yes' stickers displayed on their cars. I was therefore delighted that a Welsh Assembly was rejected by more than 80 per cent of voters, with every region of Wales voting decisively 'No'.

I was also delighted to be informed in August that I had achieved a grade 'A' in History, grade 'A' in Scripture and a Distinction in the Scripture Specialist A level examination paper. I am forever grateful to my excellent History and Scripture teachers, particularly Dafydd Pretty and Elin Phillips in the former subject, and Gareth Reynolds and Gwyn Prichard Jones in the latter, for their first class tuition.

The highlight of my time at Rhydfelen was the school's Prize Night on 1 September 1979, when I was honoured for achieving the highest A level results in the subjects I had studied. However, not everyone was pleased with the prize I had chosen to be presented to me. When the A level results were first announced in August, I was informed that I would need to choose a book to be presented to me by the headmaster Ifan Wyn Williams on Prize Night. Rather than choose a Welsh-language book as other pupils did, I chose A. J. P. Taylor's *How Wars Begin*. The expression on the headmaster's face while presenting the book was a sight to behold, as was the wry smile on Dafydd Pretty's face.

The 'paramount importance' attached to attending Aberystwyth University was emphasised so much to me in school that I rebelled against going there. Moreover, Welsh Language Society activities there had also created a negative view of Aberystwyth University in my mind. My mother was also a significant influence because she opposed the concept of exclusively Welsh-language halls of residence like Neuadd Pantycelyn. In her view, these places 'created an unhealthy delusion that you only needed to mix with your own people'.

This inherited attitude later displayed itself when I was a panellist on behalf of the Welsh Conservative Party on S4C's current affairs programme *Pawb a'i Farn* from Aberystwyth Leisure Centre on 11 March 2010. A questioner asked if the idea of a Welsh language hall of residence was an old-fashioned one for the twenty-first century. I retorted that Welsh-language halls of residence typified that 'insecure parochial introspectiveness' that is unfortunately so characteristic of large elements within the Welsh middle-class professional elite. I also stated that sharing a university hall of residence with people of different nationalities broadened one's horizons. Moreover, exclusively Welsh-language halls of residence were a 'breeding ground' for the promotion of Welsh Nationalism in general and Plaid Cymru in particular.

I decided to do a single honours degree in History at St David's University College Lampeter because of its friendly atmosphere, close personal tuition by the lecturers, and its 'not too Welsh' environment'. Becoming a student at Lampeter was a very important moment in my life. It was the first time that I had been away from home on my own for more than a week. Therefore student life at number 112 Harries Hall of Residence was novel to say the least.

Although intending to do a single honours degree in History, rules dictated that I had to study three subjects during my first year at university. I therefore took Theology plus Greek and Roman Civilization to go alongside History. I was one of the first students at Lampeter to study Welsh History through the medium of the Welsh language.

I achieved first year examination results of over 60 per cent in the three subjects I studied, which enabled me to qualify as an entrant for an undergraduate scholarship. Having sat a three hour general knowledge written examination I was awarded the John Harford Exhibition. In 1981 I won first prize in the University of Wales Inter-College Eisteddfod held at Aberystwyth, for writing a History essay. I repeated this in 1984 when I won first prize in the Inter-College Eisteddfod held at Swansea, for my Politics essay.

Before graduating with an Upper Second Class BA honours degree in History on 16 July 1982, I had encountered some enjoyable experiences of university life. There had been several girlfriends and there were also male friends such as 'Dai Brecon', the son of a farmer and 'King Paul of Tredegar', the son of a vicar whom I often socialised with.

I went to study for a Postgraduate Certificate in Education at Cardiff University in September 1982. I was there to qualify as a secondary school teacher, with History as my main subject and Religious Education as the subsidiary one. Life in a big city could not be more different to Lampeter and its beautiful rural surroundings. There were so many distractions in the metropolis that could have had adverse effects on my academic studies. There were, for example, the numerous cinemas with cheap student rates: you could spend half a day watching films like Gandhi without doing any studying. Then there was the varied night life in the city centre, with so many pubs and clubs to choose from. You could also go and experience the varied night life in Butetown.

One of the real characters of Bute Street was a rather buxom middle-aged lady by the name of Pat. She had a prominent scar on her left cheek, allegedly inflicted by a cut-throat razor. Pat was the only lady from that part of Cardiff whom I heard speaking some Welsh, albeit with a very strong 'Tiger Bay' accent. She also had a very good singing voice and was always dressed in purple and gold. Indeed, adults and students would listen to her intensely when singing her trademark 'You'll never walk alone' song at the old Custom House before she went to 'work the night shift'.

There was also a man named Byron who lived in the Cynon Valley. This loner was certainly not someone to offend. Inside that long overcoat he always wore was an assortment of knives. Byron obtained a great deal of sadistic pleasure from physically intimidating people, almost invariably women in the Cardiff Docks area. Then there was Stephen. This man was a well-known 'curb crawler' who used to lure some of the 'ladies of the night' into his car for sex but was unwilling to pay them for their 'services'. Stephen's downfall occurred when he beat up one of these women, threw her out of his car before running her over. Unfortunately for him, this very seriously injured woman remembered his car number plate and reported Stephen to the police. However, while on bail awaiting trial, Stephen suffered acute multiple stab wounds in the stomach when out drinking in Aberdare town centre. These near fatal injuries were apparently caused by some male friends of the prostitute, who had travelled up from Cardiff to give Stephen his 'just desserts'.

The History lecturer Dr David Allsobrook was a real character. This gentleman – long since deceased – who lived in Whitchurch was an 'alcoholic genius'. One of my most vivid recollections of David Allsobrook was going on a history trip to Saint Brevial's in the Forest of Dean, Gloucestershire. The 'good doctor' drove the minibus to the intended destination. He then left us to do gravestone rubbings in the church cemetery while he went on his pub crawl.

When we had completed our assignments, everyone joined Dr David Allsobrook in one of the pubs. Aferwards, our very 'merry' History lecturer insisted on driving everyone back to Cardiff. Indeed, he had to be physically restrained from crawling to the driving seat in an attempt to drive the minibus. It was left to a female student to drive everyone home, but even she would have failed the breathalyser test had she been stopped by the police. As the minibus was approaching the 'Welcome to Wales' sign on the motorway at over 80 mph, the 'good doctor' tried to open the back door and jump out. He was literally hanging out of the door but eventually we managed to drag him in safely. David Allsobrook had virtually no recollection of the events that occurred and went AWOL the following day.

A significant part of the PGCE course entailed doing teaching practice. I was sent to Rhydfelen Welsh Comprehensive School where I had been a pupil between 1972 and 1979. There had been some important changes at Rhydfelen School. Overall standards had declined because the more academic children now attended the new Welsh schools in Llanhary and Glantaf. Moreover, some of the most capable teachers had also taken flight to these new schools. All things considered, I was glad to have achieved a grade 'B' in my PGCE in History and Religious Education in June 1983.

The 'Winter of Discontent' in 1979 had a profound effect on me. I was appalled seeing television pictures of uncollected rubbish in the streets and bodies unburied in cemeteries. The 'over-mighty' trade unions needed their powers curbed, and the supremacy of democratically-elected governments of whatever political complexion had to be asserted. I therefore gave a cautious welcome to Margaret Thatcher's Conservative victory at the May 1979 general election. After all, trade union militancy had destroyed the basically-decent James Callaghan Labour Government and the Labour Party was now committing political suicide by lurching to the far left under Michael Foot's weak and ineffectual leadership.

The growth of the hard left had been obvious in the student politics at Lampeter between 1979 and 1980. Indeed, the Young Socialists, Young Liberals and Plaid Cymru were all adopting increasingly left-wing policies, particularly in supporting one-sided nuclear disarmament. Although having doubts about the new Conservative Government's employment policies, I agreed to undertake translation work for the Lampeter Branch of the Federation of Conservative Students in 1980. After all, they were the only non-Socialist body on campus. I did not actually join the Conservative Party. I hoped that a moderate anti-Socialist non-Conservative political grouping would emerge to challenge the dominance of the two main parties. I therefore welcomed the establishment of the Social Democratic Party or SDP by the 'Gang of Four' – Roy Jenkins, David Owen, Shirley Williams and Bill Rogers. Furthermore, I joined the SDP as a founder member in June 1981 after hearing David Owen speak at the Park Hotel, Cardiff.

With the benefit of hindsight, I concede that I was too young and inexperienced to stand for parliament at the time I did. Nonetheless, I was encouraged by several prominent Social Democrats to submit my name for consideration as a potential SDP parliamentary candidate. Having been interviewed at the Royal Hotel, Cardiff, by Tom Ellis, the MP for Wrexham who had switched from the Labour Party to the SDP, I was placed on the panel of approved SDP prospective parliamentary candidates on 7 May 1982. As well as helping to establish the Mid Glamorgan Branch of the SDP, I assisted Gwynoro Jones, the former Labour MP for Carmarthen, when he stood as the Social Democrat candidate in the Gower parliamentary by-election on 16 September 1982. Gwynoro Jones was a 'real character' and someone whose considerable political talents have been largely wasted. While Gwynoro Jones put up a robust fight in Gower, he was soundly beaten into second place by Labour's victorious Gareth Wardell.

I was selected as the SDP's parliamentary candidate for my native Cynon Valley constituency from a shortlist of six, at a Mid Glamorgan Area selection contest held at the Café Royal, Pontypridd, on 10 March 1983. With fewer than twenty registered SDP members living in the constituency and without any formal party organisation, it was simply the case of making the most of the very limited resources available. In order to try and test the hitherto uncharted waters in the Cynon Valley constituency, the SDP fielded two candidates in local government elections on 3 May 1983. Jack Amos stood in the Llwydcoed ward and achieved only 85 votes, two ahead of the Conservative candidate but more than 300 votes behind the Labour victor. In the Aberdare West ward, Philip Whale, although polling more than 650 votes, was nevertheless bottom of the poll. The electoral omens looked very bleak for me and I feared that I would obtain fewer votes than the 2,114 or 5 per cent of the poll achieved by Gerry Hill in the October 1974 general election (This was the first time a Liberal candidate had stood in the Aberdare constituency since 1929.).

When the June 1983 general election was called by Margaret Thatcher, the SDP, who had formed an electoral alliance with the Liberal Party was unprepared for the contest. I was given £700 from central party funds to do the best I could under the circumstances. Fighting on a shoestring budget and without any formal party organisation, I had to face the formidable Labour MP Ioan Evans who had gained a 20,263 majority over his Conservative opponent at the 1979 general election. The Plaid Cymru candidate, the highly respected Pauline Jarman, who was later to become an AM and leader of Rhondda Cynon Taf Council, was expected to poll strongly. Then there was the Conservative candidate James Arbuthnot, an Eton-educated barrister who was cutting his political teeth in the Cynon Valley. Since Margaret Thatcher had called an election in order to exploit her victory in the Falklands War, James Arbuthnot was campaigning hard to hold runner-up spot for the Conservative Party.

I was most fortunate to receive very sound advice from Glyn Owen, the very formidable Plaid Cymru candidate in Aberdare during the two 1974 general elections. He told me to concentrate my very limited manpower of less than a dozen active helpers on canvassing people on the streets where there were significant shopping centres in the constituency, primarily in Aberdare and Mountain Ash. Glyn Owen also told me to buy a powerful loud hailer in order to address the shoppers, as well as one to place on the car. These tactics proved to be quite successful and I realised there were many traditional Labour Party supporters who strongly opposed Michael Foot's policy of one-sided nuclear disarmament. I hoped that some of these would vote for me this time around. There were also Conservative voters who were considering voting SDP to try and reduce Labour's majority in the Cynon Valley. Furthermore, particularly in the northern part of the constituency where the Aubel and Beynon families were well-known, it was hoped that there would be some so-called 'personal votes' for me.

With polling day on 9 June approaching, I was increasingly confident that I would achieve the 12.5 per cent of the vote needed in order to save my £150 election deposit. I also thought I had done enough to leapfrog the Conservative candidate, but defeating Plaid Cymru's formidable Pauline Jarman was another proposition. When, however, the election result was announced at the Michael Sobel Sports Centre in Aberdare, I was delighted. The result was as follows:

Ioan Evans (Lab) 20,668 (56%)
Felix Aubel (SDP) 7,594 (20.6%)
James Arbuthnot (Con) 5,240 (14.2%)
Pauline Jarman (PC) 3,421 (9.3%)

Labour majority 13,074 (35.4%)

This was the lowest Labour vote in its Aberdare stronghold since the 1918 general election, and the party's majority had been reduced by more than 7,000 votes.

The Cynon Valley SDP Association was established at the Mount Pleasant Hotel, Trecynon, on 27 September 1983, with me elected as chairman. I was to remain in this position until June 1984. There were, however, soon to be difficulties with some neighbouring Liberal Democrat one-sided nuclear disarmers. My father's wartime experiences had taught me the importance of the concept of 'peace through strength'. This meant standing up to bullies in order to immediately neutralise their threats. As far as I was concerned, it would always be 'no' to appeasing aggressors, in this case the Soviet Union. It is for this reason I could never be a pacifist. The lessons of the Second World War had taught me that Adolph Hitler had devastated every country that was unable to defend itself against his aggression. If Great Britain had not successfully defended itself under Winston Churchill's inspirational wartime leadership, the United Kingdom would have been crushed under the 'Nazi jackboot' just like most other European countries. As Alfred North Whitehead has observed, 'The absolute pacifist is a bad citizen; times come when force must be used to uphold right, justice and ideals'.

I returned to Lampeter in October 1983 to study for the Licence in Theology. I almost certainly went back to university to have a good time. Nevertheless, I was delighted to be awarded the postgraduate Mary Radcliffe Scholarship for the academic years 1983–84 and 1984–85 as a result of me sitting two three-hour written general knowledge examinations.

During these two years at Lampeter it was a question of striking the correct balance between serious academic studies and enjoying life. Some of the pleasanter memories are the Tuesday evening socials at the King's Head, with the landlords Phil and Joyce Patterson trying to maintain some semblance of order. There were also the Friday evening Falcondale 'competitions' where postgraduate students competed in drinking and other mischievous activities with some of the local notables. This included 'competing' against a now retired policeman who was supposed to be on duty these evenings. When he was collected very much worse for wear by a colleague in a police car during the early hours of Saturday morning, it was a signal for everybody to leave the premises. Amongst the most vociferous characters that spring to memory during these evenings are Robert, 'The Philosopher King from Hornchurch'; Mark, 'The

Dynamite Destroyer from Dudley'; and Brian 'Drunkard par excellence from Barnsley'. With these apparent social distractions, I was delighted to have achieved a Merit in my Licence in Theology when I graduated on 5 July 1985.

Whilst studying at Lampeter I received the news that Ioan Evans MP for the Cynon Valley had died suddenly on 12 February 1984. On 10 March I was again selected as the SDP parliamentary candidate at the Victoria Hall, Aberdare, where I defeated eight other applicants on the first ballot. With polling day arranged for 3 May 1984, this was to prove a very difficult election to contest. It was fought in the shadow of the miner's strike of 1984–85. I remain convinced that this strike was illegal and that these brave miners and their families suffered unnecessary hardship due to the incompetent leadership of Arthur Scargill.

Being adopted as the SDP parliamentary by-election candidate for the Cynon Valley, March 1984

Only a fool would have ordered the miners out on strike without the mandate of a national ballot across all of the British coalfields. Only a fool would have started a strike in the month of April when the Government had built up very substantial coal reserves in case of possible industrial action. Only a fool would have tried to turn what was an industrial dispute into a political one in the hope that a democratically elected government would be brought down. Indeed, had Margaret Thatcher paid someone to discredit the cause of the miners she could not have had someone better than Arthur Scargill to do her bidding for her.

The Labour Party selected Ann Clwyd, the MEP for Mid and West Wales, although there was some local discontent that Ioan Evans's son or Ivor Richard, a European Commissioner, had not been the party's nominee. Plaid Cymru were also divided. The majority of the local party wished to select Phil Richards, a barrister and parliamentary candidate for Cynon Valley at the 1979 general election. Meanwhile, Plaid Cymru's National Headquarters insisted that Clayton Jones, the well-known Pontypridd bus proprietor, should stand. James Arbuthnot was re-selected by an overwhelming majority of Conservative Party members over local boy Russell Walters. There were three other candidates, Mary Winter, who had stood as a Communist candidate in 1979, Noel Rencontre, Independent, and Paul Nicholls-Jones, Independent, who had shortly before toyed with the idea of standing for the SDP.

Many political pundits believed that Plaid Cymru would provide the main challenge to Labour, thinking that the SDP vote had been just a 'flash in the pan'. How wrong these so-called experts were to be! My whole political strategy was to present myself as the most aggressive opponent to Neil Kinnock's Labour Party and the defender of democracy against Arthur Scargill and his militant revolutionaries. In so doing, I succeeded in undermining the Conservative candidate. I also portrayed Plaid's Clayton Jones as a left-wing fellow-traveller because of his unequivocal support for the strike.

However much some left-wing academics seek to romanticise the miners' strike, and claim that the mining communities were solidly behind it, I believe this was not the case. There was much underlying local opposition to the fact that no national miners' ballot had been called and a significant number of local miners had only come out on strike due to the fear of intimidation or actual bullying by left-wing militants. As a point of fact the South Wales Coalfield had earlier voted against coming out on strike in a local ballot. Their democratic decision was to be completely ignored by Arthur Scargill and his 'militant henchmen'. I was therefore able to gain the private support of some of these people who had opposed going on strike. However, my campaign was boycotted by the leadership of the 'soggy centrist' Liberal Party who opposed my strong stance against the miner's strike, my 'peace through strength' defence policy, and support for the return of the death penalty for premeditated murder in the event of the evidence being unequivocal. (Incidentally I changed my opinion on the latter issue during the mid-1990s, primarily as a result of several 'miscarriages of justice' where convicted murderers were subsequently released from custody on account of them being falsely imprisoned due to 'flawed' evidence presented against them during their trials. Had the death penalty been in existence, these 'injustices' could simply not have been rectified.) David Owen, Shirley Williams and Bill Rogers came down on several occasions to speak on my behalf. When questioned about my strong stance against the miner's strike, David Owen made a most complimentary remark when he replied, 'At least Felix has got balls!'

When the election result was announced at the Michael Sobel Sports Centre, my uncompromising stance in opposing the illegal miners strike was largely vindicated. On a considerably reduced turnout the figures were as follows:

Ann Clwyd (Lab) 19,389 (58.8%)
Felix Aubel (SDP) 6,554 (20%)
Clayton Jones (PC) 3,619 (11%)
James Arbuthnot (Con) 2,441 (7.4%)
Mary Winter (Com) 642 (1.9%)
Noel Rencontre (Ind) 215 (0.7%)
Paul Nicholls-Jones (Ind) 122 (0.4%)

Labour majority, 12,835 (38.8%)

Apart from Ann and me, all the candidates lost their election deposits. The SDP vote had held up very well considering the election had been fought during the most unfavourable political circumstances: that is, in a Labour Party stronghold at the start of a miners' strike.

The hostility often bordering on physical abuse that James Arbuthnot and myself had to endure during the election campaign from left-wing militants had created a bond between us. We were both equally fervent in our opposition to the illegal miners strike. We were both equally determined to defend the rule of law against trade union militancy. We were both equally uncompromising in the belief that a democratically elected government had to defend its authority against Arthur Scargill's revolutionary attempts to destroy it. This hostility against us both became even more prevalent during the election count, resulting in our respective supporters having to close ranks for their own safety. James Arbuthnot then told me that I was 'saying the right things but was in the wrong party'.

With the hard left howling down at us from the public gallery, I began to question whether a moderate centre party like the SDP was strong enough to withstand these people. However, with the election over I had nothing more on my mind than returning to Lampeter to sit my first year Licence in Theology examinations in June. On 14 May I received a letter from James Arbuthnot that again urged me to reconsider my party loyalty. This I ignored at the time, but things came to a head in late May when I was 'told' by some SDP members, who wished to merge with the Liberals, to tone down my hostile attitude to the miners' strike and particularly my robust views on defence. This was the final straw and on 4 June I wrote back to James Arbuthnot saying that I would accept his invitation to join the Conservative Party. The formal change of political allegiance took place on 11 June, with me writing a letter to my Cynon Valley SDP secretary Jack Amos informing him of my decision.

I then assisted the Conservative parliamentary candidate Patrick Rock in the Portsmouth South by-election, just prior to polling day on 14 June. Perhaps somewhat ironically the seat was captured by the SDP's Mick Hancock, with a majority of 1,341 votes. Such are the ups and downs of political life. On 15 June I was formally welcomed into the Conservative Party by Prime Minister Margaret Thatcher during the Welsh Conservative Conference held at Porthcawl. I was present as a delegate at the Conservative Party Conference held at Brighton in October 1984. Here I received a very favourable response amongst conference delegates and the press for my speech supporting a robust 'peace through strength' defence policy. The following morning, I heard the Brighton bomb explosion from the nearby hotel where I was staying. Moreover, I had left the Grand Hotel, where the bomb was detonated, less than two hours before the explosion.

Having successfully completed my final year Licence in Theology examinations, I went to assist the Conservative Party candidate Chris Butler in the Brecon and Radnor parliamentary by-election on several occasions. The evening before polling day on 4 July Chris Butler, who was subsequently heavily defeated by the Liberal Democrat candidate Richard Livsey, urged me to consider standing for parliament one day as a Conservative.

With David Thomas and Paul West at the Licence in Theology graduation ceremony, July 1985

I was fortunate to win a University of Wales postgraduate studentship to do a Master's degree in Theology on 21 August 1985. I was also later given the postgraduate Mary Radcliffe scholarship again for the academic years 1985–86 and 1986–87, awarded for the standard of my academic research. These financial rewards therefore enabled me to study from October 1985 to June 1987 for the two-part University of Wales higher degree of Master of Theology based on a History of the Church in Europe during the eighteenth century. Having successfully completed the first part of the academic assignment, I then proceeded to write a 20,000-word dissertation on *The Revivalist Movement in South Wales from Griffith Jones to the Schism of 1750,* under the supervision of Dr Geraint Jenkins, my former first year Welsh History lecturer. On 9 June 1987 I received the news that I had been successful in gaining the degree of Master of Theology, and I formally graduated during a degree ceremony held at Lampeter on 9 July 1987.

5

I began to appear as a Conservative Party spokesman on S4C's *Y Byd Yn Ei Le* current affairs programme in the autumn of 1985. This was the most entertaining and robust politics programme ever to be broadcast on S4C. It was recorded at HTV's Culverhouse Cross Studios, Cardiff, and presented by Vaughan Hughes, who was brilliant. In order to further heighten the already heated political atmosphere during the mid 1980s, the great Welsh jazzman Wyn Lodwick and his band would perform several musical pieces, often with a satirical theme.

In order to ensure that the invited politicians were in the mood for the politically-incorrect gladiatorial cut and thrust nature of the combat, large amounts of alcohol were placed before them to drink in the lounge before the TV programme begun. I remember a former Labour MP having to be asked the same question three times over because he was drunk. Also, for the same reason a former Liberal and then Conservative parliamentary candidate (now deceased) commented on the NHS when he was asked a question relating to unemployment. Moreover, a Liberal MP (also now deceased) had to be 'revived' in order to participate in the programme, because he had been drinking solidly from 5.30 pm to 8.00 pm. In my opinion, the real 'stars' of these programmes were Gwynoro Jones, Emlyn Thomas, Geraint Howells, and the North Wales Conservative Party agent, Elwyn Jones.

It was Elwyn Jones who was chiefly responsible for encouraging me to submit my name for consideration as a Conservative parliamentary candidate. He urged me to apply for the Caernarfon candidacy, a seat held Plaid Cymru's Dafydd Wigley, one of the finest Welsh politicians

With Elwyn Jones near Llandysul, June 1996

of the post Second World War era. In Elwyn Jones's opinion this would be a superb training ground for me. I agreed to stand for selection, to cut my political teeth on behalf of the Conservative Party. The Caernarfon Conservative Association had insisted on selecting a Welsh-speaking candidate, deciding that they wished to choose between Goronwy Parry (an experienced Ynys Môn county councillor) and me at a final selection meeting to be held at Caernarfon Conservative Club on 15 February 1986.

When Elwyn Jones heard that the Welsh Conservative agent Ted Thurgood wanted to 'persuade' the Conservative Association Executive Committee to select Goronwy Parry, he threatened to report him to Conservative Central Office for malpractice. Indeed, when this attempted 'stitch-up' was leaked to the local Conservative Association officers by Elwyn Jones, they were very annoyed and determined to make their choice on merit alone. On the day I was said to be the unanimous choice of the Executive Committee and was later endorsed by the local Conservative Party members by an overwhelming majority.

I now appeared like Daniel in Dafydd Wigley's lions' den in Caernarfon. Meanwhile, on 16 April I passed my driving test at the second attempt in Lampeter. One of the highlights of my time in Caernarfon was meeting Jeffrey Archer during a luncheon at the Royal Hotel, on 24 June 1986. Lord Archer possessed the biggest ego of any politician that I have met. Indeed, he said to me, 'Tell your audience that I am the greatest political orator since Lloyd George'.

The first half of 1987 brought mixed blessings to me. On 13 March I met Margaret Thatcher in Llandudno and was hugely impressed by her. Unfortunately, my father was diagnosed with terminal stomach cancer later that month. On 25 and 26 April the Conservative Parliamentary Candidates' Conference was to be held in Birmingham, and my dying father insisted that I should attend. His last words to me were, 'Go there and go for it!' He died during the second day of the conference. The funeral service was held on 30 April at 1 Park Lane, Trecynon, and at Aberdare Old Cemetery. Here I was assisted by Reverends D. O. Davies, Elim Chapel, Cwmdare, and David Thomas, St David's Church, Brecon. Later the following words were inscribed on my father's gravestone:

If I have made one weary life the brighter,
If I have eased another's toil and pain,
If I have made some comrade's burden lighter
I have not lived in vain.

The highly respected Conservative MP for Ynys Môn, Keith Best, had been found guilty of making illegal multiple applications in British Telecom shares on the eve of the forthcoming general election. He was now banned from standing as the Conservative candidate for the Ynys Môn constituency. I was urged by several prominent Conservatives to apply for the vacancy here, which would have meant resigning as the Caernarfon candidate if selected by the Ynys Môn Conservative Association. This was a tempting proposition, because there was a Conservative majority of 1,684 votes or 4.2 per cent over the Plaid Cymru candidate Ieuan Wyn Jones in Ynys Môn. However much Elwyn Jones wished to see me elected to Westminster, he warned me that it was 'most unlikely' that the seat could be retained by the Conservative Party in the light of the circumstances behind Keith Best's enforced departure. My decision to follow Elwyn Jones's advice was subsequently vindicated at the general election when Ieuan Wyn Jones won a decisive majority of 4,298 votes or 10 per cent over his last-minute Conservative opponent, Roger Evans, who was to become the MP for Monmouth between 1992 and 1997.

With polling day for the 1987 general election fixed for 11 June, I presented myself as the main challenger to Plaid Cymru's Dafydd Wigley, something that was assisted by my high profile in the local press and on Welsh language TV and radio. In so doing I was ably assisted by my election agent, Sophie Parry Jones, a former Plaid Cymru supporter who lived in Penygroes. Elwyn Jones acted as my election press officer and wanted to rise the political temperature by being deliberately provocative. Referring to a recent visit by Sinn Fein representatives, who had met several prominent Welsh Nationalists in Gwynedd, Elwyn Jones included the following highly inflammatory words in my election address to the voters of the Caernarfon constituency: 'It was the Welsh Nationalists who invited the Sinn Fein terrorists to

Wales. Just as the Provisional IRA is the terrorist wing of Sinn Fein, so are the vandals of the Welsh Language Society the extra-parliamentary wing of Plaid Cymru'. I readily concede that I was in awe of Elwyn Jones at the time and was therefore incapable of opposing his more extreme utterances.

There were two acts of vandalism perpetuated to sabotage the Conservative election campaign. Both of these were almost certainly instigated by some 'shadowy' Welsh Nationalist fanatics who often hid behind the more respectable cloak of Plaid Cymru. Police had to investigate the smashing of a window worth £300 at the Conservative Party's Campaign Office in Bridge Street, Caernarfon, on Sunday 30 May. Fortunately, no one was in the building when it happened and police removed a large stone found inside the main shop-front window that was shattered.

Far more serious was a petrol bomb attack on the Conservative Party's Constituency Office in 13 High Street, Caernarfon, less than twenty-four hours before polling day. Whilst I and a dozen helpers were holding a meeting upstairs, the sound of broken glass was heard from downstairs. Everyone then rushed downstairs to investigate the amount of damage inflicted and was horrified to discover that someone had thrown a petrol bomb into the lobby via the broken window. Fortunately, the bomb did not ignite, or the consequences would have been horrific. A very threatening letter written in Welsh and addressed to me was also thrown through the broken window. It is appalling that some people within the Welsh-speaking community were willing to use such extreme measures to disrupt genuine political debate in a democracy.

In order to be defended from possible physical attacks by Welsh Nationalist extremists, I was fortunate to receive the assistance of Martin Foley and his bodyguards. This South

African gentleman had recently moved to live in the constituency and ran a private security business. He and his security guards were not people to offend and proved invaluable in protecting the campaign vehicles from being attacked by political opponents. They certainly terrified at least three groups of drunken Welsh Nationalist agitators. Actions certainly spoke louder than words on these occasions, with the trouble-makers ending-up bloodied.

Elwyn Jones appointed Martin Foley and his security guards to co-ordinate the safety arrangements on my behalf on election night. The scenes inside the count and particularly outside were disgraceful, with both me and the Labour candidate Rhys Williams being the target of a torrent of abuse by many Plaid Cymru supporters. I assured Rhys Williams and his shocked female election agent that they would be protected by Martin Foley and five of his security guards at the count if their personal safety was threatened. It was remarked at the time that I was wearing a long blue trench coat while entering and leaving the election count: I had been instructed by Martin Foley to wear a bullet-proof vest for my own personal safety, particularly in the light of the threatening words written in the letter I had received only the previous day, and the trench coat hid the vest.

The election result was announced as follows:

Dafydd Wigley (PC) 20,338 (57.1%)
Felix Aubel (Con) 7,536 (21.2%)
Rhys Williams (Lab) 5,632 (15.8%)
John Parsons (Lib) 2,103 (5.9%)

Plaid Cymru majority: 12,802 (36.0%)

Although the popular Dafydd Wigley had done well to

increase his vote and majority, I was nonetheless delighted to have obtained the highest Conservative vote in the Caernarfon constituency in a four-cornered contest since 1955. I had not only comfortably defeated Labour for runner-up position in a seat held by that party up to February 1974, but was also the only Conservative candidate in north Wales to improve on the party's performance in 1983. As I later told a local journalist, 'Mission accomplished by coming second and much better than we had hoped'.

However, the scenes outside the count can only be described as 'mass hysteria'. One may have been forgiven for thinking that Adolph Hitler's Nuremberg Rallies had not ended with the end of the Second World War in 1945. Thank goodness for much of this time I was doing an interview for Radio Cymru on the Caernarfon result inside the hall. I then disappeared from the shouting mob wearing my protective body armour accompanied by two of Martin Foley's security guards. Martin Foley was later granted his request of a large signed photograph of Margaret Thatcher with 'To Martin, Thank you for your invaluable assistance during the election campaign,' written on the back of it.

I was astonished by the considerable amount of personal support for Margaret Thatcher during the election campaign, particularly in the Dwyfor area. There were many staunch Dafydd Wigley voters who hoped that Margaret Thatcher would win the election in order to keep Neil Kinnock out of 10 Downing Street. Many of these also agreed with the way the Prime Minister had curbed the power of the trade unions, especially the miners. They also believed that the country needed to be 'shaken up from top to bottom' in order to get rid of its complacency.

There were other Dafydd Wigley supporters who had no real interest in having a Welsh Assembly in Cardiff and only

*Face to face with the 'Iron Lady' at the Conservative
Party Conference in Blackpool, October 1986*

voted Plaid Cymru to express their support for the Welsh
language and culture. Some of these were hostile towards
the law-breaking activities of the Welsh Language Society.
Dafydd Wigley's grand coalition was really a mass of
conflicting political opinions. It was like having Enoch
Powell and Tony Benn in the same political party. Whilst
Plaid Cymru's election campaign in Caernarfon appeared to
be left-of-centre in its appeal, many of the party's supporters
were right wing in their political opinions and would have
voted Conservative if they had lived in England or in a more
anglicised part of Wales.

I returned to Aberdare and soon afterwards enjoyed my
Master of Theology graduation ceremony at Lampeter on 9
July. After my father's death the family business was
gradually wound down by my mother and me and it was
sold to the Post Office the following summer. I began
studying for a part-time external Master of Philosophy

Sharing a sofa with the Welsh Secretary, Nicholas Edwards,
at the Conservative Party Candidates' Conference,
Llandrindod Wells, March 1987

degree in History. My 70,000-word thesis title was *Cardiganshire Parliamentary Elections and their Backgrounds, 1921–1932.* It was supervised by Dr Malcolm Smith, the head of the Lampeter History Department and someone whom I respected academically and liked personally. The Master of Philosophy thesis was submitted for examination the following September and I was notified of my academic success on 28 November 1989.

I have been subject to a number of diverse influences emanating from Aberdare over the years. These have certainly had an effect on my character development. One such influential figure was Huw Rhys Jones, who lived in Cemetery Road, Trecynon. He was a real rebel if ever there was one. Huw's mother, Jane, was a primary school teacher who had been a friend of my mother since the early 1950s. After completing his A levels, he spent several years beginning but never completing various Business Studies and Law courses in colleges as diverse as Liverpool, Bristol, Manchester, and Swansea. Huw Jones never really earned a proper living, preferring to live off state benefits and his mother's earnings. He was nonetheless highly intelligent and a very deep thinker when sober. While I was in secondary school Huw Jones had become something of a 'cult hero' locally. He even drove his car through the main glass window of the old Tesco supermarket in Aberdare in a drunken rage. Moreover, he used to smoke over sixty cigarettes a day and spend nearly £100 a week on drink during the mid 1980s. It is little wonder that he died before his fiftieth birthday.

Whilst I could not condone Huw Jones's lifestyle, I always had a sneaking admiration for his 'happy go lucky' attitude. Huw Jones always stressed that he would allow no one to tell him what to do. He would always remain his 'own man' and would lift two fingers up to authority when the occasion arose. Huw Jones always stressed that he did not care what anyone thought about his lifestyle, as long as he was happy with things. This libertarianism would have an influence in moulding that strongly 'conservative rebel' component in my character.

Reinforcing this libertarian or free-thinking element in me was a gentleman living on the Gadlys by the name of Cliff Shott. He had spent several years during the 1950s working in Sydney, Australia, as a dog trainer. Having returned to his parents home, Cliff Shott had never really done a proper day's work, apart from lots of 'hobbles' such as taking people's dogs out for walks and training them to obey commands. When asked why he would not work, he would say: 'When you are employed by somebody, you sell your freedom to do what you like when you like for money. I would never allow someone to deprive me of my liberties through bribery'. Although this attitude may sound absurd,

Cliff Shott's pursuit of freedom at all costs certainly had an influence on me. I have generally followed Cliff Shott's advice in trying to set my own agenda in life, and attempting to maintain some freedom of manoeuvre having adopted a given course of action.

There was also Cliff Craven. This gentleman worked on the production line in Hoover's Merthyr Tydfil, and was the personification of that much-maligned figure in the south Wales valleys, the working-class Tory. Cliff Craven lived on his own after the death of his parents and was a really eccentric character. He used to dress almost like a tramp, with never any laces in his shoes, and washed and shaved only infrequently. Nevertheless, he had a superb analytical mind and a thorough knowledge of world history as a result of his prolific reading of library books. Although he admitted to voting Labour at the 1945 general election, he had afterwards been a 'true blue' Conservative. Cliff Craven always emphasised to me the importance of never being afraid to speak your mind if the occasion demands.

Then there was Dr William Simpson, who lived next door to me at 2 Park Lane. He came originally from Kirkcaldy, Scotland, and had been practising as a GP at his Trecynon surgery since 1928. Whilst initially giving the impression of someone who was aloof, in private he was a sound adviser to me. Moreover, underneath that carefully moulded public exterior William Simpson was something of a rebel. He used to drink whisky as if his life depended upon it, with seemingly no adverse effect. William Simpson also used to put five teaspoons of sugar in each of the twenty cups of tea he would drink in a day. Although well into his eighties he used to go walking around the streets of Aberdare after midnight and remained oblivious to any possible dangers of being mugged. Moreover, many of the 'drunks' while seeing him out on his own would just say 'Goodnight, Doc'.

During his conversations with me, William Simpson would emphasise the paramount importance of thinking for oneself. He was a staunch Conservative who had assisted that party's candidate Arthur Molson in the Aberdare constituency at the 1929 general election. His late wife Dorothy Simpson had stood unsuccessfully as a Conservative candidate in council elections in Aberdare. William Simpson had proposed my candidature on behalf of the SDP during the 1983 general election and 1984 by-election as a personal favour, but was delighted when I later joined the Conservative Party. He always stressed to me the importance of doing what one believes to be right and never seeking to court popularity for its own sake.

Mrs Marchant Harries, who lived at The Ivies, Trecynon, had a strong influence on me, too. She was the elderly widow of one of Aberdare's best-known solicitors, Marchant Harries. Everyone was surprised at the time that this middle-aged bachelor had a whirlwind romance and subsequently married this twice-divorced but childless Scottish lady. Mrs Marchant Harries possessed a first-class analytical mind and I learnt a great deal from her about history, politics and science.

Mrs Marchant Harries's hostility to othodox Christianity was frowned upon by my mother, who feared that she would have a bad influence on me. It is probable that my belief that science and religion ought to complement each other is due to Mrs Marchant Harries's influence. My support for Charles Darwin's theory of evolution is also largely due to her intellectual influence. Mrs Marchant Harries, who was well into her eighties, had a significant personal influence on me. She asserted that I should do what I really wanted to do in life, rather than what other people expected of me. 'Be true to oneself,' was her personal motto and she can be described as a libertarian as well as a 'conservative rebel'.

Also, Mrs Marchant Harries's rather ambivalent attitude towards marriage and family life would later influence me, her protégé.

I was encouraged by several prominent members of the Conservative Party to apply to get onto the Conservative Central Office list of approved parliamentary candidates. This would entitle me to apply for a parliamentary constituency anywhere in the United Kingdom. Having submitted my application form and been notified that I had been successful at the preliminary stage, I was asked to attend the Holiday Inn, Slough, on 3 and 4 June 1988, in order to be examined for my suitability by the designated assessors. Here I was accompanied by two other Welshmen amongst the fifty people being examined. These were Nigel Evans and Richard Lewis, who had contested Swansea West and Swansea East respectively at the 1987 general election.

Nigel Evans and I performed successfully before the assessors and were placed on the approved list of Conservative candidates on 9 July. I went on to assist Nigel Evans during the Pontypridd by-election in February 1989, where he was the Conservative candidate. I was also delighted that Nigel Evans was elected as MP for Ribble Valley at the 1992 general election. Nigel Evans would have made an excellent Secretary of State for Wales. He is a sound Welshman and someone who has clear views on the political issues of the day. This contrasts sharply with some of his 'fence-sitting' colleagues at Westminster and the National Assembly.

I was urged by the new Conservative Party agent in Wales, Martin Perry, to submit my name for consideration as the parliamentary candidate for the fairly marginal Carmarthen constituency on 27 October 1989. However, I declined this opportunity on the grounds that the seat was not winnable under the political climate at the time. Although the formidable Rod Richards had been the

Conservative runner-up to Labour's Dr Alan Williams, he was still 4,317 votes or 8 per cent behind the Labour Party's victorious nominee at the 1987 general election. The new Conservative candidate Stephen Cavenagh was relegated to third position and 8,097 votes, or 14.2 per cent, behind Alan Williams at the 1992 general election. In a letter dated 14 October 1989 I also declined an invitation to contest the Caernarfon seat again on the grounds that I could do no more than I had already done to promote the Conservative cause in that constituency. My successor Peter Fowler saw the Conservative vote drop by over 2 per cent, with Dafydd Wigley increasing his majority to 14,476 votes.

Due primarily to the influence of Glyn James, a regular visitor to my beloved Ebeneser Chapel and the first Plaid Cymru Mayor of the Rhondda, I became a lay preacher in 1982. I had continued as a lay preacher over the years, often taking four religious services on Sundays in areas as diverse as the Cynon Valley, Merthyr Tydfil and the Swansea Valley. With the great decline in the number of ordained ministers of religion my presence in chapel pulpits to conduct religious services were increasingly in demand. I was encouraged to apply to be a candidate for the Welsh Congregational ministry in March 1988. If successful I would then be officially qualified to marry, baptise, and bury people, as well as giving Holy Communion.

Having passed all the ministerial preliminaries, and with a Licence in Theology and a Master of Theology degree already, it was decided that I would not require any further formal academic training in a theological college. Instead I was asked to write a 10,000 word dissertation with the title *An analysis of the reasons for the recent decline of Welsh Congregationalism, together with a study of its sustaining factors.* This completed assignment was approved with distinction on 6 June 1989 and on 11 October I was recognised as someone eligible to be ordained as a Welsh Congregational minister. In practice, this meant having my name included in the Union of Welsh Independents Year Book.

Although one Welsh Congregational pastorate had expressed an interest in me becoming its ordained minister, my mother was adamant that I was not yet ready for the ministry. In her eyes, any potential minister should first have acquired work experience outside their chosen vocation. I followed my mother's advice and applied for several teaching appointments in south and mid Wales. I appear to have been 'over-qualified' for several teaching posts, although I did get job interviews at Brecon and Llanfair Caereinon, losing out to more experienced teachers.

I was encouraged to apply for a teaching post at a grammar school in England where I was told 'they like letters after the names of their staff'. I then proceeded to apply for a History post at Chislehurst and Sidcup Grammar School in the Outer London Borough of Bexley. Within three days of forwarding my application in early October, I was notified that I would be interviewed for the post on the following Tuesday afternoon. When I arrived I was quite surprised to discover that it would be only the headmaster, John Sennett, who interviewed me. Within ten minutes he said that he had already decided to give the advertised History teaching post to another applicant, but he was in a position to offer another job to me. This was a Religious Studies post, but John Sennett was willing to include some A level History and some A level Politics as long as I was prepared to teach GCSE Classical Studies. John Sennett then called all four heads of department into the room to give me the 'look-over', and then he formally offered me the job. On 2 November my teaching appointment at Chislehurst and Sidcup Grammar School was officially confirmed by Bexley London Borough.

I have some vivid recollections of my time in Sidcup and life in London. Under the rather austere Methodist lay preacher John Sennett, Chislehurst and Sidcup Grammar School was a well-disciplined co-educational school. Bexley Education Authority had decided to keep their grammar schools; therefore every pupil had to pass an entrance examination. There was a significant minority of ethnic pupils, particularly Indian, Chinese and Turkish. These were overwhelmingly well-behaved, with the parents very supportive of the teaching staff. One burly Turkish taxi driver, for instance, would give his son a clout for every complaint he received on parents' evenings. I recall having my second year Religious Studies classes memorising the books of the Bible and reciting them against the clock in order to see which child could do this fastest. There was one Hindu Indian girl who was so enthusiastic that she learnt all of the books backwards as well as forwards.

The worst people were non-working English mothers with wealthy husbands. These women had little better to do than telling the teachers how to do their job. Some of them could really be a nuisance and were wholly opposite to the ethnic minority parents, who trusted the teacher to know best. Also, there were some white working-class parents who felt out of their depths during parents' evenings as a result of the snobbery of some of their middle-class counterparts. One non-professional single mother, for example, broke down in tears when another parent told her that her daughter Kelly was doing poorly in school because she had no father at home.

There were six teachers from Wales on the staff, all of them with some knowledge of the Welsh language. Most of these had been teaching at Chislehurst and Sidcup Grammar School for many years, and would have found it very difficult to teach in a mixed ability comprehensive school. A rather eccentric Welshman by the name of John Davies taught French. In order to get silence from noisy pupils he would throw their exercise books out of the top floor window and order them to retrieve these books. They were also told not return to the class in less than ten minutes.

There was Noel Horrobin, the 6 feet 4 inches tall Head of Sport. He was a stern disciplinarian who would subject disruptive pupils to exhausting physical exercises in the playground. This was his way around the ban on corporal punishment. Being forced to do 100 press-ups and 100 sit-ups took the place of the cane. Under the eccentric Adele Radelat, an austere convent-educated English teacher, children were made to stand one-legged on a chair and recite nursery rhymes in order to be humiliated in front of the whole class. Although regarded as unacceptable by today's standards, these were still very effective methods to maintain classroom discipline during the late 1980s and early 1990s.

I played left-back for the Chislehurst and Sidcup teachers' football team, which competed against neighbouring secondary schools. I recall a football match against Erith Comprehensive School teachers on a Friday evening in April 1990 in which I should never have played. After finishing my school work, I returned home to my Thamesmead flat and then went out for a short run in order to be ready for the football match at Erith. However, I was bitten in the ribs by an Alsatian dog. Although I managed to fend off the dog with a large stick, I knew that I had to go for a rabies injection as soon as possible. I drove to the Sidcup Hospital some seven miles away and received my injection. The doctor then told me to go home and rest.

I rather stupidly drove to Erith to play for my school team. Everything appeared to be one large blur during the game. Although suffering from the shock of being bitten by the Alsatian dog and from the effects of the rabies injection, I somehow remained 'playing' on the pitch. Several colleagues remarked in the pub afterwards that I did not need a drink because I appeared to be drunk already. When I told them the story of what had happened before the game they all said that I must have been mad to play.

There was more than enough to do in London. I would sometimes go to the famous Portobello Road antiques market in the early hours of Saturday morning. There were also the numerous second-hand bookshops in Central London where I was a frequent visitor. It is there that I first began to collect Welsh antiquarian books. There were also the cinemas in Leicester Square where I saw over 100 films between 1989 and 1992. In September 1990 I was joined on the teaching staff by another Lampeter graduate by the name of Dan Brown, who came to teach Geography. He was a real character who lived life way beyond his financial means. Through him I met a host of other Lampeter graduates who had settled in the London area to earn their respective livings. We would sometimes go to all-night parties on the Saturday evenings and spend Sunday recovering in order to be ready for work on Monday morning.

Although I never took drugs, I was to witness their adverse affects on numerous occasions. During a party in Crayford, for example, several of the people present smoked cannabis while others took speed, with two women even snorting cocaine. The smell of cannabis smoke in a room full of people became so horrendous that I felt very faint. I managed to crawl out of the room and then collapsed in the hallway. If that was the effect that passively-smoking a banned substance had on an individual, so much more was the damage caused by inhaling! It is for this reason that I have taken such an uncompromising stance against illegal drugs. In the words of Max Boyce's famous rugby song, 'I know because I was there'.

All things considered, I had a very good time in London. I had successfully completed my probationary teaching year at Chislehurst and Sidcup Grammar School in two terms. My Religious Studies and Classics GCSE pupils were making satisfactory progress, and I was enjoying teaching A level History and Politics.

There was, however, an unforgettable incident relating to the latter subject. One of my A level Politics pupils in the Lower Sixth Form was a Turkish Cypriot girl. She had attended the neighbouring secondary modern school and on account of her progress there had been accepted to do her GCSEs in Chislehurst and Sidcup Grammar School. Like nearly all of the other 'transfer' pupils, she had difficulty competing with her 'genuine' grammar school counterparts. She had achieved five GCSE passes at Grade C and had been allowed into the Sixth Form only due to her father's persistence.

With me now teaching her, she was coming close to a minimum grade E pass in A level Politics where before she was not even reaching O level standard. She obtained an E grade in her summer Lower Sixth examinations and was becoming increasingly more confident with her work. Her father then asked me to give his daughter private tuition at home. In her next set of examinations she reached a D grade. During the next parents' evening her father told me: 'If my daughter gets a grade C, you can marry her when she leaves school'. He was completely serious. Although she achieved a C grade, I politely declined her father's offer. Nevertheless, several of my teaching colleagues said that I was a fool. One can only wonder what would have happened to me had I accepted the offer!

6

By the end of 1991 I felt that I was now ready to enter the ministry. I informed the Union of Welsh Independent Churches Headquarters in Swansea of my intention and this was then circulated to churches who were seeking a minister. I was invited to preach in the Llanfair Caereinon area of Montgomeryshire where a group of six chapels were seeking a minister. These churches voted to 'call' me as their minister and a formal written invitation was extended to me. However, the very scattered nature of the pastorate, together with some financial 'tightness,' resulted in me deciding not to accept this invitation.

An invitation to come and preach was extended by Rhosllannerchrugog and District Welsh Congregational Churches, Denbighshire. I was very well received amongst the church members and shortly afterwards a 'calling' was sent to me by the pastorate secretary Aled Roberts, the Liberal Democrat Regional List AM for North Wales since 2011.

Meanwhile, I heard that Aberaeron and District Welsh Congregational Churches were seeking a new minister. I requested a Sunday to preach in these chapels and was very well-received by the members. I was then invited back six weeks later to preach a second time. Things again went very well and a meeting with the deacons from the five chapels was later held in order to discuss terms. Although the financial package was less favourable than the Rhos one, I was more inclined to live in Aberaeron. I had spent several years studying at nearby Lampeter and had become familiar with the mid-Ceredigion area. Furthermore, my mother's health had declined after a serious fall in 1992, and Aberaeron was less than an hour and a half from her Trecynon home.

All five Aberaeron chapels voted to extend a 'calling' to me on 17 July 1992. I formally accepted the invitation and stated that I would be in a position to begin my ministerial duties in June 1993. Unfortunately, the Aberaeron chapels did not have a manse and the issue arose of finding a place to live. I eventually found rented accommodation at Flat 1 Brynaeron Nurseries, Aberaeron.

I was ordained and inducted as the Welsh Congregational minister over Peniel Aberaeron, Neuaddlwyd, Llwyncelyn, Mydroilyn and Siloh Llanon during two services held at Peniel Chapel on 19 June 1993. This was one of the proudest days of my life.

I had not been politically active during my time in London, but I retained a keen interest in current affairs. Although Margaret Thatcher was apparently becoming increasingly out of touch with people, I was annoyed at the way she was betrayed by her MPs on 22 November 1990. Although voting Conservative and welcoming John Major's victory at the April 1992 general election, I was aware that the Prime Minister had been fortunate to snatch victory from the jaws of defeat. It was the Labour Party leader Neil Kinnock who had really lost the election, particularly with his lamentable performance at the Sheffield Rally on 1 April. During his speech, Neil Kinnock gave the impression that Labour had already won the election, and like a pop star he repeatedly shouted to the assembled crowd 'We're all right'. The shot of this moment was shown repeatedly on television and this immature and un-statesmanlike triumphalism was adjudged by friend and foe alike to be disastrous for Labour's election hopes.

I began contemplating writing a doctoral thesis on the Conservative Party in order to discover what motivated its leaders, activists and supporters. Was it the pursuit of power and retaining power at all costs or any particular ideological

Dr Felix Elfed Aubel PhD! Graduating in Lampeter, July 1995

factors? My former tutor at Lampeter Dr Malcolm Smith urged me to analyse the history of the Conservative Party in Wales, as this field of study remained untouched. Any detailed research undertaken by me would have to be original and fulfil the criteria for being awarded the higher degree of PhD. Although I had undertaken some preliminary research while teaching in Sidcup, I did not decide on a title for my 100,000-word doctoral thesis until I had begun my Aberaeron ministry. The title was to be *Welsh Conservatism 1885–1935*. Having gone through over 40,000 newspapers and miscellaneous primary and secondary source material at the National Library of Wales and Cardiff Central Library, I completed the thesis by December 1994. Dr Malcolm Smith believed that the thesis was 'good enough' to be marked by Dr John Stevenson from Oxford University.

The oral examination took place at Lampeter on 28 January 1995, with Dr Stevenson and Vice-Chancellor Morris being the assessors. This was a long two hours but intellectually very stimulating. I was overjoyed to be later informed that my thesis had passed with flying colours. It was also a delight to attend my formal graduation ceremony at Lampeter on 14 July 1995. As a consequence of gaining my PhD I was appointed as an Associate Lecturer at the Lampeter History Department in September 1995. My two years there, until financial cutbacks made part-time lectures obsolete, were most enjoyable and were responsible for keeping me intellectually alert.

Although still happy with my ministerial career in Aberaeron, I was feeling a vacuum in my life after completing my PhD. This explains my 'political comeback' in November 1995. In August 1995 I was visited at Brynaeron Nurseries by Tom Raw-Rees who was the chairman of the Ceredigion Conservative Association. He told me that he wanted to know whether I would consider submitting my name as a possible Conservative Party candidate for the Ceredigion constituency at the next general election. I was flattered to be 'head-hunted' because I had not done anything of note for the Conservative Party since the late 1980s. I accepted his invitation to address the Ceredigion Conservative Association Executive Committee at the Llanina Arms, Llanarth on 5 September 1995. The meeting went well and I agreed to forward my name as an applicant for the Conservative candidature.

The selection meeting was held in Aberaeron on 21 November, with me the unanimous choice of the local Conservative Party members present. This news was greeted by Dylan Iorwerth, the editor of the Welsh-language current affairs magazine *Golwg*, as the return of 'Felix the Lion.'

On 9 February 1996 I began my long association with S4C's *Pawb a'i Farn* current affairs programme. This programme took place at Newtown Leisure Centre, Montgomeryshire. One of the panellists alongside me was the Liberal Democrat Reverend Roger Roberts, whom I have always regarded as an accomplished debater.

Several prominent Conservative Party politicians came to Ceredigion to support my candidacy. For example, on 16 February 1996 the Secretary of State for Wales, William Hague, did a tour of Cardigan town with me, before addressing a meeting at the Porth Hotel, Llandysul in the evening. This was to be the first of several visits by William

Hague, whom I regard as an excellent public speaker and someone who would have made a very good prime minister.

With Jeffrey Archer in Cardigan, March 1996

Jeffrey Archer spoke at the Moose International Hall in Cardigan, on 14 March that year. His ego had not diminished since his visit to Caernarfon the previous decade, since he now required me to introduce him as 'Jeffrey Archer, the greatest political orator since Winston Churchill'. On 27 April the feisty Home Office Minister Ann Widdecombe spoke at the Porth Hotel, Llandysul. I have always admired this lady for her willingness to speak her mind, although I may not always agree with her opinions particularly on the emotive issues of fox-hunting and abortion. Tom Raw-Rees remarked that since Ann and I were 'getting on so well together' we should become an 'item'. I whispered in his ear, 'Rather you than me'.

Unfortunately, this very enjoyable time in my life was

interrupted by the serious decline in my mother's health. Ever since her serious fall in 1992, my mother had found it increasingly difficult to look after her large home in Trecynon. She had very much enjoyed my ordination and induction services at Aberaeron in 1993 as well as my PhD graduation ceremony at Lampeter in 1995, but there were increasing signs of decline in her health. What eventually brought matters to a head was a serious fall at her home, with hypothermia turning into pneumonia. Having been admitted to Prince Charles Hospital, Merthyr Tydfil, she died on 28 September 1996, aged seventy-seven.

I now faced a dilemma: I was supposed to be preaching twice at Rhydybont Welsh Congregational Church, Llanybydder Harvest Services on 2 October, the day before my mother's funeral. Despite receiving advice to the contrary, I insisted on conducting these services. After all, I had inherited from my Slovenian father the mind set that 'things must go on' regardless of how one felt. I also insisted that I would officiate at my mother's funeral service at the Co-operative Chapel of Rest, Gadlys, Aberdare, on 3 October. I was, however, assisted by my old Lampeter friend, the Reverend David Thomas, Brecon. Another decision made by me was that after the funeral tea held at Ebeneser Chapel, Trecynon, I would return to Aberaeron in order to preside over Peniel Chapel's 'Big Meeting' at 7.00 pm. Although I am aware of the criticisms for my allegedly 'inappropriate actions' during these two days, I remain convinced that I did the right thing. After all, that was 'my father's way' of doing things.

William Hague visited Llandysul and Cardigan on 28 February 1997. Here he met representatives from the farming unions and the fox-hunting fraternity, together with spokesmen from various aspects of local government. With polling day announced as 1 May 1997, the Conservative

Campaigning with William Hague in Cardigan, February 1997

Party election campaign was launched at Tyglyn Aeron, Ciliau Aeron, on 3 April. The Conservatives locally were the victims of an anti-Tory swing across the country. There was a general feeling that Britain needed a change after eighteen years of Conservative rule, and New Labour, under Tony Blair's very effective leadership, was presenting itself as a moderate and credible alternative. Whatever I sought to do locally, assisted by my very enthusiastic election agent Paul Davies, we were just hitting our heads against a brick wall. While I concede that locally I may have defended fox hunting too strongly, and emphasised the dangers of European integration excessively, I was really in a hopeless position.

Plaid Cymru's Cynog Dafis had been an effective MP since 1992. The Labour Party candidate Hag Harries, a popular Lampeter councillor, was campaigning very hard on the tide of high national support, leaving the Liberal Democrats and the Conservatives firmly at the rear. To

*Launching my campaign as parliamentary candidate for Ceredigion
in Tyglyn Aeron, April 1997*

worsen matters, Sir James Goldsmith's Referendum Party candidate John Leaney from Newport, Pembrokeshire, was taking euro-sceptic, primarily Conservative, votes away from me. Although the Liberal Democrat candidate Dai Davies, a Cardigan accountant, was theoretically seeking to regain a seat lost by Geraint Howells to Plaid Cymru at the previous general election, the contest was clearly one between Plaid and Labour.

There had been significant boundary changes to the constituency since 1992 that make comparisons with previous results largely futile. With the removal of the North Pembrokeshire section, the now renamed Ceredigion constituency had lost an area where there were a very significant number of Conservative voters. Indeed, the boundary changes had resulted in the local Conservative Association losing 60 per cent of its financial resources and 50 per cent of its membership. Also, a number of traditional

Conservative and Liberal Democrat voters are known to have voted tactically for Cynog Dafis in order to keep Labour out. Meanwhile, some English settlers on the coast were voting Plaid Cymru in order to be 'accepted' locally.

Whilst my candidature was supported by several traditional Liberal voters, I was becoming aware that it would be essentially 'lambs to the slaughter' on election night. By the time the Ceredigion election result was announced at the Memorial Hall, Aberaeron, over 100 Conservative seats had been lost UK-wide, and things were only to go from bad to worse. The result in the Ceredigion constituency was as follows:

Cynog Dafis (PC) 16,728 (41.6%)
Hag Harris (Lab) 9,767 (24.3%)
Dai Davies (LD) 6,616 (16.5%)
Felix Aubel (Con) 5,983 (15.0%)
John Leaney (Ref) 1,092 (2.7%)

Plaid Cymru majority: 6,961 (17.3%)

The Conservative election result in Ceredigion was a disappointment, but I was largely the victim of an anti-Tory landslide not only in Wales where every Conservative MP lost their seat, but in the whole of Britain.

I was now faced with the Devolution referendum on 18 September 1997. Although I had campaigned against a Welsh Assembly in 1979, I was now increasingly attracted by the new government's proposals for the establishment of a Scottish Parliament. I was, however, very disappointed that Wales was only being offered a 'talking-shop' Welsh Assembly. With the benefit of hindsight, I should have supported the Government's proposals for the establishment of a Welsh Assembly, as hopefully the first step towards a Welsh Parliament with law-making powers. Nevertheless, I became a 'No' campaigner. However odd this political stance may appear to some people, subsequent research has indicated that at least 10 per cent of Plaid Cymru supporters voted 'No' in the Devolution referendum because they regarded a 'talking shop' Welsh Assembly' as an insult to Wales.

Having committed myself to supporting the campaign against the establishment of a Welsh Assembly, I had to defend some anti-devolutionist views which I did not agree with; however, that is the nature of politics. The campaign was to be unforgettable due to the mixture of 'characters' assembled together under one banner. Whatever their sneering middle-class Welsh Nationalist detractors may say, Rhondda's Carys Pugh and her side-kick Betty Bowen were genuine in their beliefs that a Welsh Assembly would eventually break-up the United Kingdom and lead to an independent Wales. These Labour Party stalwarts spoke for thousands of traditional Socialist voters in the south Wales valleys, particularly the wartime generation, who were 'proud to be British'. Their views were articulated on a more academic level by Beddau's very controversial Labour intellectual Dr Tim Williams.

I fondly recall campaigning in several places during the Devolution referendum campaign. One of the funniest moments was campaigning in Cardigan town on a Monday for the 'No' side, while virtually the whole main cast of S4C's *Pobol y Cwm* were doing the same for the 'Yes' side. It must have been quite a sight for the general public, with conflicting opinions being articulated via loudspeakers, leaflets, walkabouts, etc. Both sides then moved to Cardigan Mart in order to promote their views amongst the farming fraternity. On a lighter note, 'Yes' and 'No' campaigners then went for a meal in the Mart Café, where nearly all of the protagonists got on well and had a laugh recalling the more amusing moments of the day. Who says there cannot be fun in politics?

In Cardigan I was very ably assisted by Mary Davies. Meeting Mary Davies would be a turning point in my life. Whilst campaigning in the Synod Inn area of Ceredigion, I attended an auction of agricultural implements organised by Fred Davies on 11 April 1997. Mary Davies (no relation to Fred) was a registered complementary medical practitioner and psychic living in Newcastle Emlyn and was on her way to meet one of her patients in the New Quay area. We were introduced via a mutual friend, Gwilym Jenkins of Gorsgoch, who was assisting my election campaign. Within a short time Mary and I had become an 'item'.

Mary Davies came originally from Grangetown, Cardiff where her parents had a grocery and newsagent's shop. She had spent nearly twenty years working in stockbroking before moving to Carmarthenshire in order to marry a local farmer, who unfortunately died in 1994. Mary Davies was a Conservative and was a member of the Tory delegation at the election count at Aberaeron.

The day after campaigning together for the 'No' side in Cardigan, Mary and I both travelled to Cardiff, Rhondda and Pontypridd to spend three days campaigning on the open-top double-decker 'Battle Bus' with Carys Pugh, Betty Bowen, Tim Williams and their supporters. This was great fun and I learnt to appreciate a much more caring side to the much maligned and often ridiculed Carys Pugh (the self-proclaimed leader of the Labour 'No' campaign). She was completely down-to-earth, called a spade a spade, and was sincere to the point of naive in her political beliefs. Carys Pugh held no personal grudges against her opponents. For instance, in spite of her opposition to Welsh Nationalism, she spoke very highly of Rhondda's first Plaid Cymru mayor, Glyn James. Also, she had the highest personal respect for Mrs Kitchener Davies, the widow of the 'founder' of Welsh Nationalism in the Rhondda valleys. Carys Pugh was, if you ignored that unfair caricature of her, a very decent lady.

One of the funniest moments during these days was the 'Battle of Ponty'. The 'Yes' side were 'hit for six' when the 'No' Battle Bus with loudspeakers on suddenly came down Pontypridd High Street. We then disembarked to spread our message. I used two loudspeakers to address the shoppers from alongside the town's fountain. The situation became very heated with one 'Yes' male campaigner on the verge of hitting Mary, who was giving as good as she was getting. Meanwhile I and my public address system were protected by three burly Rhondda ex-miners who had been supporters of Arthur Scargill during the 1984–1985 miners' strike. After all, strange alliances can be created during one-issue referendum campaigns! In Lenin's famous words, 'My enemy's enemy is my friend'. To make an enjoyable day even better, this event was broadcast that evening not only on the BBC and HTV Welsh News, but also on national TV as well.

I was a member of the panel on S4C's *Refferendwm '97* broadcast from Llanelli on 15 September. Here I was accompanied on the 'No' side by that redoubtable Swansea Conservative, Bill Hughes. On the opposite side, were Labour's Rhodri Morgan and the Liberal Democrat Roger Roberts. The debate in front of an invited audience was chaired by Dewi Llwyd, for whom I have always had the highest regard as an objective interviewer. This was to prove a rather difficult evening because there appeared to be very few 'No' campaigners in the invited audience. Later enquiries established that it was this group's own failure to take the debate seriously enough which was responsible for this, rather than some built-in 'Yes' bias amongst the programme's producers. I have always found the Welsh-language media to be very fair in seeking to provide a balanced coverage in political debates, despite a large proportion of those working in it being Plaid Cymru supporters.

What made matters even more difficult for the 'No' campaigners was that Scotland had voted decisively 'Yes' the previous week. Now even some devolution sceptics, including privately myself, were thinking that if the Scottish people have voted for a parliament, it would perhaps be better for Wales to have an assembly than nothing. To the obvious dislike of Bill Hughes, I said that I would have been prepared to support a 'proper Welsh Parliament' if such a body had been on offer in the referendum.

I was one of the panellists on S4C's live coverage of the Referendum Result's programme, hosted by Dewi Llwyd. On going to the BBC studio in Llandaf, I was fairly certain that the 'Yes' campaign would win a decisive electoral victory. However, as the votes began coming in, everything appeared to be on a knife edge until the Carmarthen result. This ensured a wafer thin 'Yes' win by 6,721 votes. In spite of their overwhelming advantage in financial resources and manpower the 'Yes' campaign had achieved only 559,419 votes against the 'No' campaign's 552,698 votes. Nevertheless, as a democrat I pledged my support to ensure the success of this 'new Welsh democracy'.

With the National Assembly becoming a political reality, I came to the conclusion that a robust Conservative Party presence there would be essential in order to provide a moderate centre-right alternative to the other left-wing political parties. I therefore applied to get onto the approved list of potential Conservative National Assembly candidates on 8 January 1998 and was notified of my success on 3 March. On 17 April I applied for the Preseli Pembrokeshire

Conservative candidature in the National Assembly elections, scheduled for May 1999. Having got through the preliminary stages on 29 April, where the twenty original applicants were reduced to four, I had to go before the Executive Council of the Preseli Pembrokeshire Conservative Association during an afternoon meeting at the NFU Hall, Haverfordwest, on 1 May.

There were to be some long-lasting divisions as a result of the final ballot. Although I was the 'comfortable winner', my victory had not been decisive. Furthermore, I had emerged victorious by winning heavily amongst members present from the more Welsh-speaking northern parts of the Preseli Pembrokeshire constituency as well as in the more rural central belt. By contrast, Helen Stoddart, a local journalist, had polled the overwhelming majority of her votes in the southern portion of the seat, particularly around the Burton and Milford Haven area. Although Helen remained on friendly terms with me, some of her supporters found it difficult to accept the verdict of the selection meeting.

With Mary Davies and Dr Liam Fox at the Welsh Conservatives' Conference, Llangollen, June 1998

I attended the Welsh Conservative Party Conference held at the Royal International Pavilion, Llangollen, on 12 and 13 June. I now had the opportunity to again meet William Hague, who was new the leader of the Conservative Party. Two of the most memorable events of the conference were an 'after breakfast clash' between former Welsh Office Minister Rod Richards and the Conservative candidate for Ynys Môn, Peter Rogers. During a short informal meeting of several National Assembly candidates, Rod Richards, who chaired the proceedings, lit a cigarette under Peter Rogers's nose. The latter took great exception to this and some heated words were exchanged between these two very volatile gentlemen. Also, I gave a 'somewhat different' grace before the conference dinner. According to the deputy Conservative agent for Wales, Roger Williams, 'only Felix could have got away with his choice of words'.

William Hague visited Pembrokeshire on 3 August 1998, and during the evening he spoke at the Nantyffin Motel, Llandysilio. What was soon to cast a cloud over the Welsh Conservative Party was the bitter struggle for the Tory leadership in Wales. William Hague had appointed Nick Bourne, a Swansea professor in Law, as his chief spokesman in Wales. He was, however, later challenged by Rod Richards for this post, resulting in a ballot of all Conservative Party members in Wales. Between the opening of nominations on 12 October and the ballot result on 10 November there was a great deal of acrimony. On a personal level I had always admired Rod Richards for being a 'no nonsense' politician. However, I was aware that the late 1990s required a somewhat softer tone. Although Nick Bourne was somewhat aloof in his manner, the fact that William Hague had appointed him to the post was good enough to gain my support. I spoke at the launch of Nick Bourne's leadership campaign at the St Mellon's Hotel on

In Haverfordwest, December 1998, as prospective Assembly candidate for the Conservatives in the Preseli Pembrokeshire seat

20 October. Also, I took him around to meet Conservative Party members in Ceredigion and Preseli Pembrokeshire on 25 and 26 October.

What further complicated this leadership contest was the Mid and West Wales hustings for the regional AMs' list. This was held at the Halliwell Centre, Trinity College Carmarthen on 2 November, and at the Montgomeryshire Suite, Royal Welsh Showground, Builth Wells, the following evening. In these hustings I was ranked fourth out of the eight candidates, making it almost certain that I would have to win the Preseli Pembrokeshire constituency if I was to be elected to the National Assembly. Although I had hoped for third spot behind Nick Bourne and Welshpool farmer Glyn Davies, I was denied this by barrister and Carmarthenshire businessman O. J. Williams by 579 votes to 518. This was to be no long-lasting disappointment because it was only Nick Bourne and Glyn Davies who were to enter the Assembly by the 'back door' regional list. Nonetheless, they were both heavily defeated in their respective constituencies of Brecon and Radnor and Montgomeryshire.

When the result was announced on 10 November, Rod Richards comfortably won the Conservative leadership ballot by nearly three votes to two. The actual figures and percentages were Rod Richards 3,873 votes (58 per cent); Nick Bourne 2,798 votes (42 per cent). This was labelled as a 'step backwards' for the Conservative Party by the media. Rod Richards emerged victorious because he was a well-known face in the media. His right-wing views appealed to many Conservative Party activists, who had gone into a kind of 'bunker mentality' or even a state of 'self-denial' in the light of the 1997 general election disaster. He had also ran a very effective personal campaign against the generally pro-Nick Bourne Conservative Party establishment in Wales, appealing directly to the grass roots members on the slogan, 'Rod Richards, the man Labour don't want to face. The strong Welsh voice of experience'.

On 29 September my partner Mary Davies was selected as the Conservative National Assembly candidate for the Labour stronghold of Aberavon during a selection meeting held at the Port Talbot Constitutional Club. Almost a month to the day, 28 October, the highly respected Val Sanders resigned as the Conservative Party's agent for Preseli Pembrokeshire, after very heated exchanges with some of the senior Conservative Association officers, essentially over employment matters.

A petition was then signed by 218 members of the Preseli Pembrokeshire Conservative Association calling for a special general meeting, requesting Val Sanders to reconsider her resignation. On 21 November the Preseli Pembrokeshire Conservative Association Executive Committee overwhelmingly decided that it did not wish to contribute towards the employment of an agent from outside the area, preferring to have Val Sanders. The 'Haverfordwest OK Corral' was held at the Pavilion, Withybush Agricultural Showground on 5 December. The meeting passed a vote of no confidence, by 132 votes to 5, against the constituency chairman Ron Forest, an Englishman living in Croesgoch. The deputy chairman John Davies, a Welsh-speaker living in Newport, was also voted out by 129 votes to 7. With no votes against, Val Sanders was invited to return as the constituency agent. This high drama is a superb example of political assassination by grass roots members. In an attempt to steady things, the redoubtable former constituency chairman Hugh Luke, a Welsh-speaking farmer from Mathry, was elected as acting chairman until the National Assembly elections.

The Welsh Conservative Party Conference was held at City Hall, Cardiff on 18 and 19 March 1999. There was much acrimony between the Rod Richards and Nick Bourne factions. As well as a bitter personality clash between the two protagonists, there were obvious policy differences.

Three happy Tory candidates: Helen Stoddart, Mary Davies and me, in Nevern, December 1998

The Conservative election manifesto for the National Assembly elections, *Fair Play to All*, had been written by Rod Richards. In it he accused Plaid Cymru of 'linguistic apartheid' over its jobs policy in Gwynedd. Rod Richards also demanded an end to teaching Welsh to youngsters aged fourteen to sixteen where parents did not want it. All these deliberately provocative statements were reminiscent of the occasion in 1994 when he described Labour councillors as 'short, fat, slimy and fundamentally corrupt'.

The manifesto was also very hostile to devolution. It was meant to appeal to those people who had voted 'No' in the Devolution referendum, and made no attempt to appeal to the middle ground where most elections are won. In response, Nick Bourne fired a broad-side at his political rival and personal enemy when he said that 'the manifesto should be written so that it would win back support we lost last time, as well as that of other people'. He also called for 'Conservatism with a smile rather than a snarl' – which was seen by political commentators as a reference to Rod Richards's 'Rottweiler' nickname.

With polling day fixed for 5 May, the Conservative National Assembly election campaign began in Preseli Pembrokeshire as elsewhere. I was privately very pessimistic regarding the outcome. Nationally the Conservative electoral challenge under Rod Richards's leadership had been described in the press as 'little more than blue mist', while locally the divisions from the candidate selection contest, and from the 'blood-letting' during the Withybush meeting, remained serious. Plaid Cymru under Dafydd Wigley's brilliant leadership nationally were campaigning very hard locally with an excellent candidate in Conrad Bryant, the former Milford Haven Port Authority chief accountant. Although the Labour Party had witnessed local political divisions over its candidate selection, the Socialists seem to have eventually rallied round their nominee Dr Richard Edwards, a political researcher. My Conservative campaign was also further handicapped by the fact that Alwyn Luke, the chairman of Pembrokeshire County Council and brother of Hugh Luke, was standing as an Independent candidate. Some anti-Val Sanders Conservatives were supporting Alwyn Luke's candidature.

My helpers and I were swimming against an unfavourable political tide, with Plaid Cymru establishing themselves as the main challengers to Labour locally, as they were doing nationally. Nonetheless, I remain grateful to my dedicated band of helpers, ably led by Hugh Luke and Val Sanders. It was these people's unflinching commitment that was responsible for ensuring that the Conservative Party vote was to hold up reasonably well in Preseli Pembrokeshire in comparison to other similar neighbouring constituencies.

With Rod Richards in Haverfordwest, March 1999

One of the highlights of the campaign for me was S4C's *Etholiad '99* debate held in Aberystwyth and hosted by Dewi Llwyd. In what was to prove to be a very lively evening, I found it difficult to defend Rod Richards's controversial Welsh-language policy because I privately disagreed with large portions of it. Whilst it may have contributed something to stabilising the Conservative vote in some of the more anglicised 'Little England beyond Wales' southern portions of the Preseli Pembrokeshire constituency, it just played into Plaid Cymru's hands in the more Welsh-speaking northern end. I regret that I did not refute Rod Richards's Welsh language policy during the TV debate, since there was a point of principle at stake – namely the survival of the language.

The Preseli Pembrokeshire National Assembly election result was announced at the Parkhouse Centre at Withybush Showground, Haverfordwest, on Friday 6 May. It was as follows:

Richard Edwards (Lab) 9,977 (34.31%)
Conrad Bryant (PC) 7,239 (24.89%)
Felix Aubel (Con) 6,585 (22.64%)
David Lloyd (LD) 3,338 (11.48%)
Alwyn Luke (Ind) 1,944 (6.68%)

Labour majority 2,738 (9.41%)

Whilst disappointed at the time not to have come runner-up to Labour, I was relieved that in comparison to the neighbouring constituency of Carmarthen West and South Pembrokeshire where the Conservative vote had dropped as far as 18 per cent there had been only a 5 per cent drop in Preseli Pembrokeshire. I was also glad to hear that Mary Davies had saved her £500 election deposit in the Labour stronghold of Aberavon, where she had received 1,624 votes and 6.97 per cent of the poll, coming fourth out of six candidates.

7

With the National Assembly elections over, I accepted an invitation to visit my Slovenian cousins in late June 1999. Mary and I flew from Cardiff and arrived at Ljubljana airport, where I was given a welcome worthy of a king. During the fortnight holiday we travelled more than 1,500 miles visiting places of historical interest as well as tracing the Aubel family history. This proved to be a very emotional time for me, swimming in the same river where my father had swum as a boy, jumping from a high bridge into another river as a sign of courage in order to emulate my father's feats prior to the Second World War. Swimming in Lake Bled, too, proved to be an unforgettable experience, and we also visited Postoigna Caves.

My father had always claimed that Great Britain was the 'best country in the world to live in' because of its traditions of freedom and democracy. It was left to me to see these principles being applied in Slovenia after the collapse of Communism. I was hugely impressed by what I saw. One of my cousins in Zuzemberk was a secondary school headmistress and I had the privilege to be taken around the school. What impressed me was its cleanliness, well-disciplined teaching environment, and total absence of graffiti. Nearly all of the pupils could speak some English and everyone took great pride in their Slovenian national identity, without showing bigotry towards other nations.

My admiration for the quality of life in Slovenia resulted in me beginning to think of the necessity to develop a distinctive national agenda in Welsh politics. It only reinforced my belief that since Wales now had a National Assembly, that body should be given primary law-making powers in many areas of domestic policy such as health and

Receiving a warm welcome in Slovenia, June 1999

My grandparents' grave in Slovenia

education. Moreover, Ron Davies's vision that 'devolution is a process not an event' should be implemented as soon as it was practical to do so. This was simply an issue of principle because if a law-making parliament was good enough for the Scottish people, it was good enough for the Welsh. Upon returning from our Slovenian holiday, I became even more convinced that the people of Wales should no longer be regarded as second-class citizens compared to their Scottish counterparts.

This opinion was reinforced during a conversation I had with a bus driver while on holiday in Bournemouth in September 2010. I witnessed just how insecure many indigenous English people are about 'being English'. They feel themselves to be second-class citizens to the Scots and even to the Welsh. He stated that 'you Welsh have an Assembly in Cardiff, and we English have nothing'. I had much sympathy for his views. After all, the English language and culture has largely been hijacked by its American and Third World counterparts, while the Westminster Parliament, contrary to Welsh Nationalist mythology, is almost invariably viewed as a British rather than a specifically English institution.

As the conversation between us progressed, it became obvious to me that indigenous English people are suffering an acute crisis of identity. In contrast to the situation in Wales, being English without being British amounts to virtually nothing distinctive, since it has no separate culture and language to sustain it. We Welsh should therefore be thankful that we still have an indigenous language and culture, as well as our shared British identity. We Welsh therefore have the best of both worlds, while the indigenous English lack any tangible national identity. No wonder many English people wish to have a separate English parliament and are increasingly flying the flag of Saint

George rather than the Union Flag. I wish them well in their efforts to establish a distinct English national identity.

The result of a survey conducted by the anti-racist Searchlight Educational Trust in February 2011 reinforces this view. It indicated there is a 'growing assertive English nationalism' and that the 'creation of an English parliament is necessary to stop the growing unfairness of the present devolved governmental system, leading to a total break-up of the United Kingdom'.

Moreover, the *Western Mail* of 30 March 2011 cited that even former opponents of Welsh devolution, such as the Welsh Conservative MP for Monmouth, David Davies, were now calling for England to gain its own form of self-government by having a specifically English Parliament to prevent the break-up of the United Kingdom. According to David Davies:

> As a proud Welshman and a unionist we cannot possibly have a situation where we as Welsh MPs are telling the English what to do with their health service and education and they can't have a say over what goes on in Wales. Surely the answer for all unionists, all across the United Kingdom, is to give the English their own parliament with similar powers to the Welsh and Scottish parliaments and have some kind of federal structure dealing with everything else that matters to the United Kingdom.

The *Western Mail* of 21 February 2012 reported a very significant speech by Professor Richard Wyn Jones of Cardiff University. He claimed that with an increasing assertion of 'Englishness', there would be an inevitable reduction in the status of Welsh representation at Westminster. It is difficult to envisage an MP from Wales being given a ministerial role in a ministry whose affairs are devolved in the future. The growing calls for 'English votes for English laws' would create problems for Wales, because of its funding from London through the Barnett formula. In other words, any English vote with a spending commitment actually has implications for Wales and Scotland. Also, Wales could no longer presume that parliamentary debates over devolving more powers to the National Assembly would assume 'English passivity'. England broadly ignored the referendum on substantially increasing the Assembly's powers in March 2011, but it is most unlikely that it would in the future. A much stronger assertion of 'English identity' is now demonstrated by the fact that 'the feeling of benign neglect towards Wales and Scotland has been replaced by suspicion'. There is also marked resentment that they are getting more than their 'fair share'.

This research only further strengthens my conviction that there needs to be a new 'Act of Union'. This would create a genuinely 'British Confederation' of legally equal 'partner countries' within the British Isles, with the Queen being formally designated as head of state of each specific nation as well as of Great Britain as a whole.

At the very beginning of August 1999 Rod Richards was charged with causing grievous bodily harm. On 8 August he resigned the Conservative Party leadership in the National Assembly in order to clear his name. The Conservative Party chairman Michael Ancram was believed to have indicated that if Rod Richards had not stepped down, the party would have suspended his membership pending the outcome of the criminal trial he was now facing. Eight days later Nick Bourne returned as leader; this was to be the beginning of the end of Rod Richards's political career.

Although Nick Bourne was elected as leader by the Conservative group in the National Assembly he was never given an electoral mandate by ordinary Tory members. Therefore, Rod Richards would still be in a position for several years to claim that he was the 'true' leader in the eyes of the majority of Conservative Party activists.

With the issue of the Welsh Conservative Party leadership still in the background, a parliamentary by-election was called in the Ceredigion constituency because of MP Cynog Dafis's wish to concentrate his political work in the National Assembly. Polling day was arranged for 3 February 2000. Whilst I was encouraged to submit my name to be the Conservative candidate, I saw no political advantage in again contesting a seat in which I had no genuine prospect of winning. However, I pledged my support to Paul Davies, who had been my enthusiastic and very competent election agent in 1997. Having been the overwhelming choice of the members of the Ceredigion Conservative Association, I was asked to serve as Paul Davies's election minder. This was to be a short campaign, and it was unfortunate that Conservative Central Office failed to take the by-election seriously enough to provide adequate financial resources and manpower.

What disappointed me a great deal was an under-hand Conservative attempt to get me removed from the *Pawb a'i Farn* panel in Newcastle Emlyn on 28 January 2000. This made me far more suspicious of people's motives in politics, particularly within my own party. Having agreed with S4C to be the Conservative Party spokesman on the panel, that body was informed by a 'senior source' within the party that I was now unavailable due to my 'by-election commitments'. Thank goodness a female acquaintance of mine, who worked for S4C, cross-checked the accuracy of this information with me, and I was able to deny it.

Realising that something under-hand had taken place I did not mention my participation in that evening's TV programme to anyone in the Ceredigion campaign team. There must have been a few shocked faces that evening when I appeared alongside Labour's Dr Alan Williams, Plaid Cymru's Helen Mary Jones and Liberal Democrat Roger Roberts! This proved to be a lively and enjoyable debate. To this day I have not got to the bottom of this attempt to get me removed from the TV programme. However, when I returned to the Conservative Campaign Headquarters on the Monday morning, there were several sheepish-looking people who could not look me in the eye.

A somewhat devious tactic during the Conservative campaign was the publicity stunt of shooting a young calf for media attention. On 31 January Michael Ancram visited Ceredigion and was taken to a farm just outside Lampeter on a fact-finding visit regarding the difficulties facing the farming industry. In the presence of Michael Ancram, Paul Davies, my partner Mary Davies, me and the Welsh Conservative Party agent Leigh Jeffes, the farmer had a gentleman dressed in combat fatigues to shoot the calf. Photographs of the event were taken and distributed to the press. I was horrified by this barbaric media event, which cast a nasty shadow over the campaign. In the event, Plaid Cymru's Simon Thomas easily held the Ceredigion constituency over the Liberal Democrats, while we Conservatives achieved our objective of defeating Labour, ending up in third place.

On 8 February 2000 Rod Richards was expelled from the Welsh Conservative Party group in the National Assembly and had the whip removed. This was because he had abstained in the vote on the Labour Budget in December 1999, while every other Conservative voted as instructed against it. This was said to have ruined any prospect of him challenging Nick Bourne for the leadership of the Welsh Conservative Party in October 2000. In order to have a ballot of Conservative Party members he needed the support of at least two of the nine-strong National Assembly group. Rod Richards's description of his former colleagues as the 'Malevolent Seven' and Nick Bourne as a 'complete prat' only served to increase his political isolation. His bitter personal hostility towards Nick Bourne can also be seen in Rod Richards's comment, 'I don't drive a BMW like Bourne; I drive a Metro'.

I attended the Welsh Conservative Party Conference held at the North Wales Conference Centre Llandudno on 9 and 10 June 2000. Here I saw Rod Richards being frozen out by the Conservative Party leadership. According to the *Western Mail's* Clive Betts, 'the way William Hague avoided meeting the Tory right-wing *enfant terrible* was masterly. He turned sharp left and shook another hand'. One of the more positive memories I have of that particular conference was Nick Bourne's repudiation of Rod Richards's policy towards the Welsh language, which had gone down badly with many voters. Although Rod Richards was cleared of the charge of GBH on 23 June, on 22 September he was stopped from making a possible return to Westminster by Michael Ancram and William Hague.

Although I had not considered applying to be a parliamentary candidate at the next general election, an unexpected opportunity arose in the marginal Brecon and Radnor constituency in September 2000. On 20 September a Mid and West Wales Area Conservative dinner was held at the Metropole Hotel, Llandrindod Wells, with William Hague as the guest speaker. The vote of thanks was then given by the Conservative candidate for Brecon and Radnor, Dr Peter Gooderham. It was felt that the Shrewsbury doctor's 'thank you' speech was much too long at 35 minutes. One guest at the dinner later claimed that people kept looking at their watches and it was obvious that

William Hague wondered how much longer he was going to go on for. He was also allegedly slightly the worse for wear, and he made virtually no reference to William Hague. As a consequence Peter Gooderham was forced to resign his candidature, signing a prepared press release that made the preposterous claim that he wanted to 'explore other professional developments'. However, Peter Gooderham had only played into the hands of his numerous critics within the Brecon and Radnor Conservative Association, who regretted having selected him in the first place.

The subsequent advertisement for a new parliamentary candidate for Brecon and Radnor provided the prospect of me getting selected in a winnable seat. Although there was a Liberal Democrat majority of 5,097 votes in 1997, when Richard Livsey had defeated the Conservative MP Jonathan Evans, the highly respected Livsey was retiring at the next general election. He had been replaced by local (Talgarth) farmer Roger Williams, making the constituency arguably more marginal. I was one of thirty-seven applicants and was delighted to receive a letter from the very formidable Conservative Association chairman, Edna Walters, inviting me for an interview before the Selection Committee at the Nothcote Conservative Club, Brecon, on 7 November 2000. I was fortunate that I was one of six people, from the twelve applicants interviewed, to face the Executive Council on 14 November at the same venue. On both occasions the questioners were very rigorous, with some people, particularly from Radnorshire, quite hostile. However, I got the impression that I had gained the private approval of Edna Walters and her treasurer Michael Sandford.

On 16 November I was informed that I had been invited to appear before a final selection meeting to be attended by the full membership of the Brecon and Radnor Conservative Association, which was to be held at the

Metropole Hotel, Llandrindod Wells on 20 November. The build-up to this event was to make many spy stories appear tame. Information was passed to me stating that while I had only come fourth out of six successful applicants in the Selection Committee interview stage, I had been catapulted to the first position after addressing the Executive Council. I was, however, informed that while I had very strong support amongst Conservative Party members in Breconshire, my support in Radnorshire was a great deal weaker. Moreover, the fact that the final selection meeting was to be held in Radnorshire was clearly going to be to my disadvantage. Nevertheless, the anonymous source told me not to be too despondent because 'what Edna wants, Edna usually gets'.

The final selection was a three-cornered contest between myself, O. J. Williams and Andrew Phillips. I had been informed that the fight was really between me and Andrew Phillips, a farmer and Herefordshire county councillor who lived just across the English border in Kington. His geographical proximity to Radnorshire would result in a great deal of support there. In order to ensure that the Breconshire members would attend the Llandrindod Wells meeting, Michael Sandford, on the instruction of Edna Walters, organised two coachloads of people, as well as carloads, with the military precision associated with his being a retired army major.

I was said to have 'pulled out all the stops' in my speech and in 'the assertive and knowledgeable way' that I answered questions. O. J. Williams was only an interested spectator, as several of his prominent supporters had already promised to vote for me in the event of a second ballot. Andrew Phillips had therefore to win a majority of the votes on the first ballot if he was to be selected. To the dismay of his very vocal supporters, Andrew Phillips was 'considerably behind' me when the first ballot result was announced. In the second vote, I gained the overwhelming majority of the less than thirty votes cast for O. J. Williams in the first round, plus some additional votes from the Llandrindod Wells area of Radnorshire, who now wanted to pick the strongest candidate to fight the Liberal Democrats.

Having achieved a 'decisive victory', I was unveiled as the Conservative parliamentary candidate for Brecon and Radnor. With less than six months before an expected general election I knew that I would have much work to do in what was geographically the largest constituency in England and Wales.

Mary and me with David Davies, Nick Bourne, William Graham and David Melding, Conservative Assembly members, Llandrindod Wells, February 2001

I attended the Welsh Conservative Party Conference held at the Brangwyn Hall, Swansea, on 8 and 9 March 2001. One of the most memorable events was at the conference dinner, hearing Falklands War veteran Simon Weston speaking of his horrendous wartime experiences.

However, there was much tension between Nigel Evans, the Shadow Secretary of State for Wales, who opposed granting more powers to the National Assembly, and some of the AM's such as David Melding, Jonathan Morgan and Glyn Davies, who favoured greater devolution. In politics, it is sometimes difficult to distinguish between personal and policy loyalties. For example, while policy-wise I supported a Welsh Parliament, I could strike up a far better rapport with a devolution sceptic like Nigel Evans than with some pro-devolutionists.

Since Brecon and Radnor was considered to be a fairly marginal constituency, several prominent Conservative politicians visited it during the 2001 general election campaign. These included Timothy Yeo speaking in Brecon, Michael Ancram in Knighton, Peter Walker in Rhayader, Michael Portillo in Llandrindod Wells, David Hunt in Llyswen, and Ann Widdecombe in Brecon. The last visit aroused much controversy as her well-known anti-hunting views were not popular with many traditional Conservative voters. Nonetheless, I was delighted to meet Ann again. The two of us had a very good-natured 'battle royal' over the controversial issue of fox-hunting where we held such diametrically opposed views.

This contest was a straight fight between me and Roger Williams, the LibDem candidate. Although both of us had been in the SDP during the early 1980s, we had both found new political homes within a short time of each other. Nevertheless, there remained mutual respect between us and friendly words were exchanged on several occasions during the election campaign. The Labour candidate and future government minister Huw Irranca-Davies was also a pleasant political opponent, as was Plaid Cymru's Brynach Parry. The Independent Business candidate Ian Mitchell was also quite amiable. However, there was considerable ill-feeling

With Edna Walters and others on the campaign trail, May 2001

Campaigning with Ann Widdecombe in Brecon, May 2001

between the other candidates and Liz Phillips of the United Kingdom Independence Party, and it seemed to me that her antagonistic attitude towards her political opponents did her more harm than good. Unfortunately, her attitude became even worse towards me, because her supporters were increasingly deserting her for the Conservative Party.

On 7 June, with polling day soon approaching, some political pundits were suggesting that the contest was 'wide open' and that there was still 'everything to play for'. Indeed, while one commentator predicted a Liberal Democrat win, he conceded that the Conservatives may have won the 'poster war'. The name 'Felix Aubel' was displayed on nearly a thousand placards, especially in Breconshire. The highly-respected election agent Brecon's Merfyn Jenkins, although well into his eighties, did an excellent job in ensuring that postal votes had been given to Conservative voters who were unable to vote on polling day.

I emphasised that a vote for the Liberal Democrats amounted to voting Labour as the two parties were in a coalition government in the National Assembly. There was also the traumatic issue of foot and mouth disease, on which I had been very supportive of local farmers and had campaigned vigorously alongside them during the Eppynt protests. I had also strongly promoted William Hague's campaign to 'Save the Pound', although the local response to this had been mixed. By contrast, the Liberal Democrats had emphasised Roger Williams's 'local man' credentials, with one eve-of-poll leaflet describing me as 'Hague's man from Aberaeron'. The other candidates all campaigned on their national manifestos.

The scenes at the election count in Brecon were dramatic, with the result finely balanced until the end. With Roger Williams less than 800 votes ahead of me, I called for a recount. When the final figure was announced there were only 751 votes between us. The result was:

Roger Williams (LD) 13,824 (36.85%)
Felix Aubel (Con) 13,073 (34.85%)
Huw Irranca-Davies (Lab) 8,024 (21.39%)
Brynach Parry (PC) 1,301 (3.47%)
Ian Mitchell (Ind) 762 (2.03%)
Liz Phillips (UKIP) 452 (1.2%)
Robert Nicholson (Ind) 80 (0.21%).

I had polled very strongly in the rural areas of Breconshire, with the towns favouring the Liberal Democrats. A similar pattern had occurred in Radnorshire. In Llandrindod Wells the Conservative vote had increased since 1997, but Roger Williams had won very decisive victories in the urban centres of Knighton and Presteigne. Many English incomers to East Radnorshire were known to have voted Liberal Democrat. Furthermore, many traditional Labour Party supporters in the former mining areas of Ystradgynlais and Aber-craf, where a fifth of the electorate resided, voted tactically Liberal Democrat in order to 'keep the Tory out'.

I have often been asked whether I was disappointed in not having been elected as the MP for Brecon and Radnor. Although publicly I was 'fighting to win', the election result was closer than I had expected. Privately I had anticipated that Roger Williams would win by around 1,500 votes, due primarily to the poor national Conservative opinion poll ratings and tactical voting by some Socialists who regarded voting Labour as a 'wasted vote'. By reducing the Liberal Democrat majority from 5,097 votes to a mere 751 votes, the Conservatives in Brecon and Radnor had defied the national trend. This became even more apparent when one considers that the Conservative vote locally had risen by nearly 6%, something which had been achieved in only one other Welsh constituency: this was by the very enthusiastic Stephen Crabb in Preseli Pembrokeshire.

Having failed to gain any Conservative parliamentary representation in Wales and making virtually no impact nationally, William Hague resigned the leadership of his party. The consequent Conservative leadership contest was to reveal underlying tensions between Nick Bourne and me. By the time Conservative MPs had decided that party members would have the choice of electing either Kenneth Clarke or Iain Duncan Smith as their new leader, Nick Bourne had endorsed the former on 3 July while I had plumped for the latter. Although I recognised that Kenneth Clarke had many leadership qualities, I simply could not accept that someone who supported further European integration, the Euro single currency, and who had shared a 'Britain in Europe' platform with Tony Blair in 1999, could become leader of the now largely Euro-sceptic Conservative Party. I therefore endorsed the comparatively unknown Iain Duncan Smith due to his principled opposition to closer political and economic links with the European Union. I was assisted by the fact that former Michael Portillo supporter Nigel Evans was also now endorsing Iain Duncan Smith for the same reason.

I was appointed on 27 July as Iain Duncan Smith's leadership campaign manager for Mid and West Wales, and was now responsible for ensuring that this region would defy the expressed wishes of Nick Bourne. On 21 August I organised a meeting at the Bishops Meadow Motel, Brecon, where more than 300 members of the Brecon and Radnor Conservative Association assembled to hear Iain Duncan Smith speak. This event was to achieve national press coverage, with the *Daily Mail*'s Quentin Letts, who covered the proceedings claiming that 'lots of those present had already decided to support Mr Duncan Smith'. Moreover, he echoed my private opinion that 'If Mr Duncan Smith does win this leadership contest it may be not because people think he is a whizzo but because they have graver doubts about the other bloke, Kenneth Clarke'.

When the result of the ballot for the Conservative leadership was announced on 14 September, I was delighted that Iain Duncan Smith had defeated Kenneth Clarke by 155,933 votes to 100,864 on a 79 per cent turnout. However, I concede that I put my scepticism towards the European Union before the electoral revival of the Conservative Party in promoting Iain Duncan Smith's candidature. Kenneth Clark was far more popular with potential Conservative voters and more likely to revive the party's electoral fortunes nationally than his more ideological and right-wing victorious opponent.

A most welcome distraction from this bruising Conservative leadership contest was the BBC *Week In Week Out* TV programme recorded in Caernarfon on 10 September 2001. The subject to be debated was 'Immigration into Wales and its effect on the Welsh language and culture'. I had been invited to attend as a member of a selected audience who were to be questioned by Betsan Powys. I was rather conveniently placed in the front row to sit alongside Welsh Nationalist firebrand Seimon Glyn who had recently made inflammatory remarks regarding 'English immigrants who are destroying Welsh-speaking communities'. The BBC had hoped to orchestrate a televised confrontation between us for the purpose of 'media entertainment'. What Betsan Powys and her colleagues had failed to realise was that I, particularly after my visit to Slovenia in 1999, shared many of Seimon Glyn's concerns relating to the survival of native Welsh-speaking communities. Protecting an indigenous language and culture was an inherent component of a native Welsh

Conservatism, which I was seeking to develop.

Before the recording of the *Week In Week Out* programme both Seimon Glyn and I had exchanged friendly words and there appeared to be a rapport between us. Unknown to Betsan Powys, we had agreed to outmanoeuvre the interviewer by jointly attacking 'anti-Welsh' elements in the audience. These were personified by the *Daily Mirror*'s Paul Starling, who had been ferocious in his criticisms of Seimon Glyn and of Cymuned, the cultural group established to support Glyn's views. This strategy worked perfectly and the look of surprise on Betsan Powys's face was a sight to behold! As a consequence of my actions on this TV programme, I was to begin an informal association with several 'cultural Welsh patriots'.

My strongly-held views regarding the dangers of the encroachment of the European Union on the sovereignty of the British Parliament led me to assist the non-party Democracy Movement in west Wales. I was strident in my opposition to the Nice Treaty that promoted further European political integration, and I attended a House of Commons lobby of MPs on 17 October 2001 in an attempt to persuade them to oppose its ratification. On 28 October I went on the London 'Stop the Euro Treaty 2000' march and rally organised by the Democracy Movement, which was attended by Euro-sceptics of all political persuasions from Britain and abroad.

The obvious internationalist nature of the opposition to further European integration clearly demonstrates that Euro-scepticism has nothing to do with xenophobia, as many of its critics suggest. Rather, it is a diverse collection of people who believe that it is democratically elected national governments that should be responsible for making laws for their respective citizens. It is for this reason that I have never been able to understand the Plaid Cymru policy of separating Wales from the United Kingdom and then allowing the EU to dictate policy to a so-called independent Wales. To me, 'Independence in Europe' is a contradiction in terms. Moreover, if Westminster is said by Plaid Cymru leaders to be too far from Wales to legislate in its interests, surely Brussels and Strasbourg are even more remote?

The underlying tensions between Nick Bourne and me extended beyond who both of us wanted to lead the Conservative Party. In the immediate aftermath of my general election result in Brecon and Radnor, there were several prominent local Conservatives who suggested that I should replace Nick Bourne as the National Assembly candidate in that constituency. It was stated that while Nick Bourne had lost to the Liberal Democrats by 5,852 votes in the 1999 National Assembly elections, I had only recently been defeated by 751 votes. It was therefore argued that I would be better placed to fight the Liberal Democrats. This possibility attracted press speculation, and Nick Bourne issued a statement claiming that 'Felix Aubel's political interests lay with Westminster' without even consulting me.

Whilst I had no intention in seeking the National Assembly nomination in Brecon and Radnor, I was annoyed that Nick Bourne had assumed my political intentions without consulting me regarding this matter. There was therefore some 'coolness' between us when we opened the new Conservative Party Office in Llandrindod Wells on 26 August. Nick Bourne also objected to the fact that I was using the Conservative office in Brecon as the address for campaign literature promoting Iain Duncan Smith's candidature for the leadership of the Conservative Party. I had also persuaded Edna Walters to chair the Iain Duncan Smith meeting in Bishops Meadow Motel on 21 August, compromising her supposed public political neutrality.

When Iain Duncan Smith was elected by a decisive

With Nick Bourne in Clyro, June 2002

majority over Kenneth Clarke on 14 September, there was press speculation that Nick Bourne would 'find it very difficult' to work with the new leader due to his strong support for Kenneth Clarke. The situation was further heightened when Iain Duncan Smith appointed the Eurosceptic Nigel Evans as the Shadow Secretary of State for Wales. *Wales on Sunday*'s Martin Shipton wrote on 16 September that 'Bourne faces Tory chop!' Whilst this was certainly an exaggeration, I was persuaded by a very senior person working in the Welsh Conservative Office at 4 Penlline Road, Whitchurch, to allow my name to be included on the new approved list of potential Conservative National Assembly candidates on 5 December. This now made it possible for me to seek the Conservative Party nomination in Brecon and Radnor, or anywhere else for that matter, if I so wished.

In the event, Nick Bourne was to go unchallenged for the

Conservative Party candidature in Brecon and Radnor when nominations closed on 9 January 2002. Furthermore, I pledged my support to Nick Bourne during his unopposed Selection Meeting at Bishops Meadow on 23 January. I therefore turned my attention towards Westminster instead, and was successful in having my name included on the new approved list of potential Conservative parliamentary candidates in March 2002.

Running parallel with the 'local difficulties' between Nick Bourne and me in Brecon and Radnor, was the final demise of Rod Richards's political career. On 12 December 2001 it was reported that Iain Duncan Smith had refused to intervene personally in order to try and force Nick Bourne to re-admit Rod Richards into the Conservative National Assembly group. This was in spite of the fact that Rod Richards had supported his campaign for the leadership of the Conservative Party. Nonetheless, the Welsh Conservative Party chairman Henri Lloyd Davies handed Rod Richards a political lifeline when he stated that he would be allowed an interview in order to try and become an approved potential National Assembly candidate.

The 90-minute interview took place at Cardiff's Quality Hotel on 12 December. It was reported on 16 December that the decision to reject Rod Richards was taken by three votes to two, with the deciding vote against him being cast by the panel's chairman Paul Valerio, a strong supporter of Nick Bourne. Rod Richards was found drunk in Llandaff Fields on 18 December. It was said that a passer-by dialled an ambulance because Rod Richards was in a collapsed state and not moving. He was then taken in a semi-conscious condition to the University of Wales Hospital in Cardiff.

Responding to this event Rod Richards made the somewhat ironic statement in the *Welsh Mirror* that 'I now accept that Rod the so-called Rottweiler is in need of real help from the RSPCA'. The *Western Mail*'s Toby Mason well summed up Rod Richards's predicament when he wrote on 20 December:

> For seldom in modern politics can one man have engineered such a fall from grace in a career marked by a legion of second chances. Whatever the future for Mr Richards now, he is a shadow of the politician who once walked the .corridors of powers and led the Conservatives in Wales.

One of the most interesting events around that time was the defection of the prominent Plaid Cymru member Guto Bebb to the Welsh Conservative Party. Whilst his change of allegiance was not formally announced until 22 January 2002, he had been seen by me 'keeping a very low profile' at the Welsh Conservative Policy Forum held at the Fairwater Conservative Club, Cardiff, on 1 December 2001. I was astonished that he had not been 'recognised' and later 'revealed' by the *Western Mail*'s Clive Betts who was covering the event. For once, Clive Betts was inexplicably blinkered. I had debated on S4C's current affairs programme *Maniffesto* on several occasions with Guto Bebb, who had come across as a conservative with a small 'c'. Indeed, he was always vociferous in his condemnation of Plaid Cymru's policy of supporting the European Single Currency.

Whilst I welcomed Guto Bebb's defection to the Welsh Conservative Party, Plaid Cymru's Elfed Williams wrote in the *Daily Post* of 30 January 2002:

> Guto Bebb is obviously a career politician who, after losing in the selection process for being a Plaid Cymru candidate in the last general election in both Caernarfon

and Clwyd West, has gone scuttling round Wales to find a party and a constituency that will select him as a candidate. He has now been selected as a candidate for the Conservative Party in the Ogmore by-election. I wish the Conservatives well with Mr Bebb – they will need it.

With polling day fixed for 14 February I was asked to serve as Guto Bebb's minder for the last week of this short election campaign. Mary and I stayed with the Owen Williams family, prominent local Conservatives, in Llanharan House. Although we were shown much hospitality I had difficulties with an unfriendly ghost who resided in the bathroom opposite our bedroom. On the first evening at Llanharan House, I went to wash in the very deep Victorian bath. I felt my head being pushed below the water level as I relaxed in the bath. The room became very misty and I again sensed that horrible choking feeling that indicated the presence of a hostile entity. Also, words were being telepathically communicated to me which amounted to: 'Get out of this room; you are not welcome here. I was a sailor who drowned at sea during the Second World War. You are now experiencing what it was like for me when I drowned!'

I eventually raised myself from this very deep enamel bath, and I ran into the corridor naked as fast as a lightning strike. Henceforth, I washed myself in a standing up position. I also telepathically insulted the hostile spirit before it could again communicate with me, thereby carrying out Napoleon Bonaparte's famous dictum that 'the best form of defence is attack'. Although this ghostly presence remained there during my visits to the bathroom, it was now rather subdued.

I recall how several Plaid Cymru helpers used to call Guto Bebb a 'traitor' to his face during the Ogmore election campaign. He was equally vociferous in his response, which only served to heighten the ill-feeling between the Conservative candidate and his former party. Labour's Hugh Irranca-Davies was the decisive winner in the election with 52 per cent of the vote and Guto Bebb trailed a distant fourth place with 7 per cent. Plaid Cymru was said to be privately very disappointed to have achieved only 21 per cent of the poll at a time when it was expected to pick up many protest votes from disillusioned traditional Labour Party supporters who were unhappy with Tony Blair's 'New Labour' Government. Plaid Cymru therefore appears to have allowed itself to be distracted from its objective of attacking the Labour Party by its public hostility towards Guto Bebb.

Another interesting event was Ann Widdecombe's visit to the Pantyrathro Mansion House, Llansteffan, on 5 April 2002. While coming to address a meeting of Conservative Party members, the former Shadow Home Secretary was confronted by more than fifty placard-waving pro-hunting demonstrators. Things became very heated in the exchanges between Ann Widdecombe and her opponents, while I attempted to direct her into the hotel. Whilst disagreeing with her opinions concerning hunting, I have nothing but admiration for this lady, who is one of the few politicians who is prepared to speak her mind regardless of the consequences.

The Welsh Conservative Party Conference was held at the North Wales Conference Centre, Llandudno, on 24 and 25 May. There I became even more aware of the deepening political and personal rivalry between Nigel Evans and Nick Bourne. The Swansea-born Nigel Evans regarded himself in his role as Shadow Welsh Secretary as the leader of the Conservative Party in Wales. Meanwhile, Nick Bourne, the Conservative National Assembly leader, argued that matters of policy relating to Wales should largely be in his hands.

Clive Betts summed up these differences very astutely when he wrote:

> The clashes are deep and bitter. One is Welsh while the other is very English – although he obtained a Law degree in Aberystwyth twenty years ago. Both have very different versions of the value of the Assembly. Mr Bourne was one of the first Tories to accept it after the referendum. Mr Evans remains a prominent sceptic. Mr Evans inclines towards a Thatcherite political vision, while Mr Bourne is a One-Nation supporter. Mr Bourne's politics is cerebral, while Mr Evans shoots from the hip.

The deep rivalry between Nigel Evans and Nick Bourne was to be demonstrated in Brecon and Radnor. Nigel Evans wanted me to be fast-tracked as the Conservative parliamentary candidate there by the summer of 2002. Edna Walters also favoured this course of action. Whilst I was on holiday in Jersey, a meeting of the Brecon and Radnor Conservative Association Executive Committee was held at the Nothcote Conservative Club on 17 June to discuss this matter. It was decided that I would be the only name placed before a special meeting of the Brecon and Radnor Conservative Association to be held on 3 July at the Metropole Hotel, Llandrindod Wells. According to the *Western Mail*'s Nick Speed, 'Spies at the meeting report that not everyone was pleased with the decision, with Assembly group leader Nick Bourne arguing it would be sensible to concentrate on the next poll in the electoral cycle first'. Nick Bourne was 'told' by Edna Walters to propose the motion at the Llandrindod Wells meeting adopting me as the Conservative candidate for Brecon and Radnor at the next general election. Here he claimed that 'Nick without Felix would be like Tim Henman without Greg Rusedski, or Ant without Dec'.

The year 2002 witnessed the career of Rod Richards reaching new lows. On 7 January he admitted to the press that he was an alcoholic and said that he would die unless he managed to break his addiction. He now intended to check into a 'drying-out' clinic for a fourth time in a bid to beat his booze problem. Rod Richards resigned his seat in the National Assembly on 10 September in order to begin a fight to 'beat the booze'. Clive Betts greeted this news by claiming that 'Talent, aggression, wit and misfortune are the defining characteristics of Rod Richards's political career'.

It was reported on 4 October that Rod Richards was 'fighting a bid to declare him bankrupt' arising from debts of around £100,000 owed to brewers Whitbread. He retorted by saying, 'How ironic would it be for a brewery to make an alcoholic bankrupt?' On 2 February 2003 he was declared bankrupt with debts of over £300,000 at the High Court in London. By late May 2003, Rod Richards was now bankrupt, unemployed and divorced thus bringing his once promising political career to a very sad end. Rod expressed his frustrations in the *Welsh Mirror* of 3 June under the prominent heading, 'Bunch of Bastards'. He defiantly asserted that 'The bunch of bastards that have been running the Conservative Party over the last two or three years, when I have finished with them are going to feel as though they have been f….d by a train!'

One of the most amusing recollections I have of the year 2003 was attending a meeting at the Blackwood Miners' Institute on 11 February, where Arthur Scargill was the guest speaker. As leader of the Socialist Labour Party, Scargill combined his opposition to the Iraq war with support for the firefighters' industrial dispute. He accused George Bush and Tony Blair of 'war crimes' and doubted that it was Al-Qaeda that was responsible for the 11 September catastrophe. He even suggested that the US Secret Service was behind the destruction of the twin towers in order to discredit the 'Islamist freedom fighters'. Arthur Scargill then brought his nonsensical speech to a close by announcing that he would stand in May's National Assembly elections in the South East Wales electoral division!

In interviews for the BBC's *Dragon's Eye* and HTV's *Waterfront*, I rather humorously welcomed Arthur Scargill's candidature for the National Assembly. Despite the obvious way that I had mocked Arthur Scargill, I was surprised by the negative way my comments were greeted by several prominent members of the Conservative Party. For example, the Welsh Conservative Party chairman Carol Hyde asked what this 'born-again Scargilite Communist' (me!) was doing attending the Conservative Party Conference? I believed that my comments in Blackwood were 'just good fun'. People should not be involved in politics unless they have a sense of humour!

The Welsh Conservative Party Conference was held at the City Hall, Cardiff, on 7 and 8 March 2003. Although serving as a build-up to the National Assembly elections on 1 May, this event was over-shadowed by the resignation of Ron Davies as the Labour AM for Caerphilly. This was the culmination of a week of allegations about the former Secretary of State for Wales's visit to Tog Hill, a notorious gay haunt near the M4 in Somerset. Just as in the case of his 'moment of madness' on Clapham Common in 1998, Ron Davies fell from grace not so much because of his activities but owing to the inept way he tried to 'explain' these embarrassing situations by being economical with the truth. He admitted to Paul Starling afterwards: 'Whether I've been the architect of my downfall is something I'll have to consider'. It was a tragic irony that the man who did more than anyone else to secure the National Assembly should find himself on the political scrapheap for almost a decade.

In my opinion both Ron Davies and Rod Richards possessed self-destruct mechanisms in their personalities. Soon after one personal or political mess was cleared-up, even bigger ones appeared on the horizon. It seems to me that neither person was able to learn from their mistakes, regardless of how many second chances they were to have in life.

(I was nevertheless delighted that Ron Davies was subsequently selected as the Plaid Cymru candidate for the Caerphilly constituency at the May 2011 National Assembly elections, since he has still much to contribute to Welsh politics. It was with sadness that I heard the news of his defeat, which deprives the Assembly of a great visionary.)

Although I assisted Nick Bourne's campaign to get elected to the National Assembly in Brecon and Radnor, I felt that I was not being utilised as much as I should have been. I was given no campaign schedule and was not even notified of election strategy meetings if they existed. It seemed inevitable that the Welsh Conservative leader would have to campaign outside his own constituency, therefore I felt that I should have been more involved in the proceedings. However, I regarded Nick Bourne's strategy of visiting every seat in Wales as a time-wasting exercise, which would have an adverse affect on his efforts to dislodge the formidable Liberal Democrat AM Kirsty Williams. This proved to be the case, as Kirsty Williams trounced Nick Bourne by a majority of 5,308 votes or 19.77 per cent. Upon hearing this very disappointing Conservative election result, I was devastated. It appeared that all my work in reducing the Liberal Democrat parliamentary majority to a mere 751 votes, or 2 per cent had been in vain. Had it not been for Mary Davies and Edna Walters, I would have immediately resigned my parliamentary candidacy.

8

For the ensuing municipal year I was delighted to be appointed, on 16 May 2003, chaplain to Councillor Stan Thomas, the new chairman of Ceredigion County Council. His Induction Sunday Service was held on 1 June at Neuaddlwyd Chapel where Stan Thomas was a nominal member. I soon learnt there were certain perks to being chaplain to Stan Thomas. There was plenty of free food and drink for the councillors and the chaplain to consume while attending various social functions.

During these events, I was told various anecdotes. For instance, it was always worth attending social events organised by Neath-Port Talbot and Merthyr Tydfil councils because of their 'generosity'. It was ironic that the self-styled party of the working-classes, Labour, was the most extravagant in spending the taxes of ordinary people on social entertainment. On the other hand, Independent-controlled Powys County Council was labelled 'mean' for not handing out lots of free booze as gifts. It therefore seems that several Ceredigion councillors only attended events organised by other local government authorities if the 'corporate hospitality' was generous enough to make it worth while for them to do so. I was therefore understandably disappointed when my year as chaplain came to an end on 25 May 2004.

Unfortunately, Edna Walters had to relinquish her position as constituency chairman in Brecon and Radnor on 20 March 2003, because her three-year term had come to an end. She was replaced by Mary Fellowes from Hay-on-Wye, a very pleasant lady but who lacked Edna's political astuteness.

Writing in the *Western Mail* on 16 May, I claimed that,

'By granting the Welsh Assembly powers of primary legislation in those areas such as health and education, which are already devolved, the process of devolution will be strengthened'. I elaborated on this theme on 19 June, asserting that 'Wales can only manage without a full-time Secretary of State if we have a Welsh Parliament with real powers, as in Scotland'. I had recently had a holiday in Jersey, and I concluded by saying that Wales had much to learn from the system of government in operation there. On 7 August I outlined in the *Western Mail* that: 'Constitutionally, Jersey is a dependency of the Crown, owing allegiance to the Sovereign. Effectively, it is self-governing in internal matters but the UK Government is responsible for defence and international affairs generally'.

Outside the Jersey Parliament, June 2005

These pro-devolution comments resulted in a very hostile response from Peter Weavers, the newly-elected vice-chairman of the Brecon and Radnor Conservative Association. This ardent anti-devolutionist, who wanted the Conservative Party to adopt a policy of abolishing the National Assembly, also attacked Nick Bourne for merely supporting the status quo. Things escalated further after I had attended a meeting of the pro-devolution Conservative Ymlaen group. This was held at David Melding AM's house in Barry. Here I was also accompanied by Jonathan Morgan AM and several other pro-devolutionist Conservatives from west Wales, such as

Paul Davies who had contested Preseli Pembrokeshire at the 2003 National Assembly elections.

On 27 October David Melding claimed, in a speech to the Institute of Welsh Politics at Aberystwyth, that the Conservative Party's policy of opposition to further powers for the National Assembly was unsustainable. He argued that 'The Welsh Conservative Party should no longer defend the Labour Party's flawed settlement'. David Melding ended with the challenge to his party that 'the people of Wales should now be offered the real choices given to Scotland and Northern Ireland in 1997/98'.

Peter Weavers was very annoyed with David Melding's comments and would become even more annoyed with me, when I defended the AM in the *Western Mail* of 3 November. I said: 'David Melding is a patriotic Welsh Conservative who rightly believes that the National Assembly needs to gain full primary legislative powers if it is to deliver better public services to the people of Wales'. Aiming my fire-power at those anti-devolutionists who had called for Nick Bourne to expel David Melding from the Welsh Conservative group in the National Assembly, I asserted that 'The time has come for those Assembly sceptics within the Welsh Conservative Party to accept that devolution is a process rather than an event. The next stage of this process is parity with Scotland'. Glyn Davies now stated that he favoured greater powers for the National Assembly – yet he would prefer to see the Assembly abolished than remain as it is.

Tensions were high at the Welsh Conservative Party Policy Forum held at Fairwater Conservative Club, Cardiff, on 8 November. Here Nick Bourne tried to defend the indefensible by claiming that 'the settled will of the people in 1997 was for devolution in its current form. That is our policy; that is our message. Any other message is not the party's message'. Nick Bourne had pleased neither the anti or pro-devolutionists and had arguably defended the worst of three possible options. I was annoyed with Nick Bourne, because he had refused to take the anti-devolutionists head on. Whilst I believed that Nick Bourne was privately more sympathetic to devolution, his public hesitancy displayed a lack of principle and courage in politics. This only added weight to Rod Richards's view that 'the only political principle that motivated Nick Bourne was the self-preservation and self-promotion of Nick Bourne'.

On 21 January 2004 I resigned as the Conservative parliamentary candidate for Brecon and Radnor. In a letter to Mary Fellowes, I wrote:

> I have become increasingly disillusioned by the very hostile attitude of one or two prominent Conservative officials in Brecon and Radnor regarding my views on the National Assembly. Whatever one's opinions the National Assembly is here to stay and it is our duty to make it work for the benefit of everyone in Wales. Unfortunately, the current devolution settlement is not delivering better public services for the people of Wales and the National Assembly can only be improved if it is granted real power. Why should we in Wales continue to be treated as second-class citizens in comparison with the Scottish people who have a proper parliament with primary legislative powers over large areas of domestic affairs? It is also a Europe-wide phenomenon that smaller nations like the Basques and Catalans have been granted greatly increased powers over their affairs, while remaining part of a federal Spain. Why should Wales be treated any differently?

In order to preserve Conservative Party unity, I issued a

press release declaring that 'work commitments' were responsible for my resignation. There was also much truth to this because as I told the *Western Mail*'s Martin Shipton and *Dragon's Eye*'s David Williams: 'My significant employment commitments as a Welsh Congregational minister, chaplain to Ceredigion County Council, freelance lecturer and broadcaster, place considerable restrictions on the time I can devote to nursing such a large constituency as Brecon and Radnor'.

Recent guidelines issued by Conservative Central Office had demanded an amount of time from candidates in marginal constituencies that I simply could not fulfil due to my various work commitments. I also stressed that I would continue to remain active in promoting the Welsh Conservative Party.

While differences over devolution were a contributory factor behind my resignation, together with the difficulties in trying to fit in campaigning around increasing work commitments, the overriding reason for my resignation was that I did not believe that I could win the seat at the next general election. Nick Bourne's crushing defeat in the National Assembly elections and its acute effect on local Conservative morale had convinced me that there was no point spending so much time on a lost cause. This decision was vindicated at the 2005 general election. Roger Williams defeated his new Conservative opponent Andrew R. T. Davies, a Vale of Glamorgan farmer and then Welsh Assembly abolitionist, by 3,905 votes, or 10.18 per cent. The Liberal Democrat majority had been increased by more than five-fold.

Meanwhile, there were growing question marks over Iain Duncan Smith's leadership of the Conservative Party. He faced a vote of no confidence from his fellow Conservative MPs on 29 October 2003. I accepted an invitation from

Dragon's Eye's David Williams to accompany him to Westminster in order to comment on the outcome. Whilst the amiable David Williams attempted to 'persuade' me to say that MPs should ditch Iain Duncan Smith before the vote of no confidence, I was to remain a loyal supporter of Iain's until the end. After all, I had organised his successful leadership bid in Mid and West Wales, and I also shared his Euro-scepticism.

In a desperate attempt to get me to change my mind, David Williams utilised the services of the formidable Quentin Letts of the *Daily Mail*. Quentin Letts even tried appealing to my self-interest by claiming that I would have a better chance of winning Brecon and Radnor with Kenneth Clarke at the helm! Whilst privately I agreed with Quentin Letts, my verbal comments continued to display outward loyalty. When Iain Duncan Smith was deposed by 75 votes to 90 votes by his fellow Conservative MPs, I stuck to my line that this was a 'tragedy'. After all, loyalty is highly prized amongst most ordinary Conservative Party members. I also supported Ian Duncan Smith's endorsement of Michael Howard as his unopposed successor.

I continued to be a spokesman for the Welsh Conservative Party on television and radio. Nick Bourne was attempting to close down debate within the Conservative Party on the recently published Richard Commission Report on granting more powers to the National Assembly. This was blatantly obvious during the Welsh Conservative Party Conference held at the North Wales Conference Centre, Llandudno on 2 and 3 April 2004. In an article published inthe Welsh-language periodical *Barn* that month, I stated that I saw no necessity for a referendum on granting limited primary legislative powers to the National Assembly, as suggested by Lord Ivor Richard. This was because it amounted to little more than a tidying-up process to improve the workings of that institution. I then challenged Nick Bourne to begin taking the initiative on the issue of the National Assembly's powers, rather only accepting political changes when they had occurred!

About this time, Ceredigion County Council's Unitary Development Plan or UDP envisaged building 6,500 new houses by 2010, many of which were beyond the reach of ordinary people to afford. Various groups were formed in 2002 and 2003 to oppose this plan, one of which, a cross-party group, took the name Llais y Cardi (*Voice of the Cardi*). As a means of trying to scuttle the UDP, they gathered a petition with more than 8,500 signatures, demanding that the county be run by an elected mayor, rather than by the ruling Independent-Liberal Democrat coalition. Llais y Cardi's hope was that if a majority of people voted for an elected mayor, a subsequent mayoral election would result in someone being elected to that position who opposed the UDP. This could then serve to scuttle the current UDP and result in a new one being drawn up that was more favourably disposed to preserving the indigenous language and culture. The hard-working group – including a substantial number of Plaid Cymru members – gathered the required number of signatures, and presented the petition to the County Council offices in Aberaeron in November 2003. The County Council verified the signatures, and all was set for the referendum on having a mayor.

Up to that day, Llais y Cardi was simply a campaigning group collecting signatures, and a very successful operation it was. But later in the month things changed when, at a meeting in Lampeter, members of the group, led by Gwilym ab Ioan, voted to turn Llais y Cardi into a political party, with the new name of Llais Ceredigion. This was announced to Plaid Cymru in a private meeting a little later, and they responded with shock, seeing the potential of vote-splitting, particularly in future Council elections.

With polling day fixed for 20 May, an all-party pro-mayoral grouping was established to campaign for a 'Yes' vote. The campaign launch was held at the Feathers Royal Hotel, Aberaeron on 5 April. Speakers included Emyr Hywel, chairman of Llais Ceredigion and a former chairman of the Welsh Language Society; Siôn Jobbins, former mayor of Aberystwyth and Plaid Cymru National Assembly candidate for Preseli Pembrokeshire in 2003; and me on behalf of the Welsh Conservative Party. A message of support was passed on to the campaign by Labour representative Howard Williams.

During the campaign, I sought to link a genuinely Welsh Conservatism with the preservation of the Welsh language and culture when I stated in the *Cambrian News* of 14 April that:

> It is a fundamental Conservative principle to protect and nurture traditional rural communities and values. This is best done by ensuring there are affordable homes available for those people who wish to live and work in the communities where they were born and bred. There is nothing inherently nationalistic about this, since Conservative councillors in Shropshire, for example, are at the forefront of the attempt there to provide affordable houses for local people.

One of the most interesting events of the Ceredigion campaign for an elected mayor was S4C's TV debate from the Mwldan Theatre, Cardigan, on 10 May. This was between Emyr Hywel and me on the one side and Ceredigion Council leader Dai Lloyd Evans and local Plaid

Cymru AM Elin Jones on the other. It was a very significant event in Welsh politics seeing a Welsh Nationalist and a Welsh Conservative standing shoulder to shoulder in an attempt to preserve indigenous Welsh-speaking communities. However, nearly all of the nationalistic movements in Eastern Europe who rebelled against Soviet Communist oppression were Conservative in their political orientation. Nationalism and Conservatism therefore went hand in hand without the need for Socialism. This is something Plaid Cymru's current very left-wing leadership would be wise to remember.

With the approach of polling day, it became clear that the proposal for an elected mayor in Ceredigion would be overwhelmingly defeated. The leadership of all the established political parties, including Plaid Cymru, had decided to support a 'No' vote. Plaid Cymru had made a huge tactical gamble here, hoping that they would win control of Ceredigion County Council after the elections on 10 June and thereby be able to modify the UDP in order to be more sympathetic to local needs. After all, Plaid Cymru would have to nearly double their council representation from the current twelve members to twenty-two in order to gain an overall majority on the local authority!

The mayoral campaign had become highly personal, with the 'No' side adopting a policy of character assassination on some of their 'Yes' opponents. For example, Dai Lloyd Evans compared Llais Ceredigion members to the British National Party. The prominent 'Yes' campaigner and former chairman of Plaid Cymru in Ceredigion, Gwilym ab Ioan, was smeared in the press for allegedly being declared bankrupt on two occasions. Emyr Hywel was unfairly blamed for the financial collapse of the Cnapan cultural festival, which he had helped organise for several years. Simon Brooks of Cymuned was branded a political extremist and had to endure much personal abuse from several Plaid Cymru members in the village of Talybont where he and his young family lived (at least one of whom had been out collecting signatures for the earlier petition!). It was also alleged that I was only supporting the 'Yes for Mayor' campaign because I wanted the job myself. Nothing could have been further from the truth.

The referendum result was declared at Aberaeron Memorial Hall on 21 May. Ceredigion voters rejected plans for Wales's first ever directly-elected mayor by 14,013 votes to 5,308 on a 36 per cent turnout. In percentage terms this proposal had been rejected by 72.5 per cent to 27.5 per cent.

This result came about because all the major political parties closed ranks and got their supporters out to vote 'No'. Many of the Plaid Cymru supporters who had signed the petition calling for a mayoral referendum in the first place were apparently persuaded by the well-oiled Plaid machine to fall into line by voting 'No' – it seems that this attitude was taken to snub Gwilym ab Ioan, who had left the Plaid Cymru National Executive some years before. Had Plaid Cymru campaigned for a 'Yes' vote, the referendum result may well have gone the other way. I was also convinced that a turning-point in the campaign was when it was revealed that an elected mayor would legally have been unable to overturn the UDP without the support of the majority of county councillors.

It is perhaps ironic that the majority of the 'Yes' voters were English incomers living in the Ceredigion coastal belt. Some of these people apparently cared more about the preservation of the indigenous culture than large numbers of the native Welsh-speakers themselves. Unlike many of the indigenous Welsh-speaking landowning interests who were influential in the ruling local authority group, these incomers did not stand to gain financially by selling their land to housing developers. Some of them may also have suspected that prominent natives of the county stood to gain financially from the building of more than 6,500 new homes in Ceredigion.

With the referendum now over, Simon Thomas MP called for Llais Ceredigion to disband and support Plaid Cymru's attempt to win control of the county council. In the light of his bitter attacks on the 'Yes' campaign during the referendum, Llais Ceredigion decided to field their own county council candidates who would stand on the platform of opposing the UDP. When these results were declared at Aberaeron Memorial Hall on 11 June, one witnessed the demise of those people who put principle first. Although Llais Ceredigion and Llais Aberaeron candidates polled well over a thousand votes in the six wards they stood in, none came close to being elected.

My partner Mary Davies, who stood under the Llais Aberaeron designation because she was still a member of the Welsh Conservative Party, was the only candidate to gain second position in a contest where there were more than two candidates. She achieved a creditable 27 per cent of the vote in the Aberaeron ward. By contrast, former Ceredigion Conservative Association vice-chairman David Williams, who had left the party to join Llais Ceredigion, secured only 15 votes and 2 per cent of the poll in the Llanrhystyd ward. Meanwhile, Gwilym ab Ioan was defeated by Dai Lloyd Evans in the Lledrod ward by 682 votes against 319. Emyr Hywel had to suffer the indignity of coming bottom of the poll in the Aberporth ward, where he had come within forty votes of winning when standing as a Plaid Cymru candidate there only a year or so previously. His brother Glyndŵr Howells also came bottom in the Beulah ward, as did Michael Dawe, a former Welsh Conservative Party branch chairman, in the Penparc ward.

Although Plaid Cymru made an overall gain of four council seats, the local authority remained under the control of Dai Lloyd Evans's Independent-Liberal Democrat administration. Simon Brooks wrote the following words in the *Cambrian News* of 24 June:

> The cruel fact is that Plaid Cymru gambled with the future of Ceredigion and lost. They backed up Dai Lloyd Evans, wrecked the referendum campaign for an elected mayor, and made cast-iron promises to their supporters that they would win control of the council. Dai Lloyd Evans has acted in a rational way over the past two months seeking to defend his own political power base. Plaid Cymru has spent the past two months misleading its own supporters, and batting for the opposition. The mayoral Campaign could have given Plaid Cymru control of Ceredigion County Council on a plate. By persuading Plaid supporters to vote 'No', council group leader Penri James snatched defeat from the jaws of victory.

Emyr Hywel was even more scathing in his condemnation of Plaid Cymru's antics when he wrote in the *Daily Post* of 26 June: 'Both Plaid Cymru and the Welsh Language Society must take responsibility for what has happened. They are responsible that the UDP has been given the go-ahead, and they are responsible that Welsh faces wipe-out as a community language in the county'.

The European parliamentary elections were also held on 10 June. Being a Euro-sceptic I was impressed by the excellent election campaign run by the prominent TV celebrity and former Labour MP Robert Kilroy Silk on behalf of the United Kingdom Independence Party, which emphasised how Britain was paying £5 billion year membership fee to the EU which could rise to more than £11 billion by 2014.

I voted Conservative in the European parliamentary elections, out of personal loyalty to Jonathan Evans MEP. Although we sometimes disagreed on Britain's relationship with Europe, I have always admired Jonathan Evans's political skills as well as liking him personally. He had also been very supportive of my candidature in Brecon and Radnor. I was therefore delighted that Jonathan Evans defeated Plaid Cymru's Jill Evans for the third out of four Welsh seats in the European Parliament.

During a meeting of Llais Ceredigion held at the Llanina Arms, Llanarth, on 24 June, it was decided to carry on as a separate political entity. Morale, however, was very low amongst the members and supporters. On 24 July a social gathering was held at Rhydybroga, Llangoedmor, the home of Michael and Marian Dave, for all of the Llais Ceredigion helpers. This was little more than a funeral wake. One of the very few constructive things to emerge from this get-together was the desire of some of those present to establish a Welsh think-tank in order to stimulate debate on the major political issues affecting Wales.

The idea of establishing the Machynlleth Group was proposed by Gwilym ab Ioan. His proposal was supported by me and given a qualified endorsement by Simon Brooks. By contrast, Emyr Hywel was sceptical when he said: 'I must now accept that everything that I have ever fought for politically will now never happen'.This was to be a sad truism, because Llais Ceredigion had its last political meeting on 30 October. It was to remain in a 'nominal' state of existence under the new chairmanship of Gwilym ab Ioan, but it was really almost as dead as the dodo.

The Machynlleth Group was established in Owain Glyndŵr's famous Parliament House on 6 November. This

Welsh political think tank was to be little more than the 'walking corpse' of the Ceredigion 'Yes for Mayor' campaign with a north Wales input. Amongst those present were the former Ceredigion Conservative Association stalwarts David Williams and Michael Dawe, together with present Welsh Conservative Party members Mary Davies and me. There was Simon Brooks and Gwilym ab Ioan from the Ceredigion Branch of Cymuned, as well as that organisation's new chief executive, Aran Jones, who ran Cymuned nationally from Pwllheli. Wyn Hobson from Bangor was another Cymuned stalwart and one of the sharpest minds that I have ever encountered. Then there was Royston Jones, a former member of the Free Wales Army during the 1960s. Royston Jones wore a gold ring on his finger with the FWA insignia engraved upon it and I was surprised that he could not speak Welsh.

The majority of the members present agreed that this discussion group should follow the example of the Fabian Society, but without the socialist aspirations of that body. Gwilym ab Ioan commented that 'Wales needs yet another socialist body as badly as a slug needs salt'. He also claimed there was a vacuum in Welsh politics to the right of centre of the present political spectrum that the Machynlleth Group could fill. These comments resulted in a bitter disagreement between Simon Brooks and Gwilym ab Ioan, with the former walking out of the meeting!

Simon Brooks accused Gwilym ab Ioan of wanting to establish a new Welsh political party. This underlying tension went back to two years previously. Gwilym ab Ioan wanted Cymuned to become a political party to fight for the allegiance of traditionally Welsh-speaking communities, rather than being merely a language pressure group like the rival Welsh Language Society. By contrast, Simon Brooks successfully opposed this idea because he believed that the purpose of Cymuned was to create a non-party organisation to fight for the civil rights of Welsh-speakers in an increasingly anglicised Wales.

Gwilym ab Ioan had been a former vice-president of Plaid Cymru but had resigned from the party in January 2002 to join the Independent Wales Party (IWP). Prior to this, Gwilym had refused to be silenced by Plaid Cymru in 2001 after complaining that parts of Wales were being invaded and colonised by an element of 'English drop-outs, scroungers and retired people who are destroying the indigenous communities'. At the launch of the IWP he accused Plaid Cymru of 'selling out' to the English political establishment and of having no more concern for the indigenous population than the other three political parties represented in the National Assembly. In a venomous attack on his former party, Gwilym ab Ioan said:

> Plaid is just Old Labour with a Welsh face. Plaid has been hijacked by a left-wing socialist clique desperate for personal power at any price, even though this has reduced a once proud party into a spineless, establishment-friendly, favour-begging-bowl carrier, run by a handful of quasi-Welsh, liberal-minded, cap-doffing Uncle Toms.

After the collapse of the IWP due largely to internal dissent, Gwilym ab Ioan, along with Royston Jones established the short-lived Plaid y Werin. One of Royston Jones's favourite books was *Sons of the Romans – The Tory as Nationalist*, written by the right-wing Plaid Cymru member from the Rhondda, H. W. J. Edwards, which had a foreword by Enoch Powell.

Like the nineteenth-century Irish Nationalist leader Daniel O'Connell, Royston Jones regarded the indigenous language as an obstacle in the struggle to achieve political independence. Royston Jones wrote in his journal *Ein Gwlad*, in December 2005:

> In terms of our national interest the Welsh language is subversive to our progress towards independence. Division by language merely plays into the hands of those loyal to the status quo. Plaid Cymru has been so corrupted by left-liberalism, political correctness and attendant follies that it will no longer speak up for the nation. A new kind of nationalism, one that lives up to its name by being a political movement for the entire nation, not just those whose primary concern is the Welsh language is needed.

In other words, Royston Jones believed that the 'respectable' Welsh-speaking middle-class elite who are at the heart of Plaid's electoral support would always place campaigning for the preservation of the Welsh language above the struggle for political independence.

Whatever may have been Gwilym ab Ioan's real motives in establishing the Machynlleth Group, there was no appetite for forming yet another political party amongst the clear majority of members present. The Conservative or ex-Conservative Party members wanted a genuine policy forum to begin possible co-operation between Welsh cultural patriots and the pro-Welsh element within the Welsh Conservative Party. Indeed, I wished to build on the rapport I had established a couple of years previously with people like Seimon Glyn and Gwilym Euros Roberts.

With attendance figures declining from meeting to meeting the Machynlleth Group was becoming a 'corpse waiting to be buried'. A decision was made to 'suspend' group meetings on 11 November, although one or two discussion papers were circulated via the internet, until even that came to an end in 2006. It appears that several prominent members of Plaid Cymru feared that this centre-right grouping could one day challenge Plaid's monopoly of the nationalist vote in Wales. The Machynlleth Group may therefore have been undermined from within by the more pro-Plaid element within the new leadership of Cymuned after the departure of Simon Brooks, Wyn Hobson and Gwilym ab Ioan from prominent positions within that organisation.

I also believe that this was one of the reasons why Plaid Cymru made the strategic decision to scuttle the campaign for an elected mayor in Ceredigion. If Llais Ceredigion had won the referendum and had established a presence on the county council, other groups of Welsh patriots in other parts of Wales would be encouraged to do likewise, thereby breaking Plaid's hold on the political allegiance of Welsh Nationalist voters. This was to occur in May 2008 in Gwynedd, when Llais Gwynedd succeeded in denying Plaid Cymru a majority of seats on Gwynedd County Council, primarily as a result of a 'people's rebellion' against the policy of closing small rural schools approved by the Plaid administration.

A special *Pawb a'i Farn* TV programme relating to English immigration into Wales and hosted by Dewi Llwyd, was recorded at Aberaeron Leisure Centre on 2 December 2004. During that week a series of excellent programmes produced by Euros Lewis of Cribyn had been broadcast on S4C called *Croeso i Gymru*. They related to the experiences of three different English-speaking families who had moved to live in largely Welsh-speaking communities. A panel of politicians and an invited audience were asked to discuss these programmes and the effects of English immigration into Wales. The panel included Plaid Cymru's Simon

Thomas MP, Ross Hendry from the Labour Party, Nick Bennett from the Liberal Democrats and me representing the Welsh Conservative Party. I was fortunate, because several people connected to Llais Ceredigion, Gwilym ab Ioan, David Williams, Mike and Marion Dawe, Mary Davies and Simon Brooks, agreed to be members of the audience.

This was one of the most enjoyable out of more than a dozen *Pawb a'i Farn* TV programmes that I have done over the years. The agreed strategy between me and my supporters in the audience was to give Simon Thomas a difficult time. This was because of his very hostile attitude towards Llais Ceredigion during the Mayoral referendum. He was accused of hypocrisy when he attempted to express his support for the Welsh language and the importance of preserving traditional Welsh communities. Plaid Cymru was attacked for now being a left-wing socialist party whose prime interest was to seek to win disillusioned Old Labour voters in the south Wales valleys, rather than defending the linguistic and cultural interests of its traditional primarily rural supporters. This message seemed to strike a chord with several members of the audience and I received more rounds of applause than the MP for Ceredigion. The very lukewarm reception Simon Thomas received that evening may well have been a bad omen for his future!

The year 2005 opened with tensions within the Welsh Conservative Party over the issue of the powers of the National Assembly. On 6 January the *Western Mail* reported that Nick Bourne had expressed his qualified support for limited law-making powers for the National Assembly. Here he declared:

I am in favour of the Assembly getting law-making powers, but that should happen over a period of time. We and other non-Labour parties should be prepared to be pragmatic and work to achieve an agreed programme to provide an alternative government to the Labour administration in the Assembly. This can only be achieved if the Welsh Conservative Party comes into line with the other opposition parties in supporting more powers for the National Assembly.

Political self-interest was obviously the motive behind Nick Bourne's statement, in the sense that he hoped one day to be in the Cabinet of a non-Labour coalition administration in Cardiff Bay. He had, however, now attempted to move the Welsh Conservative Party forward in a more progressive direction. This move was therefore welcomed by me and other pro-devolutionist Conservatives like David Melding, Jonathan Morgan and Glyn Davies. By contrast, Bill Wiggin, the Shadow Welsh Secretary appointed by Michael Howard, declared on 20 January his personal preference for abolishing the Welsh Assembly. His comments angered several senior Welsh Conservatives and exploded an uneasy truce within the party over the National Assembly's powers. To further complicate matters, Michael Howard favoured a so-called 'Preferendum', where voters would be able to list in order of preference their opinions from a list likely to include independence, an Assembly with law-making powers, the status quo and abolition. Yet Michael Howard refused to reveal which option he would personally support, although privately it was said that he favoured abolition.

This idea of a 'Preferendum' only resulted in worsening Conservative divisions over the issue of devolution. At one end of the spectrum were abolitionists like Bill Wiggin, the 'Monmouthshire Mafia', and former North Wales AM David Jones. Meanwhile, at the other end were those favouring law-making powers in line with the recommendations of the Richard Report, such as David

Melding and myself. Nick Bourne characteristically put himself somewhere in the middle – favouring law-making powers but on a slower timetable than the 2007 deadline suggested by Lord Richard.

It appears that Michael Howard's idea of a 'Preferendum' was really an attempt to abolish the National Assembly by the back door. This was certainly the interpretation of Peter Davies, chairman of the South-East Wales Area of the Welsh Conservative Party and father of Monmouth AM David Davies. In a letter published in the *Western Mail* on 27 January 2005, Peter Davies wrote in his characteristically forthright way:

> After five years, whether it's health, education, social services, local government, or indeed anything else it touches, the Assembly is seen to be a complete and utter failure. Michael Howard is right to promise us another referendum, thereby giving us a chance to get rid of this monstrous leech on the Welsh taxpayers.

These divisions became even more obvious at the Welsh Conservative Party Conference held at the Millennium Stadium, Cardiff, on 4 and 5 March. Bill Wiggin urged delegates to campaign for the abolition of the National Assembly and received some of the loudest applause of the conference's first day. A further party split opened up as Glyn Davies rubbished Nick Bourne's vision for a coalition with Plaid Cymru and the Liberal Democrats to challenge the Labour-led administration in the National Assembly. He said: 'Nick has his personal opinion. It's not been discussed within the Assembly group and I don't agree with it. I don't really want a coalition. Neither do I want to be talking about a coalition before a general election'.

With polling day for the 2005 general election on 5 May,

I assisted the very energetic Stephen Crabb's campaign in the now much more marginal constituency of Preseli Pembrokeshire. Conservative morale locally was very high, with the constituency Labour Party divided over the issue of an imposed all-woman short-list of applicants to replace Jackie Lawrence, who was not seeking re-election. I was delighted that Stephen Crabb was elected with a majority of 607 votes over his Socialist opponent. I was also very pleased that Wales could no longer be regarded as a 'Tory Free Zone' because there were two other Conservative victors on the night, David Jones in Clwyd West and David Davies in Monmouth.

Whilst I had campaigned for a Conservative Party victory nationally, there were very important local considerations at stake in the Ceredigion constituency where I lived. Plaid Cymru MP Simon Thomas, in the words of Gwilym ab Ioan, had made 'vindictive, untrue and vitriolic attacks' on Llais Ceredigion during the Mayoral referendum and County Council elections in 2004. As far as many of these people who had been on the receiving end of these attacks were concerned, the 2005 general election brought an opportunity for 'payback time'. It is known that several prominent members of Llais Ceredigion did not vote Plaid Cymru for the first time in their lives. Also, dozens of erstwhile pro-mayoral supporters voted for the Liberal Democrat candidate, Mark Williams, as being the most likely person to unseat Simon Thomas. These votes may have been crucial to the election's outcome, since Simon Thomas was to lose to the Liberal Democrats by only 219 votes.

In a letter published in the *Cambrian News* of 12 May, and headed 'The wages of betrayal is rejection,' Gwilym ab Ioan analysed the factors behind Simon Thomas's election defeat. Some of the most thought-provoking extracts are quoted below:

What seems to have slipped under the radar in Ceredigion is the resentment felt after Plaid Cymru spectacularly stabbed Llais Ceredigion and Cymuned in the back during last year's Mayoral referendum. The Plaid leadership has a short memory, not so the ordinary electorate, many of whom are still seething over the way Plaid jumped into bed with Dai Lloyd Evans and co. Llais Ceredigion got decimated and Cymuned got weakened, much to the glee at the time of the arrogant Plaid leadership. The chickens have come home to roost. If you sow thorn seeds you reap thorns during your harvest.

During the election campaign Simon Thomas had laughed off suggestions that Ceredigion would fall to the Liberal Democrats, saying the party was a 'spent force in the area'. Simon Thomas was also a bad loser, blaming 'student voters from England' and 'tactical voting by Tories' for his completely unexpected defeat. Meanwhile, I was delighted with the result in Ceredigion.

One of the most enjoyable evenings I had during the latter part of 2005, was attending 'An Audience with George Galloway MP' at the Aberystwyth Arts Centre on 3 October. This one-man show by the controversial left-wing anti-Iraq War MP was to prove to be excellent entertainment and well worth the £9 admittance fee. However much some people have questioned George Galloway's sincerity, he proved to be a first class public speaker who could combine humour with devastating criticisms.

George Galloway described Tony Blair as 'the sanctimonious vicar, his voice catching with fake sincerity, sounding like a TV evangelist caught sleeping with hookers and paying for them by skimming the collection'. Gordon

Brown was said to be 'an ascetic son of the manse, awkward, shy and bookish. To a working-class boy like me, he seemed a bit of a weirdo'. John Prescott was described as 'big, ugly, rough and tough. He is a nodding dog in the rear window of Blair's New Labour limousine'. George Galloway showed utter contempt for Neil Kinnock, calling him a 'shallow, insubstantial individual'. Afterwards, I reiterated my views about George Galloway's 'brilliant entertainment value' to *Dragon's Eye* and *Waterfront*, which were later broadcast on those TV programmes. Needless to say, I was delighted that George Galloway won a sensational parliamentary by-election victory by a majority of more than 10,000 votes in the supposedly safe Labour Party seat of Bradford West, on 29 March 2012. Give Labour hell, George!

With Michael Howard resigning as the Conservative Party leader three months after the general election defeat, the campaign for his successor began in August 2005. I, like many other Conservatives, believed that the contest would be between Kenneth Clarke and David Davis, the Shadow Home Secretary and bookies' favourite. With the EU now less of a political hot potato because of France's rejection of the European Constitution, I wrote an article in the September edition of *Barn* saying that I tended to favour Kenneth Clarke because David Davis could easily be portrayed as a right-wing reactionary. However, I also spoke very highly of David Cameron, the Shadow Education Secretary, as a 'true modernizer' who wished to make the Conservative Party relevant to the present age. Against many expectations Kenneth Clarke was eliminated in the first round of voting on 18 October, eventually leaving David Davis and David Cameron as the two names for ordinary Conservative Party members to decide upon.

David Cameron was now clearly the favourite, having achieved 90 votes in the final round of voting amongst MPs against 57 for David Davis and 51 for Shadow Foreign Secretary Liam Fox who was eliminated from the contest. I was astonished how in less than a month since his superb Conservative Party Conference speech, David Cameron had been catapulted into a seemingly unassailable position. This demonstrated that the Conservative Party now wanted to elect a leader who could be an election winner rather than someone who was in tune with beliefs that were held by the majority of the party faithful, as was the case with Iain Duncan Smith. Political pragmatism had returned to the Conservative Party.

The six-week campaign between the two Davids was very predictable, with Nick Bourne and the Welsh Conservative Party establishment heavily supporting David Cameron. I also promoted David Cameron's candidature amongst Conservative Party members, especially since he had declared his support for a more distinctively 'Welsh' Conservative Party. He was also much more favourably disposed towards granting the National Assembly more powers than the far more sceptical David Davis, who was heavily supported by the anti-devolution element within the Welsh Conservative Party. Indeed, David Davies, MP for Monmouth, and his father Peter, were organising David Davis's campaign in Wales.

When the Conservative leadership ballot result was announced on 6 December, David Cameron had won a decisive victory over David Davis by 134,446 votes to 64,398. I was delighted with the result, asserting that the Conservative Party could now become more in tune with the aspirations of the modern age. I also welcomed David Cameron's decision to remove the anti-devolutionist Bill Wiggin as Shadow Welsh Secretary, replacing him with Cardiff-born Cheryl Gillan. Unlike her predecessor, she was given a seat in the Shadow Cabinet. This indicated that

David Cameron was far more sympathetic to Welsh aspirations than Michael Howard had been.

Nick Bourne stated on 10 January 2006 that the Conservative Party had ditched its policy of offering a referendum on scrapping the National Assembly as part of the Preferendum. In future any referendum held regarding granting more powers to the National Assembly would simply be a yes or no. Writing in the *Western Mail* of 20 February Cheryl Gillan stated: 'Conservatives do not oppose more powers for the National Assembly. But those powers should only be granted if that is what the people of Wales want. The right way to test opinion on that would be through a referendum'.

During the Conservative Party Conference in Bournemouth on 2 October, David Cameron endorsed this new progressive policy. These statements by the leadership of the Conservative Party were welcomed by me. After all, I had been campaigning for the Conservative Party to take a more pro-devolution position ever since the narrow 'Yes' vote in the referendum of September 1997.

9

In 2004, I was given an opportunity to utilise my media experience in another direction. I received a telephone call from S4C's afternoon chat show *Prynhawn Da*, asking if I would present a slot on antiques at the Tinopolis studio on 10 August. This came as a pleasant surprise and I gladly accepted the invitation. Although I had spoken on antiques to various organisations such as branches of the Women's Institute, Merched y Wawr, Rotary, Round Table, business clubs and chapel societies on several occasions, doing a live TV slot on the subject was completely different. I decided to speak on Staffordshire pottery, particularly the flat back figures of famous political, religious, military and royal notables produced during the Victorian era. This was because I had been collecting examples of these over the past several years and therefore had items to exhibit while talking about the subject on TV. The 'powers that be' must have been satisfied with my performance because I was asked to do *Prynhawn Da* TV slots between 16 August and 29 September on Welsh pottery, weapons, carnival glass, places to buy antiques and spotting fake antiques.

A new opportunity arose that was to prove very challenging. I mentioned to the producers that a very large antiques fair with more than a thousand stalls was being held at the Builth Wells Showground on 9 October. I was then asked to present a Welsh-language version of the well-known BBC One antiques programme *Bargain Hunt* from this venue. Coincidentally David Dickinson was filming *Bargain Hunt* from the same place that day. Who would have thought that the relatively inexperienced me would be sharing the same stage with the 'Duke' himself?

Prior to broadcasting the events from Builth Wells, I was

given several miscellaneous antiques slots on *Prynhawn Da*. Between the beginning of January 2005 and the end of February, I spoke on collectables, tea sets, portraits of prime ministers and children's annuals. Here I was able to strike an excellent rapport with Elinor Jones, whom I have the highest regard for. Elinor Jones's professionalism and sense of timing in asking questions and making appropriate observations has proved to be invaluable in making the antique slots a success over the years. I am also most grateful to John Hardy for his assistance in often co-hosting these slots with Elinor Jones and occasionally doing a one-to-one interview with me.

With Elinor Jones and Hywel Jones on Wedi 3*, April 2011*

On Saint David's Day 2005, the *Prynhawn Da* programme came to an end. It was replaced by *Wedi 3* which, although broadcast from the same Llanelli studios, was to be considerably different in its format. The duration of the programme was virtually cut in half, from nearly two hours to barely one hour. A new more modern-looking studio format was also established and the programme was intended to be far more 'slick' in its presentation than its predecessor. I was delighted to be informed that I had been appointed as the 'antiques expert' for the new programme.

As a consequence, I have averaged at least twenty antiques slots on *Wedi 3* per year to date. One of my favourite TV slots took place in May 2005. I had bought a fascinating autograph book at an auction in Henllan, Llandysul. A gentleman who came originally from Stockport had died and his possessions were sold by Stephen Jones in his Henllan Auction Rooms. At the bottom of a box full of worthless books was a leather-bound book originally dating from the early years of the twentieth century. This included the autographs and occasional comments from some of the most prominent Labour Party politicians and trade union leaders of the day. For example, Ramsay MacDonald, Arthur Henderson, George Lansbury, Clement Attlee, Ernest Bevin, Herbert Morrison, Aneurin Bevan, Hugh Gaitskell, Harold Wilson, Michael Foot, Barbara Castle, A. J. Cook and Tom Mann. To get all these signatures in one book is very rare and certainly worth the £50 I paid for the whole box. This important autograph book was certainly worthy of a slot on *Wedi 3* on 9 June 2005, and the programme was very well received.

My first filming assignment in England on behalf of *Wedi 3* took place at the Antiques for Everyone fair held at the NEC Birmingham in November 2007. This is a four-day event, with more than 400 stalls packed with antiques of the highest standard from all over Britain and Europe. Amongst some of the most memorable events was seeing a serious collector of Nantgarw porcelain from the Neath area pay £20,000 in cash for three superb plates decorated by

Thomas Billingsley between 1813 and 1820. Most serious collectors of antiques pay in cash for items in order to maximise discounts from dealers. There must surely have been several million pounds being discreetly carried and hidden by the thousands of people visiting this event. I also witnessed a magnificent early eighteenth-century open-bottom Welsh dresser in immaculate condition from north Wales being purchased for £15,000. It was bought in cash by a Brecon farmer. Who says that farming isn't generally profitable?

I was filmed walking around several stalls dressed in a seventeenth-century Cromwellian suit of armour, one of the best-preserved that I have ever seen. It was shortly afterwards sold for £16,000 to a Sussex gentleman, who was delighted with his purchase. When questioned why he was prepared to spend what appeared to be over the odds for such an item, he retorted, 'Where do you get a better example outside the Tower of London?' He was correct in his assessment and fulfilled the criteria that a serious collector of antiques should buy the best example he can afford. I followed this guidance by purchasing a lovely mid seventeenth-century Welsh coffer in excellent condition, which was a real bargain at £750. It is often cheaper to buy an item relating to Wales in an English antiques fair than in Wales because the demand is less.

I returned to England in March 2008 to present two antiques slots for *Wedi 3* from the British Antiques Association Fine Art Fair from the Duke of York Square, Chelsea. On 13 March I dealt with items for sale on a Welsh theme, while the following day I explored the topic of 'quirky' things. I was astonished by the high prices dealers were asking for their stock. For example, a pair of nineteenth-century Staffordshire Prussian soldiers on horseback, which normally fetch around £400, had an asking price of £960. Nevertheless, several very expensive items were sold in front of me. The outstanding one being an oil painting that was purchased by a Chinese lady for £40,000 from an art dealer living in the Welshpool area. Amongst the 'quirky' items, was a load of recycled chrome, which had been taken from aeroplanes and later converted into mirrors, chairs and even a settee. The least expensive item on his stall was a cool £3,500.

In October 2008, I spent two days filming at the Decorative Antiques and Textiles Fair at Battersea Park, London. This was a very expensive fair, with little room for haggling. What astonished me was the way people would wander around this fair, sit down for tea and then consider in a very relaxed manner the pros and cons of buying a specific antique. It was not usually the cost of the object that was discussed, but its suitability for the home decor. This contrasted sharply with the very intense way people bargained with the dealers in the early morning antique markets in the Bermondsey, Portobello, Angel, and Spitalfields areas of London. The difference in styles can be explained by the fact that most of the people present at the Battersea fair, just like the one in Chelsea, had more money than sense.

The highlight of the 2010 *Wedi 3* antiques trail was doing a slot on Fakes, Mistakes and Discoveries by way of paintings held at the National Gallery, London on 29 June. The intention of the exhibition was to celebrate the remarkable collaboration of scientists, conservators and art historians at the National Gallery. It explored this pioneering work by presenting the varied and fascinating stories behind more than forty paintings in the National Gallery's collection. The exhibition was arranged over six rooms, representing some of the major challenges faced by Gallery experts: Deception and Deceit; Transformations and Modifications; Mistakes; Secrets and Conundrums; Redemption and Recovery; and a special focus room relating to Botticelli. The exhibition also featured works by Raphael, Durer, Gossaert, Rembrandt and others. Presenting an antiques slot on this fascinating exhibition proved to be an unforgettable experience.

Undoubtedly one of the most controversial and emotive slots that I have ever done on *Wedi 3* was broadcast on 7 November 2011. It related to the very contentious 'art' of taxidermy, where animals, birds and fish are killed and afterwards skinned in order to be stuffed and displayed as trophies. Several collections, both old and new, of stuffed animals and birds, were brought to the studio in order for me to discuss their history and elaborate upon their financial value. Their very presence in the studio set aroused strong emotions from several employees. It was difficult for me to avoid the conclusion that those people, both male and particularly female, from the Welsh-speaking urban 'social elite', tended to view these items with shock and horror. Conversely, people from a rural background, as well as some more working-class urban-dwellers from both sexes, enjoyed viewing or even collecting stuffed animals and birds.

There have also been interesting expeditions to places in England with S4C's evening chat show *Wedi 7*. On 8 September 2008, for instance, I previewed a Toys and Dolls auction to be held at the Bonhams Auction House in Knowle, near Solihull, the following day. I have never before seen so many teddy bears assembled together. These teddy bears included some rare examples of the German Steiff varieties dating from the beginning of the twentieth century. Several of these had auction catalogue estimates of approximately £1,000 and most of these estimates were exceeded by enthusiastic bidders eager to acquire part of early children's history. There was also a straw-filled pink mohair Steiff pig c1910, which, although a little worn in places, nonetheless made more than £900. In this case, the buyer was correct to purchase an example in only fair condition. It would be virtually impossible to acquire one in a better state unless someone was prepared to pay a fortune at one of the great American international antique toy fairs.

I visited the Clocks and Watches Exhibition at the British Museum, London, on 5 January, 2009. This proved to be a real eye-opener, with all those beautiful sixteenth-century clocks forever remaining in my memory. The highlight of the exhibition was Hans Schlottheim's automated clock in the form of a galleon. This piece was made in Germany and dates from around 1585. The hours were struck on bells in the crows' nests at the top of the masts, and the time was shown on a dial at the front of the ship. It also played music and as a finale it fired a canon. On board were life-like miniature figures of the Holy Roman Emperor and members of his court. Whilst all this was happening the galleon, which had very small wheels built underneath it, would move along the table in a very regal way. It is incredible that such technology was available over 500 years ago to produce a toy as well as a very accurate clock. When commenting on the value of such an exhibit, I stated that it was 'priceless'.

However, one of my most controversial slots I did for *Wedi 7* took place on 14 November 2006. The subject was Clogau gold, and here I made the controversial remarks that it would be better if people bought ordinary 22 carat gold rather than spend considerably more money on alleged Welsh gold. I stated that for something to be labelled as 'Welsh gold', it only needed to have 10 per cent of its content coming from Wales. Moreover, the only remaining unused 100 per cent Welsh Gold, all 2.5 KG of it, was in the hands of the Royal Family for the purpose of making wedding rings. Although not everyone was pleased to hear these remarks, I 'stuck to my guns'.

Another controversial and very enjoyable slot I did for *Wedi 7* was broadcast on 4 April 2011. This was in relation to the commemorative-ware produced to celebrate the wedding of Prince William and Kate Middleton on 29 April. I was astonished to hear of the very hostile reaction amongst several members of the Welsh-speaking professional 'chattering classes', who immediately contacted the Tinopolis studio in Llanelli to convey their strong opposition to this programme.

Indeed, they even accused *Wedi 7* of 'glorifying the foreign English Royal Family'! Thank goodness these anti-British Welsh Nationalist Republican extremists represent only a small minority of the population of Wales. After all, if they opposed the Royal Wedding, they did not have to buy any of this commemorative-ware – which, incidentally, has proved to be very popular amongst the general public.

Wedi 3 and *Wedi 7* came to an end on 29 February 2012, as part of the re-organization of S4C in the light of the Westminster Coalition Government's reduction in funding for the Welsh language TV channel. I was nevertheless delighted to learn that my antiques slot would continue in the new *Prynhawn Da* afternoon magazine programme, which replaced *Wedi 3*. I did my first seven new *Prynhawn Da* slots between March and September 2012, when visiting guests brought their miscellaneous antiques and collectables to be valued by me.

I was given another opportunity to utilise my knowledge from studying antiques by Antur Teifi in September 2006, when I was appointed as a field officer for the Square Mile Project which was intended to revitalise communities in Carmarthenshire by getting people involved in miscellaneous corporate activities. This was the beginning of over forty Antur Teifi-sponsored antique evenings throughout Carmarthenshire. It continued until February 2009, when funding for this excellent project unfortunately came to an end.

I have encountered several rather 'difficult moments' while lecturing on antiques on behalf of the Square Mile Project in Carmarthenshire. During an event in the Talley area in January 2007, I was the only sober person present. There were also several people intoxicated as a result of smoking illegal substances. Such was the strength of the toxic smoke in this small upstairs room that I found it difficult to value the miscellaneous items brought. With all of these people laughing and joking, I felt that I would have been better doing a stand-up comedy act rather than pricing antiques.

Whilst I was talking about swords and bayonets at the Urdd Eisteddfod in Carmarthen in May 2007, with the children and young people clearly enjoying examining the items on the table, one lady rushed forward to express her anger that people were being exposed to the 'glorification of British imperialism'. This was none of her business, since she had no connection with the children and young people who were enjoying themselves. Moreover, most of the military items displayed were French and German.

It appeared to me that this lady represented that anti-British and anti-militarist attitude that is characteristic of many people within the 'respectable' Welsh-speaking middle class. These are often the same people who describe the blood-thirsty Owain Glyndŵr as a Welsh patriotic hero, while at the same time labelling themselves pacifists largely because they oppose any military action in the name of the British state. Likewise, they have turned a blind eye to the terrorist atrocities of so-called 'freedom fighters' in southern Africa, while condemning as 'un-Christian' Great Britain's heroic defensive war for survival against Nazi Germany.

There was a more unpleasant experience to come. When I accepted an invitation to do an antiques valuation evening in the Llandovery area in October 2008, I felt that I might as well have been speaking in London. Upon entering the venue, I was informed by a rather domineering 'Hyacinth Bouquet' type of lady with a distinctive cockney accent: 'We want no Welsh here'. This hostile attitude towards the Welsh language is far more prevalent amongst some people who have come to retire in Welsh-speaking Wales than is acknowledged in the media. Indeed, this was one of the most difficult antiques evenings that I have had to undertake, due to the 'anti-Welsh' atmosphere. There were some derogatory remarks expressed concerning my 'unfortunate strong Welsh accent', even while speaking in English. I retorted that 'Thank goodness, doctorates are rewarded on ability, not on accents'. To worsen matters further, the audience ignored the smoking ban in public places and the room was covered with the haze and nasty smell of cigarette smoke. Departing from this place was a truly liberating experience.

People have often asked me to suggest potentially good investments when beginning to collect antiques. I have always responded with the stock phrase, 'Always buy what you like.' It is my opinion that a financial appreciation in a specific item's value should be regarded as a secondary reason for buying it in the first place. Antiques should be enjoyed for what they really are, decorative items in one's home. I have also urged people to buy the best possible example of an antique they can afford. It is far better to have a smaller collection of good quality antiques closely related to each other, than an assortment of 'damaged tat'.

During my valuation evenings, I have been frequently asked to define the factors behind what makes an antique valuable. I have argued that the three main factors are

Pontargothi Antiques Evening, November 2010

condition, rarity and desirability. Whilst the first is self-explanatory, there is in practice a considerable difference between the second and third factors. For instance, an item can be categorised as 'rare' because few pieces were made at the time of production. The reason behind this may be that it did not sell well because it was considered to be unattractive in its appearance. Such items should be avoided by antique collectors. Then there is the question of desirability. An item could have been produced in large numbers at the time, but because it is considered to be attractive and therefore desirable by later collectors, it has become rare. Although one has to pay more for antiques belonging to this latter category, these are really the items to collect.

Too many people have become obsessed with the monetary value of antiques. Most people living in the 1960s or early 1970s upon viewing an antique they had not seen previously would say 'What is it?' Meanwhile, they would say today, 'What's it worth?' One can measure 'value' several ways. There is the monetary value of an antique, although prices can fluctuate from one area of Britain to another. Then there is the historical value of an antique. Something may be 'priceless', as far as the history of a specific locality is concerned, while in financial terms not valuable. Similarly, an object handed down from one generation to another may be deemed 'priceless' as a family heirloom. Yet in financial or

Llanddarog Antiques evening with Angela Skyrme, January 2011

historical terms be worth virtually nothing. Antique collecting is therefore a funny old world.

It is my experience that auctioneers gain the most financially from selling antiques. When someone asks an auctioneer to sell an item for them, the latter has everything to gain and nothing to lose. The auctioneer usually charges the vendor 20 per cent commission for selling the item on their behalf. He often also charges a 20 per cent 'buyer's premium' on top of the hammer price paid by the winning bidder. For example, if a Welsh dresser is sold for £5,000, the purchaser has to pay £6,000 for the item. Conversely, the vendor only receives £4,000 from the auctioneer. In other words, the auctioneer has made a profit of £2,000 on an item that has cost him nothing financially to purchase. On the other hand, an antiques dealer has to pay for an item before selling it to a member of the public. It is my experience that the more expensive the item the less the percentage profit. For instance, a Royal Worcester vase purchased by my partner Mary Davies for £400 was sold by her for £480 at an antiques fair in Johnstown, Carmarthen, in October 2010. This was a profit of only 20 per cent on the item, approximately half what an auctioneer would have made without 'digging into his pocket' in the first place.

One must also be very careful when wanting to buy an item at auction. Not only is the 'buyer's premium' to be taken into account when bidding, but also very questionable methods used by some auctioneers in order to 'inflate' the selling price of the item for sale. For example, if a grandfather clock has a reserve of £2,000 on it, the auctioneer has the legal right to take 'phantom bids' against a genuine bidder in order that the reserve is met. Also, when an auctioneer says that the bidder in the room is bidding against a 'commission bid' – that is, when someone has allegedly left a bid in his absence – you have only the auctioneer's word for that. My advice is to stop bidding when you see genuine bidders stopping bidding in the auction room.

Another unscrupulous practice some auctioneers allow is for the vendor to bid for his own item in order to force a prospective purchaser to pay much more for the object he wishes to buy. For instance, in one Carmarthenshire auction house the auctioneer would allow a gentleman to bid for over 200 items he had himself put into the auction. This gentleman would often stand at the back of the auction room and 'push' the bidding higher in order for his profit as well as the auctioneer's to be maximised. Occasionally, however, he would get too greedy and genuine bidders would withdraw from the auction. The auctioneer would then have to knock down the hammer in the name of the vendor in order to pretend that he had bought it.

Another auction house in Carmarthenshire would

exploit the fact that a bidder had left a 'bid on the book' for a particular item because he was genuinely unable to be present on the day of the auction. If you leave, for instance, a bid of £100 for a particular item, you are really telling the auctioneer that you are prepared to pay up to that figure for it. Therefore, if the actual bidding in the room stops at £45, you should get it for £50. However, this particular auctioneer would start the bidding on the top figure left on the 'book', that is £100. In other words, the winning bidder was paying double the amount of money for the item that he had purchased due to his absence being exploited by the auctioneer.

It is also important to remember that in a 'general auction', where there is no catalogue of the items for sale issued to the public prior to the bidding, a prospective buyer has no legal redress if the item he has purchased is defective in any way. Auctioneers cover themselves by saying before the commencement of the auction that every item offered for sale is 'sold as seen'. In other words, it is up to the prospective purchaser to decide for themselves regarding the accuracy or otherwise of the description of the item made by the auctioneer.

However, even in a 'catalogue auction', the purchaser has only very limited redress in the event of a dispute with the auction house regarding the accuracy of its description of an item in the catalogue. For example, if a painting is described in the auction catalogue as in the 'manner' or 'style' of Sir Kyffin Williams, you can be certain that the auctioneer believes that it is a fake or reproduction. Also, if a prospective purchaser has any doubt regarding what the catalogue description is meant to convey, he should ask for a written statement of authenticity from the auctioneer prior to bidding for it. If the auctioneer is unwilling to provide this, he has in practice indicated that he is unsure of its authenticity.

If someone has any doubt about the authenticity or condition of an item they have an interest in purchasing, they should refrain from bidding. Likewise, it is easy for anyone to be caught up in 'auction fever' and to bid way over the value of something in order to stop someone else from getting it. This should be avoided at all costs, with the potential bidder setting in advance how much he is prepared to bid for the item. In the event of it going beyond this carefully thought-out figure, there is always another day to buy a similar item. Also, someone should never show the auctioneer that he is too keen to purchase a particular item otherwise he will believe that you are determined to buy it at whatever the price. He might therefore be tempted to 'run the bidding' in order to get you to pay more and gain him additional commission from the increased 'buyer's premium'.

When accepting an invitation to do an antiques evening, I really do not know what to expect. For example, while addressing a Merched y Wawr branch in the Lampeter area, I referred to the fact that a lady living in the near-by village of Cribyn owned a pair of rare nineteenth-century Staffordshire greyhounds with the name 'Master McGrath' impressed upon the left one and the name 'Pretender' impressed on the right one. This pair of figures, which were in superb condition, was worth in excess of £5,000 to people involved in greyhound racing. One lady sitting in the audience was determined to try and find out where in Cribyn the owner of these figures lived. There followed a 'public dialogue' between she and me that went something like this:

She: Does the owner of the greyhounds live in Cribyn or outside it?

Me:　She lives in the village.

She:　Does she live in a house or a bungalow?

Me:　She lives in a house.

She:　Is it a privately-owned house or a council-owned property?

Me:　It is a privately-owned dwelling.

She:　Does she live on the Lampeter side of the village or on the Aberaeron side?

Me:　I am close to giving you sufficient information to identify the owner of these beautiful greyhounds, who wishes to remain anonymous. I am therefore not willing to provide further information regarding their location.

She:　I know why you are not willing to tell me who the owner is.

Me:　You seem to think that you know my thoughts better than me. Please tell us all why I am not prepared to reveal the owner's identity.

She:　Oh that's easy. You won't identify the lady, because you hope that she will leave them to you in her will!

Me:　What a good idea! I can only live in hope!

Undoubtedly, there will be new 'antiques adventures' on the horizon. These cannot come quickly enough for me.

10

From June 1993 until March 2006, I spent nearly thirteen generally happy years as the minister for Peniel Aberaeron, Neuaddlwyd, Llwyncelyn, Mydroilyn and Siloh Llanon Welsh Congregational Churches. One of the most important turning-points in my life was the decision to leave my position as a Welsh Congregational minister in the Aberaeron area in March 2006, in order to minister over three churches in the Trelech region of Carmarthenshire. After almost thirteen years in the same pastorate, I needed a change in order to revitalize my energies. Ministers who spend almost their whole careers in the same churches usually become 'stale', since new challenges are an essential requisite for an eventful life.

My induction service as the minister over Capel y Graig, Penybont and Ffynnonbedr Welsh Congregational Churches took place at Capel y Graig, Trelech, on 25 March 2006.

The prolonged 'saga' of expanding my pastorate between December 2006 and July 2007 to include Bwlchnewydd and Capel Cendy churches, demonstrated to me how a minister needs to be simultaneously thick-skinned, diplomatic, patient, and determined in the pursuit of achieving a fixed objective. I was once told that one needs broad shoulders in the ministry. All the heavy weightlifting exercises that I have done, and continue to do, over the years to stay fit has ensured that! But on a more serious note it means a minister needs a temperament that is not easily hurt in public, together with strong faith in God. I am also forever grateful to my parents for instilling in me the following precepts from a young age, something my father once described as the 'Alphabet of Life'. The relevant section reads:

A = Application
B = Bloody mindedness
C = Commitment
D = Determination
E = Enthusiasm
F = Fortitude
G = Grit

The service eventually uniting Bwlchnewydd and Capel Cendy chapels under the same ministry as Capel y Graig, Penybont and Ffynnonbedr was held on 17 July, 2007 at Bwlchnewydd Chapel.

Being inducted as the minister of Bwlchnewydd and Capel Cendy, July 2007

If the current trends continue, in less than two decades there will be only approximately twenty Congregational ministers in Wales. With the average age of worshippers considerably over seventy, more than half of the chapels in Wales will unfortunately close by 2020. There has also been a huge decline in the membership of Welsh Congregational churches. In 1953 they had a total membership of 119,000, but this had declined to 54,000 by 1988. Ten years later the membership had fallen to 38,000 and by September 2012 there were fewer than 24,000 Welsh Congregationalists. In reality, these statistics are much worse because only around a quarter of the actual members are reasonably regular worshippers during Sunday services. It is therefore hardly surprising, though unfortunate, that people do not want to be associated with an apparently 'sinking ship' by entering the ministry.

In an article published in the Welsh-language periodical *Y Faner Newydd* in 2005, the Reverend Goronwy Evans, Lampeter, recalls receiving very sound advice from the Reverend Jacob Dafis when beginning his ministerial career. The famous Welsh Unitarian minister told his young protégé:

> Be a shepherd to your parishioners, but don't be a lapdog to them. Mix with them, but never allow them to trample over you. Remember that some of those very people who heap praise on you today will be the ones who will knife you in the back tomorrow. And I had numerous experiences of this occurrence during my ministerial career. Remember, you are a servant of God and to some extent to your members, but never be servile to them.

I have endeavoured to follow these astute precepts throughout my ministerial career and would commend them as an essential part of a minister's 'survival kit'.

Whilst staying at the Wadham Guest House, Weymouth in September 2009, I noticed the following verse on the wall. This may well summarise the sometimes thankless work of ministers. It reads:

We the willing,
Led by the unknowing,
Are doing the impossible

For the ungrateful.
We have done so much
For so long for so little,
We are now qualified
To do anything for nothing.

Fundraising for the Air Ambulance Service, Talog,
February 2011

During my ministerial career in both Aberaeron and Trelech, I have encountered many dubious people, strange customs and questionable habits. Upon beginning my ministry in 1993, I heard the story of a quite recently deceased undertaker who used to visit very sick people from his locality at Bronglais Hospital, Aberystwyth. Whilst speaking to them, he would place one hand in front of the other alongside the patient's bed in order to measure the length required for a coffin. Several different people have confirmed the accuracy of this story, including one gentleman who was 'measured', but recovered to outlive the undertaker.

Another undertaker who lived to the north of Aberaeron, upon hearing of the death of a native of the town, would get changed into appropriate mourning clothes and drive his hearse past the deceased's home. He hoped that members of the family would see him, call him inside and ask him to take the funeral. If no one saw him along the street, this undertaker would knock on the deceased's door in order to sympathise with the family. He calculated that this would gain their favour and achieve his objective of 'getting' the funeral. Another one of his tricks upon 'getting' the funeral was to tell the widow or widower to leave all of the funeral arrangements to him. In practice, this meant that he was given a blank cheque.

A trick played by one dubious undertaker was to inflate his funeral costs. In 1993 I officiated over the funeral of a non-chapel member and I charged the usual £30 for conducting the service. Some six weeks later, the family of the deceased said that I had been rather expensive in charging £70 for officiating at the funeral. I showed the family my bank statement in order to prove that I had charged £30. I then telephoned the undertaker to get him to justify the grossly inflated 'minister's fee' on the funeral bill. I received the unapologetic answer that he had charged the family a non-itemised administrative fee of £40 for obtaining a minister to conduct the funeral!

A trick sometimes used by another unscrupulous undertaker was to order the funeral flowers on behalf of the family. He would then pay for them and afterwards bribe the shop assistant to provide another much higher-priced invoice for him to present to the family on his itemised bill. The same principle can also be applied in relation to arranging food for guests after the funeral service. An undertaker had been asked to book food for at least fifty guests at an Aberystwyth hotel in 2003. After a female employee had received the correct payment of £400 from him, he gave her a £50 bribe to write out another invoice for £600 in order for him to present to the family on his funeral bill.

One solicitor in mid Ceredigion used to send the immediate family of the deceased a large bunch of flowers out of 'sympathy' for their predicament. He then charged the family for the flowers at a grossly inflated price when the time came to settle legal fees. Several people complained to me concerning this dubious practice, especially when no family should be expected to pay for flowers they had not ordered in the first place.

Whilst attending a Rotary Club function in the mid Ceredigion area, I recall overhearing how two solicitors present at the event worked out a way for their respective clients to pay them the maximum amount of money for writing solicitors' letters. One solicitor would write a letter on behalf of his client to someone who had allegedly caused offence to them. The other solicitor would then seek to persuade his client to ask him to write an official reply to the other solicitor's letter that he had received. It was then just a case of almost perpetual solicitor's letters from one client to the other. Both solicitors had a good laugh behind their gullible clients' backs while at the same time filling their pockets with money.

A comparatively recent development during my time as a minister has been the desire of some men living locally to marry oriental women. These men often have the wrong impression that these women will be more 'submissive' to them than many so-called 'independent' Welsh or English women. Almost invariably in my experience, nothing could be further from the truth. For instance, during my Aberaeron ministry a businessman in Ceredigion married a Thai woman. Soon afterwards, she began staying in Swansea for so-called weekends with fellow 'Thai friends'. In reality, she was working as a prostitute and drugs dealer. When her somewhat naive husband eventually accepted that the stories relayed back to him of his wife's life 'on the streets' were true, she continued to rob him financially. This cunning woman's tactic was to use 'their' young son as a 'bargaining chip'. When the couple were eventually divorced, this businessman's financial assets were very considerably depleted. Afterwards, this gentleman was too afraid to have a DNA test to prove that he was the father of the child, because he feared that the 'real' father may well have been one of his former wife's street clients.

In April 2010 I met a retired widower in a Carmarthen supermarket who had recently married a Chinese woman. She was quite well-spoken and of a seemingly pleasant disposition, judging by her Welsh husband's very complimentary remarks. She told me that she was looking forward to the fact that *fourteen* members of her family would be staying with her and her husband in three weeks' time.

After officiating at a Sunday service not far from my current pastorate shortly afterwards, I spoke to quite a wealthy farmer in his early seventies who said that he wished that his two very shy sons would find themselves a wife each who would look after them and their father-in-law, who was a widower. Rather tongue in cheek, I related the story of my conversation with the above-mentioned gentleman and his Chinese wife. Upon hearing this, the farmer was clearly keen to learn more. Indeed, he wanted me to find out when and where exactly the fourteen Chinese people were staying in order for him and his sons to be somehow introduced to them via me. He clearly believed that a minister's work knows no boundaries and that I could apparently perform 'miracles'. In other words, it appeared that he wished to find a wife for each of his sons and possibly one for himself amongst these visitors.

However, this farmer appeared to become slightly more hesitant when I related the following story to him. During a holiday in Tenerife in January 2010 I met a retired businessman from just outside Carmarthen who had been completely 'ripped off' financially by his cunning and wholly unscrupulous Thai wife. For example, when they had been living in Thailand she doubled the price of goods bought by her and paid for by her husband, who was not familiar with the local Thai currency. To worsen matters further, he was expected to pay all of the bills incurred not only by his wife, but also her parents, as well as her extended family of a dozen people. This came to several thousand pounds. Furthermore, he was 'persuaded' to spend over £60,000 to build a house for his wife's parents on top of the £10,000 'bond' he had to pay the woman's father for giving permission for him to marry his fiancée. To add insult to injury, he later discovered that under Thai law no 'foreigner' could own land in Thailand, which meant that he had no legal rights whatsoever over the property paid for entirely by him.

The marriage lasted less than two years, when the gentleman divorced his wife for adultery on account of her affairs with several other men. Finally, just prior to the divorce, she emptied all of their joint bank accounts and stole his Jaguar car. As a consequence of these personal and financial disasters, this very generous although somewhat naive gentleman was attending Alcoholics Anonymous and receiving psychiatric treatment in an attempt to overcome his traumatic experiences.

There seems to be an unusual connection between Christianity and witchcraft in some chapel circles. For example, Tony Roberts, in his book *Myths and Legends of Pembrokeshire*, gives an account of witchcraft in the Gwaun Valley. He states that during the early part of the twentieth century one well-known family of witches wanted to become members of Caersalem Baptist Chapel, and were admitted. However, this made no difference to their behaviour. One witch, even on the day she became a chapel member, bewitched a young servant girl working at Gelli Fawr farm. The witch was sitting on a pew behind the servant girl, who rushed out of the chapel and ran wildly about the roads. Her father, having tried every means of pacifying her, went to Cwrt y Cadno to consult Dr Harries, the famous Carmarthenshire wise man. Dr Harries told the father what had happened and even showed him the scene in a mirror. He gave him a piece of paper with some words written on it that the girl had to wear on her breast. This apparently proved sufficient to bring her back to her normal state.

A witch who lived in the Pennant area of Ceredigion in the early 1990s would occasionally attend the local chapel. Also, a deacon of mine in the Aberaeron area had a grandmother buried in the chapel cemetery who had been a well-known witch locally. I have been told that a coven of witches still meet in the Trelech area. Furthermore, there is a witch living in the nearby village of Talog who advertises her 'services' in the local paper.

Some people in the Aberaeron and Trelech areas are known to have used 'poppets' or effigies to try and bring bad luck to other people. After all, this is one of the services offered by the witch of Talog. In folk-magic and witchcraft, a poppet is a doll made to represent a person, for casting spells on that person. These dolls may be fashioned from such materials as a carved root, grain or corn shafts, a fruit, paper, wax, potato, clay, branches, or cloth stuffed with herbs. The intention is that whatever actions are performed upon the effigy will be transferred to the subject.

Amongst many cultures throughout the world, a poppet or effigy would be used with very sharp needles stuck into its 'heart' as a way of doing evil to an enemy. It was this evil type of poppet that was used on a chapel member of mine in the Aberaeron area in 1994. It took an experienced Anglican exorcist to 'raise' this curse, which had been placed by a witch on the instruction of another former church member. The motivation behind this 'evil' was envy that had turned into jealousy. Enmity then evolved into paranoid hatred that was exploited financially by an English witch living outside Lampeter.

I have also encountered a case of the 'evil eye' during my ministerial career. This is an ancient belief in the existence of a malevolent power in the glance of some people, which is almost invariably provoked by envy or jealousy. In this instance, a lady who had given birth to a baby boy was apparently 'wished bad luck' by the 'evil glance' in the eye of a childless spinster neighbour. Both mother and child were subsequently taken ill due to acute breathlessness for no apparent medical reason and had to be hospitalised.

The spinster even visited the mother and child in hospital while I was, coincidentally, speaking to them. It became obvious to me that the spinster was praising the baby to its mother in a very 'false' and patronising way. Indeed, this is one of the most noticeable characteristics of the utilisation of the 'evil eye'. Realising this, I asked the spinster to say, 'God bless you' to the baby, having just said what a beautiful child the mother had. Therewith, the spinster immediately walked away without uttering another word. As a precautionary measure, the mother later placed an amulet, in this case a horseshoe, in the porch of her home in order to protect her baby son and herself from the malevolent effects of the spinster's 'evil eye'.

A phenomenon in Welsh rural culture that never ceases to amaze me is that of the 'family meeting'. As someone brought up in the south Wales industrial valleys where the words 'family' and 'household' are synonymous, the idea that someone who does not live under the same roof as you can make decisions on your behalf is incomprehensible to me. During my years in the ministry I have witnessed several of these 'family meetings'. Usually a 'family meeting' is called to discuss the consequences of a death and its resulting implications for the family. This can entail making the funeral arrangements but more often relates to the distribution of assets within the family.

Whilst resident in Aberaeron, I was told of an incident in upland Carmarthenshire during the mid 1990s where a 'family meeting' was called to discuss the implications of the death of one of the brothers who rented the family farm from his relations, at a very high rent for the acreage. The meeting was chaired by the 'family head' and it was immediately decided that the family farm was to be sold. The widow, a non-Welsh speaker, was then unsuccessfully 'pressurised' to sign a form written in Welsh whose contents she did not understand. By all accounts, had she acquiesced to this rather intimidating pressure, the newly bereaved widow would have signed away her rightful financial entitlement from the sale of her late husband's business, leaving her with substantial debts to pay. In the event, the proceeds of the sale of the farming business were sufficient to pay any outstanding debts, which had been incurred solely by the deceased.

In the nearby vicinity I was called to attend one of these

'family meetings' in 2008. To my astonishment the gentleman who now farmed the 'family farm' was not even invited to sit around the table to discuss the implications of his in-law's death. As the minister responsible for the funeral arrangements, I insisted upon chairing the 'family meeting'. It was obvious that some of the people present were surprised that I had taken this role away from the 'family head,' who had travelled several miles to be present. However, once the business relating to the funeral arrangements involving me were settled, the 'family head' was then responsible for chairing the remainder of the proceedings.

I shall never forget how submissive or even servile the gentleman who farmed the 'family farm' was to his in-laws. Had it been me, I would have insisted that, as the person responsible for farming the farm, and in whose residence the 'family meeting' was held, I would not only have been sitting at the table during the discussions but also responsible for chairing them. This demonstrates a fundamental 'clash of cultures'. On the one hand, one has an essentially rural deference being given to one's elders even if they do not live in the same household. On the other hand, one has a primarily urban individualism that believes that people who do not live under the same roof as you have no business to tell you what to do in the residence that you reside in. In the latter context, I was brought up to believe that your 'real' family is who you share your household with. Also, that your home is your castle and no one else's outside the household.

11

It was Enoch Powell who wrote, 'There are no friends in politics, only acquaintances'. Whilst referring to debates in the House of Commons, Lloyd George observed that 'Your opponents are in front of you, but your enemies are behind you'. Over the years I have learnt to appreciate the accuracy of these appraisals. In September 1998 I was promoting Nick Bourne's candidature for the leadership of the Welsh Conservative campaign for the National Assembly elections, due to be held in May 1999. Whilst in the Glen Hotel, Haverfordwest, Nick Bourne received a mobile telephone call from Karen Lumley, the Conservative National Assembly candidate for Delyn.

Karen Lumley informed Nick Bourne that she had spoken to her 'good friend' Stuart Andrew, who had contested Wrexham at the 1997 general election on behalf of the Conservative Party. Stuart Andrew had told her in the 'very strictest confidence' that he was on the verge of joining the Labour Party, largely because he felt that he was being discriminated against in National Assembly selection contests as a consequence of his homosexuality. Nick Bourne then told Karen Lumley to continue the façade of 'friendliness and trustworthiness' towards Stuart Andrew in order to continue maintaining his confidence in her. This would enable Nick Bourne to know exactly when the political defection was to take place. I was horrified with what I saw as Karen Lumley's 'betrayal' of the trust that Stuart Andrew had placed in her, and the cold calculating way that Nick Bourne had responded.

There is no way that I would have betrayed a confidence bestowed upon me as a friend for the sake of political favour. After all, there are far more important things in life than politics. As a postscript to this story, Stuart Andrew later returned to the Conservative fold under David Cameron's more socially liberal political agenda and was elected as the MP for Pudsey at the 6 May 2010 general election. Meanwhile, during the same election Karen Lumley defeated the former Labour Home Secretary Jackie Smith in Redditch at her third attempt.

I faced a similar situation in the Cynon Valley during the mid 1980s. A gentleman by the name of David Ball had fought several local government elections on behalf of the Conservative Party in very hostile territory. He was a member of the Cynon Valley Young Conservatives when I was chairman of that organisation between 1985 and 1987, and we became friends. With Margaret Thatcher seemingly becoming more extreme in her political actions, David Ball, who was really more of a 'One-Nation' Conservative, decided to join the Liberal Democrats. While I urged him on numerous occasions to remain a member of the Conservative Party, I never once disclosed to anyone David Ball's decision to change political allegiances. Personal friendships should always be given priority over political beliefs. Indeed, I have often preferred the social company of people from different political persuasions than those from my own party.

Unfortunately, there are now very few genuine 'characters' in the National Assembly who are prepared to speak their mind and say what many people are really thinking. There are far too many politicians residing in Cardiff Bay who speak like ventriloquists' dolls. They are almost all singing from the same hymn sheet, even when they claim to represent different political parties. 'Political Correctness' has also gone mad, with the deliberate 'gagging' of the open debate of really contentious issues in the National Assembly Chamber. A soggy consensus rules, with genuine radicalism both from the left and right seemingly in retreat. I believe that the National Assembly has still not recovered from the departure of some of the genuinely political heavyweights from that institution.

Both Plaid Cymru's former President Dafydd Wigley, and the late Dr Phil Williams (who was AM for South East Wales) were original thinkers who could have made an immense contribution to Welsh politics. Ron Davies, former Labour Secretary of State for Wales, had a genuine vision of how he wished to see devolution develop over the years. Rod Richards and David Davies provided a strong right-wing counter balance and were willing to ruffle feathers in order to stimulate political debate. There has been no real 'alternative' political agenda, although the new Welsh Conservative Assembly Group leader since July 2011 Andrew R. T. Davies and his deputy Paul Davies are thankfully displaying an increasing willingness to challenge this 'soggy consensus' during Assembly debates. Plaid Cymru threw its traditional hostility towards the Labour Party overboard, in order to go into coalition with Rhodri Morgan in 2007. Rhodri Morgan and later Carwyn Jones could then claim the credit for any successes achieved, while at the same time lay the blame on Plaid Cymru's Ieuan Wyn Jones for any economic failures. The Liberal Democrats forfeited a golden opportunity to form a non-Labour coalition government by linking-up with the Welsh Conservative Party and Plaid Cymru after the 2007 National Assembly elections. However, divisions within the Welsh Liberal Democrats, and anti-Tory sentiments amongst some Plaid Cymru grass-roots members, made this impossible.

Nick Bourne deserves much credit for making the Welsh Conservative Party acceptable as a potential coalition partner for Plaid Cymru and the Liberal Democrats. This may, however, be the result of diluting Conservative policies so much that the Tory Party had possibly become under his leadership somewhat indistinguishable from the 'soggy' left-of-centre consensus that predominates in Cardiff Bay. Looking back over Nick Bourne's leadership era in the *Western Mail* of 13 January 2012, Rod Richards asserted:

> So far as I am concerned, he is not a conviction politician. He moved the Conservative Party into a pro-devolution stance because he thought it would make him popular. Nationalists describe him as a 'modernizer' because he says things they agree with.

Whatever the merits or otherwise of Rod Richards's assessment, it must be conceded that Nick Bourne succeeded, with a great deal of assistance from David Cameron, in making the Welsh Conservative Party a genuine 'political player' in Wales again.

The Welsh Conservative Party increased its constituency representation in the National Assembly from one to four on 3 May 2007, although its overall total increased by only one to twelve as a consequence of the rather complex system of proportional representation. Moreover, the Conservative Party topped the poll in Wales for the first time since 1874 in the European Parliamentary elections held on 4 June 2009. This was to be the first national contest since the 1918 general election that the Labour Party had not come first in terms of the popular vote in Wales.

I was delighted with the Welsh Conservative Party's performance in the general election held on 6 May 2010. The Welsh Conservatives saw the percentage of the votes cast for them increase to 26 per cent and their parliamentary representation rose from three seats to eight. I was especially pleased to see the very able Jonathan Evans elected for Cardiff North, Guto Bebb for Aberconwy and

Alun Cairns for the Vale of Glamorgan. In my own constituency of Carmarthen West and South Pembrokeshire, it was good to see Simon Hart, the Head of the Countryside Alliance, unseat the incumbent Labour MP Nick Ainger by 3,423 votes. The almost total collapse of the Plaid Cymru vote here demonstrated that Welsh-speaking farmers, in upland Carmarthenshire in particular, were prepared to desert Plaid on a large scale by voting Conservative in order to get rid of Labour. It only adds further credence to my view that once you scratch a farmer's skin, you usually find a Conservative.

One other general election result brought much satisfaction to me. That was Glyn Davies's magnificent victory over the colourful Liberal Democrat incumbent Lembit Opik in Montgomeryshire by 1,184 votes. This is especially the case when one considers that apart from at the 1979 general election Montgomeryshire has been a Liberal stronghold since 1880. Glyn Davies achieved a huge swing of 13.2 per cent from the Liberal Democrats to the Welsh Conservatives to emerge victorious, and this must be largely attributed to his personal popularity and campaigning ability. On a national level, Glyn Davies and Guto Bebb in particular are valuable assets in strengthening the 'pro-devolutionist' element within the Welsh Conservative Party.

Whilst all of this is commendable, I believe that Nick Bourne should have taken more of the initiative in Welsh politics during his time as the Welsh Conservative National Assembly Group leader. Unfortunately, his public profile always remained low and he needed to present himself as a potential leader of a new government in waiting. Indeed, an opinion poll undertaken in March 2011 for HTV revealed that only 5 per cent of those voters interviewed could identify Nick Bourne as the 'leader' of the Welsh Conservative Party.

The failure of Glyn Davies to be re-elected to the National Assembly in May 2007 was detrimental to the Welsh Conservative Party. He had many admirers outside his party and would have made a major contribution to attracting into the Conservative fold more right-wing Plaid Cymru supporters who regarded their party's coalition with their old enemy, Labour, an act of betrayal. However, Glyn Davies's election to the Westminster Parliament in May 2010 has provided him with a platform to help attract to the Welsh Conservative Party even more of those 'Welsh conservative' elements who have usually voted Plaid Cymru but who have no sympathy with that party's increasingly left-wing socialist aspirations.

This political re-alignment in Welsh politics is quite possible, since Plaid Cymru was so comprehensibly rejected by the electorate at the May 2010 general election. Plaid was victorious in only three constituencies out of forty and trailed a poor fourth place in terms of the popular vote, polling a mere 12 per cent of those people who voted. Not only did Plaid fail to recapture Ynys Môn from Labour at a time when Gordon Brown was the most unpopular leader of that party since Michael Foot, but also Plaid Cymru were humiliated in their number one 'target seat' of Ceredigion. Here the very conscientious and hard-working Liberal Democrat incumbent Mark Williams increased his majority from a miniscule 219 votes in 2005 to a massive 8,324 votes over the lack-lustre Plaid candidate, Penri James.

Plaid Cymru also saw its parliamentary majorities reduced significantly by Labour in Arfon and Carmarthen East and Dinefwr. Even in the Plaid Cymru stronghold of Dwyfor Meirionnydd, the Welsh Conservatives polled more than half the votes secured by Elfyn Llwyd. Although Plaid succeeded in reducing the Labour majority in Llanelli, they still lost by 4,701 votes to Nia Griffith. Meanwhile, in the south Wales valleys, where Plaid Cymru had hoped to gain substantial support from disillusioned Labour voters as a result of its socialist policies, the party was overwhelmingly defeated. Substantial election expenditure by Plaid Cymru in Cynon Valley, Rhondda and Caerphilly came to nothing, with the party trailing in third place behind the Welsh Conservatives in the latter constituency. To add insult to injury, Plaid Cymru was even out-polled by the extremist BNP in the Newport East and Newport West constituencies. So much for Plaid Cymru's coalition with Labour in the National Assembly as far as electoral success for Plaid is concerned.

One of the most significant consequences of the success of the Welsh Conservative Party at the May 2010 general election was that Alun Cairns, one of the Regional List AMs for the South Wales West area since 1999, was elected as the MP for the Vale of Glamorgan constituency, situated in the South Wales Central electoral division. The mistaken assumption amongst political commentators was that Alun Cairns would relinquish his Assembly seat, and that Porthcawl's Chris Smart, who had been ranked second by Conservative Party members in the South Wales West region, would serve as a Regional List AM until the National Assembly elections in May 2011.

However, the thought of having the die-hard anti-devolutionist, friend and confident of Peter Davies, and former Rod Richards right-wing political henchman Chris Smart as a member of the Welsh Conservative Assembly Group, was anathema to Nick Bourne and his supporters. I was later told by a Welsh Conservative AM that Nick Bourne's alleged private view was that Chris Smart was 'unfit' to be a Tory AM. If this was so, the AM argued, Chris Smart should not have been placed on the list of approved Welsh Conservative National Assembly candidates in the first place. The fact that he had been approved surely meant he had been adjudged 'fit' to hold public office. As a means of denying Chris Smart his alleged 'democratic right' to a National Assembly seat, a wholly unscrupulous Machiavellian-type means was seemingly devised that arguably flew in the face of 'natural justice'.

In practice, this 'Keep Chris Smart out of the National Assembly at all costs' campaign, entailed Alun Cairns 'offering' his 'resignation' from the National Assembly to the Board of Management of the Welsh Conservative Party. However, the *Western Mail* of 29 May reported that this apparent resignation was refused, with Alun Cairns being asked to remain in the National Assembly until the 2011 elections to that institution. During several media interviews Chris Smart was understandably furious and pointed out with some plausibility that it would simply not be practical for Alun Cairns to carry out his political work effectively as an AM in Cardiff Bay for one electoral region while at the same time representing another constituency at the Westminster Parliament. He also said, 'This decision is an insult to the 30,000 people in the region who voted Conservative and will now not be properly represented at the Assembly. The people responsible for this decision have not even bothered to tell me. I heard about it from the media'. Furthermore, it is difficult to avoid the conclusion that if he seriously wished to resign his seat in the National Assembly, Alun Cairns would have submitted his resignation to that institution's Presiding Officer Lord Dafydd Elis-Thomas, as Rod Richards had done in September 2002, rather than to the Welsh Conservative Party's Board of Management.

The presence of the very independently-minded 'true Tory' figure of Chris Smart as a member of the Welsh Conservative Group in the National Assembly would certainly have posed a threat to Nick Bourne's alleged 'grand design' of co-habiting with Plaid Cymru and the Liberal Democrats in a possible non-Labour 'rainbow' coalition government sometime in the future. This view was given much credence by an article in the *Western Mail* of 29 March 2011. Here it was even suggested by 'an influential Conservative source' that Nick Bourne would possibly be prepared to serve as Deputy First Minister under a Plaid Cymru-led Welsh Assembly government, even if the Welsh Tories won more seats than the Nationalists in the elections on 5 May. With such potentially 'high stakes' at play, it is therefore hardly surprising that Chris Smart had to be cold-bloodedly assassinated politically in the name of personal ambition and calculated expediency on the part of Nick Bourne, even if that meant denying the people of South Wales West full-time representation in the National Assembly for a year. This was also the price that Nick Bourne was seemingly prepared to pay in order to exorcise the last prominent 'living presence' of the Rod Richards leadership era from exercising any power within the higher echelons of the Welsh Conservative Party.

I generally supported David Cameron's Government's attempts to reduce public expenditure as announced in the October 2010 Public Spending Review. After all, it was nothing short of recklessness and the abdication of fiscal responsibility for Gordon Brown's Labour Government to have spent £4 on public spending for every £3 that was raised from taxation. Also, it was sheer economic madness for Gordon Brown to sell Great Britain's gold reserves for $275 an ounce when gold is now worth over $1,800 dollars an ounce. Taking over £6 billion pounds out of pension funds and thereby jeopardising the well-being of our senior citizens is a further indictment of the Tony Blair–Gordon Brown era.

In contrast, there is no way that Margaret Thatcher would have got the United Kingdom into this economic mess of spiralling monetary borrowing resulting in escalating debt for decades to come had she still been Prime Minister. Being a 'good housewife' Margaret Thatcher would have spent only what the country could afford. As one of my oldest chapel members in Trelech told me in January 2011, 'Every Labour government has left office with the country poorer'. There could be no more accurate truism.

After all, as a consequence of Labour's sheer economic incompetence between 1997 and 2010, the people of the UK are now faced with an all-time high debt of more than £155 billion to repay. This horrendous Labour legacy in more than doubling the National Debt means that we now have to pay £120 million a day just to keep up with the interest payments on this debt. Extending debt repayments over a longer period of time, as proposed by Labour and Plaid Cymru, makes no economic sense whatsoever. Anyone who has got into credit card debt should realise that the slower the repayments are made, the more interest one has to pay. One simply cannot play Russian roulette with the finances of the UK.

I also welcomed the contents of George Osborne's budget on 23 March 2011 as a means of seeking to stimulate economic growth without jeopardizing the overriding priority of reducing the nation's acute financial debt. In the Welsh context, 10,000 people on low incomes have been taken out of tax altogether and the fiscal changes have benefited 1.13 million Welsh taxpayers.

This general theme was further developed in George Osborne's latest budget on 21 March 2012. From April 2013, 42,000 further people in Wales will be lifted out of paying income tax altogether, since the threshold when people start paying tax on their income will be increased to £9,250. This measure will also help 1.1 million Welsh taxpayers. As a consequence of this budget, Wales is getting in cash terms an extra £11.7 million, which is surely something to be welcomed. Welsh Secretary Cheryl Gillan rightly described it as 'a budget for enterprise and a budget for low and middle earners in Wales'. Commenting on the budget announcements, Welsh Conservative Assembly Group leader Andrew R. T. Davies stated: 'This is a budget that rewards work, backs business and will support the economy, while benefiting tens of thousands of families the length and breadth of Wales'.

Nonetheless, splitting differences on policies, and often agreeing on the least disagreable course of action is, unfortunately, an inevitable feature of any coalition government. According to the *Western Mail* of 4 June 2012, the Conservative and Liberal Democrat power-sharing coalition has made at least twenty-one prominent climb-downs or U-turns since taking power in May 2010. It is, therefore, hardly surprising that the plain-speaking and highly-principled Monmouth Tory MP David Davies told the Prime Minister David Cameron in early May 2012, during a conversation with him in the House of Commons tea-room, about his concerns regarding the UK goverment's recent general direction.

Echoing the sentiments of many erstwhile grassroots Conservatives who instinctively dislike the coalition with the Liberal Democrats at Westminster (according to my experiences in speaking to them), David Davies later wrote in a letter published in the *South Wales Argus* of 10 May:

> I must acknowledge there has been incompetence at the highest levels of government over the last few months in a number of departments. Meanwhile there has been an

emphasis on issues such as gay marriage and reform of the House of Lords, at the expense of explaining the financial situation; a failure to deport dangerous terrorists because of concerns about human rights; and an apparent unwillingness to listen to the concerns of electors and the backbench MPs who represent them.

There also appears to be a tremendous waste in the public expenditure undertaken by the Welsh Government. Those numerous recently-built Assembly offices located in major municipal centres across Wales have cost millions of pounds from taxpayer's money to construct. This money could have been better spent on providing well needed additional funding to the NHS or education in Wales. The so-called 'devolving' of jobs from Cardiff Bay to the various Welsh regions has resulted in virtually no new local jobs being created. In reality, many people who had hitherto been employed in the National Assembly have been relocated to work in these new expensive Assembly offices. Indeed, the *Western Mail* of 14 May 2012 reported that more than £2m in relocation expenses will have been paid out to Welsh government workers over the past four years. In today's age of information technology, all that was really needed was not nearly twenty expensive and grandiose Assembly offices, but a room with the appropriate IT facilities in each County Council office across Wales to download and upload relevant information from and to the National Assembly.

Why do we need so many bureaucrats working for the Welsh Government across Wales? What are these people actually *doing* to justify their employment? These are questions many ordinary people are asking, since it is obvious that Wales is being stifled by an increasingly over-bearing state bureaucracy. Indeed, there are more than 4,000 extra civil servants employed in Wales after thirteen years of devolution. It was reported in the *Western Mail* of 21 May 2012 that almost four out of five staff working for the Welsh government are designated as managers. The Welsh Conservative Assembly Group leader, Andrew R. T. Davies, commented: 'Categorising almost 80 per cent of the Welsh government workforce as "managers" appears excessive and taxpayers will rightly question whether the civil service in Wales is top-heavy.' It is little wonder that Wales's over-dependence on the public sector to provide employment in practice obstructs any significant growth in the private business sector in Wales. A genuinely entrepreneurial free enterprise Welsh economy will be created only when the present largely 'state-dependent jobs culture' is swept away.

The *Daily Post* of 26 February 2011 reported that Wales got nearly £1.6bn from the EU between 2000 and 2006 and has received another £1.5bn since 2007. With match funding, it represents an investment of more than £6bn, most of which has gone to west Wales and the valleys, which covers two-thirds of the nation's land mass. Nevertheless, the economic performance of these areas has fallen further behind the European average with Wales the only UK region to see an area fall below 75 per cent of the average GDP (Gross Domestic Product). Furthermore, it was reported in the *Western Mail* of 14 March 2012 that GDP in west Wales and the valleys had fallen from nearly 71 per cent to only 68.4 per cent of the EU average. Surely with all this money available, a 'golden opportunity' to revitalise the Welsh economy has been squandered, due in part to the apparent reluctance of the Welsh Government to champion a significant growth in the private sector, where that seemed to them to be detrimental to 'public sector trade union interests'.

Although Cheryl Gillan deserves some praise for her work as the Secretary of State for Wales, there have been some arguably 'questionable happenings' within the Welsh Conservative Party. A good example was the lengthy 'Mohammad Asghar saga'. In December 2009, Mohammad Asghar, the Plaid Cymru South Wales East Regional List AM since 2007, defected to the Welsh Conservative Party on the grounds that he did not believe in Plaid's policy of an independent Wales outside the United Kingdom. Mohammad Asghar was, however, quoted in the *Western Mail* of 15 December as conceding that the 'final straw' for him was when he had been stopped by Plaid Cymru leader Ieuan Wyn Jones from employing his daughter, Natasha, as a press officer in the National Assembly. Moreover, the same newspaper article written by Martin Shipton quoted a Plaid source as claiming that 'Mr Asghar voted in the Assembly to support independence on July 7 this year'.

There were also several prominent Welsh Conservatives who were privately very critical of Nick Bourne's decision to accept Mohammad Asghar into the Tory Assembly Group owing to his rather 'fluid' political affiliations. This was particularly so when one considers that he had been a member of the Labour Party in Newport, prior to joining Plaid Cymru. Even Naz Malik, the then – but now 'sacked' – Chief Executive of the All Wales Ethnic Minorities Association, said of Mohammad Asghar's defection to the Welsh Conservative Party: 'This unprincipled decision is a bad day for the black and minority ethnic communities of Wales. We want to be trusted by political parties and this unprincipled action has done nothing for our cause'.

On 27 August 2010, Mohammad Asghar was selected as a Welsh Conservative candidate for one of the top two places on the South East Wales Regional List. It appears however, that considerable pressure was put on the South

Wales East Area Executive of the Welsh Conservative Party to endorse him. David Fouweather, the Chairman of the Conservative South East Wales Area Council, claimed in the *Western Mail* of 16 September: 'I was told that failure to re-adopt Mr Asghar could result in my possible suspension from the party'. It was also revealed that telephone calls were made from highly-placed Conservatives in London to members of the area executive to try and influence the voting process. Moreover, it is understood that there were fears of embarrassment at the forthcoming Conservative Party Conference if the first ethnic minority member of the National Assembly had been de-selected. Another Conservative source said: 'I would be very surprised if Mohammad Asghar was not given certain assurances about selection as a candidate before he agreed to defect'.

There was considerable opposition to the new Conservative policy of positive discrimination in favour of women when selecting candidates for the May 2011 National Assembly elections. It was decided that in cases when a Conservative AM was not seeking re-election, the replacement would have to be a woman. The *Western Mail* of 14 October 2010 reported that Suzy Davies had been selected to stand to replace Alun Cairns as the Conservative's top candidate on the South Wales West Regional List. This positive discrimination policy can, in this instance, be interpreted as intended to prevent Chris Smart from entering the National Assembly. In other words, Nick Bourne and his supporters may well have feared a 'grassroots' members' revolt in this region against the very unfair way that Chris Smart had been treated in the aftermath of the May 2010 general election. This Conservative policy of positive discrimination towards women applicants appeared to be out of step with current selection procedures in Wales, since both Plaid Cymru and the Liberal Democrats have abandoned this rather patronising practice in favour of selection on merit.

I received a letter dated 28 October from a former highly-placed salaried official within the Welsh Conservative Party which appeared to 'open a can of worms' on certain alleged unscrupulous practices amongst the then leadership of the Welsh Tories. A section read: 'As for Wales, I'm disgusted with all the gerrymandering going on to accommodate the likes of women candidates and Mohammad Asghar and to thwart people like Chris Smart. It's a disgrace'.

There were also apparently serious tensions within the Welsh Conservative Group in the National Assembly. The *Western Mail* of 30 November reported that the formidable South Wales Central Assembly Member, Andrew R. T. Davies, resigned as Shadow Health Minister because the Tory AM for Cardiff North, Jonathan Morgan, had allegedly received Nick Bourne's support to become chairman of the Assembly's Health Committee. This rather unexpected resignation followed the previous week's return of Conservative AMs Jonathan Morgan – long seen as a potential successor to Nick Bourne – and William Graham to the Shadow Cabinet as Shadow Ministers for local government and regeneration respectively. It has been alleged that these latter two gentlemen had been less than wholly supportive of Nick Bourne during his 'Assembly expenses crisis' in December 2008. Indeed, Martin Shipton claimed, in the *Western Mail* of 28 February 2009 that just before Christmas 2008 Jonathan Morgan had lobbied colleagues to back him in calling for a leadership election as a prelude for an attempt to displace Nick Bourne as the Welsh Conservative Assembly Group leader. However, Jonathan Morgan found there was insufficient support and the attempt was abandoned. As a consequence, Nick

Bourne removed him from the Shadow Health portfolio, with William Graham, who allegedly supported Jonathan Morgan's candidature, refusing to serve as a shadow minister.

Andrew R. T. Davies now used his newly found freedom to articulate his views from the backbenches in order to raise his profile as a possible successor to Nick Bourne sometime in the future. In an interview in the *Western Mail* of 16 October 2010, Andrew asserted, 'If you have ambition, ambition means you want to be at the top of anything you do'. Moreover, Andrew R. T. Davies is one of the Welsh Conservative Assembly Group's most capable speakers in the Assembly's debating chamber and has gained respect for his forthright debating style. In a possible criticism of Nick Bourne's more 'wishy-washy offend nobody' public speaking manner, Andrew R. T. Davies was quoted as saying on 30 November 2010, 'There is nothing I love more than a good bare-knuckle political fight. Seriously, that's something we should be seeking to do'.

Indeed, Andrew R. T. Davies had to deny in the *Western Mail* of 19 February 2011, that he was planning to oust Nick Bourne after a glossy ten minute video posted on You Tube was widely seen as the start of a leadership campaign. It showed the South Wales Central AM both at work and at home, not only visiting a rehab clinic in his constituency and working in his Assembly office, but also talking about his farm and being with his family. Cardiff Bay rumours suggested that he had fired the starting gun on a post-Assembly election leadership bid. Furthermore, Andrew R. T. Davies's denial appeared to be somewhat less than wholly unequivocal, since he merely said there was 'no vacancy' for the Tory Party leadership in the National Assembly.

The Conservative Party leadership decided that every member would be given the freedom to campaign as they wished in the Devolution referendum on 3 March 2011, with the Tory Party electoral machine remaining officially 'neutral' during the campaign. I was hardly surprised to discover that every Welsh Conservative AM publicly supported to various degrees the 'Yes' campaign to allow the National Assembly to have direct law-making powers without the permission of the Westminster Parliament in the 20 subject areas where it already has limited law-making powers. After all, once elected politicians in any particular institution have had a taste of exercising influence and power, they invariably want more!

During the official 'Yes for Wales' launch in Cardiff on 4 January 2011, Nick Bourne, while sharing a platform with the leaders of Welsh Labour, Plaid Cymru and the Welsh Liberal Democrats, declared: 'I believe in the premise and promise of devolution. We must embrace devolution in the good times and the bad times. The successes and failures should be our responsibility. With the devolved power, real and long-lasting improvements can be made in people's daily lives'.

In contrast to the public unanimity of Tory AMs, the Welsh Conservative Party MP's were clearly divided on granting the National Assembly more powers. The *Western Mail* of 20 January reported that the outspoken die-hard anti-devolutionist Member for Monmouth, David Davies, would be voting 'No' in the referendum. In a statement, he claimed that: 'The Assembly has done nothing to justify giving it more powers. The NHS in Wales is in a deplorable state. We have longer waiting lists than England. Council Tax bills have gone through the roof since the Assembly was established. I am not confident that laws passed by the Assembly would be scrutinised by Cardiff Bay as fully as laws passed by Westminster. If there is a 'Yes' vote, then it won't be long before AMs want even more powers'.

Two more Welsh Conservative MPs came out and confirmed they were backing the 'No' campaign in the *Western Mail* of 27 January. The well-known devolution sceptic and Member for Preseli Pembrokeshire, Stephen Crabb, stated that 'Pembrokeshire is just not a priority for Cardiff Bay. Until that attitude changes, I cannot support moves to strengthen Assembly powers'. Meanwhile, his neighbour, Simon Hart, the Welsh Conservative MP for Carmarthen West and South Pembrokeshire, said: 'What I have found telling is the number of passionate and patriotic Welsh people who are voting 'No' because they feel that rather than increase our influence, Wales risks falling behind our neighbours, becoming less competitive. Now is not the time for further powers so I will be voting 'No' in March'.

The public 'No' pronouncements of Stephen Crabb and Simon Hart put them at logger-heads with the respective Welsh Conservative AMs for the same constituencies. The AM for Preseli Pembrokeshire, Paul Davies, has for many years favoured more powers for the National Assembly while Angela Burns, the AM for Carmarthen West and South Pembrokeshire, has seemingly been a more recent convert to devolution. It was therefore hardly surprising that the divisions within the Welsh Conservative Party over the issue of strengthening the powers of the National Assembly should be displayed most publicly in west Wales. A very good personal rapport between Stephen Crabb and Paul Davies appears to have avoided any bitter divisions between members of the Preseli Pembrokeshire Conservative Association, although it seems that the clear majority of grassroots Tory activists supported the 'No' stance of their MP. Meanwhile, the allegedly somewhat less than wholly 'hunky dory' general working relationship between Simon Hart and Angela Burns may well have 'spilled over' during the devolution referendum campaign in this area.

The *Carmarthen Journal* of 2 February reported that Simon Hart was apparently 'playing the start of the slippery slope towards Welsh separatism card' while campaigning for a 'No' vote. He claimed that 'Wales needs to be part of the United Kingdom if it wants to be a world force and compete with everyone else. To my mind, the biggest threat to Wales is a gradual drift towards forcing the independence issue. We have an opportunity to put a marker in the sand now'.

This theme was further developed by Sir Eric Howells, the very prominent Pembrokeshire Tory and former chairman of the Conservative Party in Wales during the pre-devolution era. In the *Carmarthen Journal* of 16 and 23 February, he claimed that 'the political establishment in Wales is pushing for a constitutional change that will take us a further step towards separation from the United Kingdom'. 'The 'Yes' Campaign might not be open about it but their ultimate aim is one thing – an independent Wales. If Wales were to separate from the UK then we would lose the £9.1 billion a year that we receive from the UK treasury. If we were self-funding in Wales, that would amount to £3,100 each per year for every man, woman and child in the nation'.

Another indication of the deep internal divisions within the Welsh Conservative Party was the presence of Carmarthenshire's Henri Lloyd Davies, a former Welsh Tory chairman between 2000 and 2003, at the 'True Wales' 'No' Campaign launch at Newbridge Rugby Club on 19 January. During an interview with the BBC's David Williams for *Yes Butt, No Butt: An Insider's Look at the Referendum*, broadcast on 6 March, Henri Lloyd Davies said: 'I fear that a lot of the politicians in Cardiff Bay are too comfortable. They're looking for the grand coalition, the easy life, the limousine for ministerial work. I think we have got to have a more radical right-wing agenda. There is no effective opposition in the Assembly at the moment'. I was astonished to hear these remarks, since Henri Lloyd Davies had been a former Plaid Cymru candidate and a Conservative 'Yes' supporter during the 1997 Referendum. Meanwhile his son Harri, a former Tory Parliamentary candidate, and two-time Assembly candidate, was actively campaigning for a 'Yes' vote in Carmarthenshire on 3 March 2011.

My personal experiences in championing the 'Yes' campaign in this area, together with miscellaneous anecdotal evidence, appear to indicate that a clear majority of Welsh Conservative Party activists in the West Carmarthenshire and South Pembrokeshire constituency seem to have supported the view of Simon Hart and Eric Howells rather than that of their AM, Angela Burns. Traditional British Unionism therefore appears to have had far greater appeal to Tory activists and voters than the more pragmatic stance of their AMs and Welsh Conservative 'progressives' like me.

The sharp differences of opinion within the Welsh Conservative Party also became obvious in north Wales. The former Tory agent in Clwyd, John Broughton, led the nominal 'True Wales' 'No' campaign in north Wales. However, the group's official campaign launch at Prestatyn was attended by fewer than two dozen people. Nonetheless, this put him at logger-heads with the local Welsh Conservative AM, Darren Miller, who actively campaigned for a 'Yes' vote in the referendum. Similarly in Monmouth, Tory AM Nick Ramsay campaigned very vigorously for a 'Yes' vote, explicitly opposing the well-known views of the constituency's anti-devolutionist Conservative MP David Davies.

These divisions between Nick Bourne and his pro-devolutionist Welsh Conservative AMs on the one hand

and the majority of ordinary Tory Party supporters on the other were brutally exposed in a You Gov poll for S4C published on St David's Day. Whilst the poll suggested that 67 per cent of those voting would back the 'Yes' campaign, with 33 per cent voting 'No', the reverse was true for Conservative Party supporters. Despite the backing of all Welsh Conservative AMs for a 'Yes' vote, party supporters split 75/25 per cent in favour of a 'No' vote. Moreover, 40 per cent of those Conservative voters interviewed wanted to see the National Assembly abolished.

In an apparently desperate last-minute attempt to 'turn opinion around' within his own party Nick Bourne made a speech at an event hosted by 'Yes for Wales'. In the speech, he claimed that he had been 'wrong' in 1997 about devolution being used as a means of perhaps fragmenting the UK long-term. Nick Bourne now declared: 'I do think that it's important that Wales should have the ability to decide on domestic issues in Wales. So it is my strong belief that we do need these additional powers; we do need this next level of decision-making in relation to powers that we've already got to ensure we can effectively do the job'. The speech was reported by the *Western Mail* of 1 March.

On 21 January 2011, I was asked by the BBC's Elin Cadifor to present a slot on S4C's current affairs programme *CF99* on my recollections of the 1997 devolution referendum campaign. This involved re-visiting the locations of the 'Scuffle' in Cardigan and reminiscing over the 'Battle of Ponty', etc. The extensive filming took place on 2 and 3 February and proved to be really great fun. This programme was broadcast on 2 March, the evening before Polling Day. My extensive comments and the accompanying BBC film archive clips of these occasions, reminded me of the genuine 'blood and guts guerrilla warfare nature' of the 'No' campaign in 1997. We may not have had many helpers, but we fought with a genuine passion and rugged determination to disrupt and embarrass our overwhelmingly wealthier and far more numerous 'Yes' opponents by utilising every means at our disposal.

Things could not have been more different in 2011. The 'No' campaign now basically involved a large inflatable pink pig being carried along the streets of Blackwood by half a dozen or so *Last of the Summer Wine* type male characters! There was no real 'No' organization, hardly any zeal, with their campaign hopelessly divided between UKIP and Conservative Assembly abolitionists on the one hand, and so-called 'anti-establishment real devolutionists' personified by Labour's amiable Rachel Banner on the other. They were correctly described by the broadcaster David Williams on 6 March, as 'strange bed-fellows; a mixture of the disaffected and the disillusioned'. Moreover, 'True Wales's' refusal to seek official status as the legally designated 'No' lead campaign actually denied them £70,000 in government money to promote their cause. This state funding could have been used to communicate their message via TV and Radio broadcasts, together with paying the costs of a leaflet to be distributed across Wales by private courier companies which would have compensated somewhat for their lack of 'foot-soldiers'. They could also have bought several dozen large inflatable pink pigs to parade around Wales if they could find enough people to carry them!

By contrast, the 'Yes' campaign had the support of the whole well-to-do political establishment and the Welsh-speaking *crachach* social elite. Their campaign organisation was 'slick', professional, media-friendly, and with an abundance of helpers from all four major political parties together with many with no publicly held political affiliation. They also had the financial resources to print and distribute over 1.5 million glossy leaflets with public endorsements from numerous 'celebrities', particularly from the sporting world in general and international Welsh Rugby Union players in particular. The enthusiastic, urbane, suave and persuasive Roger Lewis, Chairman of the Welsh Rugby Union and successful capitalist businessman who chaired the 'Yes' campaign, reminded me somewhat of New Labour's 'holier than thou' trio of Tony Blair, Peter Mandelson and Alastair Campbell during their 'Teflon touch non-stick' heyday!

It therefore came as no surprise to me that when the referendum results were announced on 4 March, the 'Yes' campaign had achieved a decisive victory. With 21 of the 22 local authority areas recording a 'Yes' majority, 517,132 people (63.5 per cent) voted to give the National Assembly primary legislative powers, against 297,380 (36.5 per cent) who voted 'No'. Even in Monmouthshire, the 'No' majority was only a miniscule 320 votes. At 35.6 per cent, the turnout was higher than the 34.1 per cent achieved in the referendum to set up the London Assembly. I was naturally delighted with the result and First Minister Carwyn Jones's words 'An old nation comes of age' captured the mood of this truly historic occasion. Moreover, Carwyn Jones announced on 8 March that the new powers of the National Assembly would become effective from 5 May.

It appears that the 'Yes' campaign's argument that 'laws affecting Wales should be made in Wales,' just as the equivalent already occurs in Scotland and Northern Ireland, had been much more effective in gaining people's votes than the 'No' campaign's criticism of the National Assembly's generally 'poor record of achievement' since its inception in 1999. The 'give us the tools to do the job properly' argument was indeed far more persuasive than the 'vote No to keep everything as it is' contention. It has also been claimed that the almost two to one 'Yes' vote represented 'the triumph of faith and reason over the politics of despair'.

The prominent and very outspoken 'No' campaigner Len Gibbs from Tai Bach later conceded to the BBC's David Williams: 'We always were a forlorn hope. We had sticks and staves to fight against the might of the Welsh establishment. We never had a chance'. Len Gibbs also seemingly displayed many of the more 'extreme' political beliefs associated with some of the die-hard National Assembly abolitionists in the 'No' camp, who usually hid behind the more respectable Rachel Banner during the actual referendum campaign. According to Len Gibbs, 'There are lots of people in Wales who would like to blow this place up. We'd get told everyday, burn it down!'

However, seeing Nick Bourne and some of his Welsh Conservative Assembly cohorts during the time of the official declaration of the referendum results 'cosying-up' so closely to their socialist and nationalist political opponents, only served to give credence to the sentiments expressed by a 'true Welsh Tory' like Henri Lloyd Davies. Also, I just could not help thinking that some of those smiling Plaid Cymru members in the audience were privately really thinking 'silly useful idiots Carwyn Jones, Nick Bourne and Kirsty Williams; you've just helped to put another nation-building block in place on the road to Welsh independence!' The remarks of the National Assembly's Presiding Officer, Lord Dafydd Elis-Thomas, in the *Western Mail* of 7 March that in the light of the overwhelming 'Yes' vote, the Wales Office should be scrapped 'the sooner the better', thereby abolishing the post of Welsh Secretary in the British Cabinet, only served to give even more credibility to this view. Somewhat predictably, the Secretary of State for Wales, Cheryl Gillan, responded to these comments by saying, 'He's singing to a separatist tune and I don't think that's what the people of Wales want'.

With David Cameron's coalition government having to implement generally unpopular cuts in public expenditure in order to reduce the country's acute debts, the National Assembly election on 5 May 2011 was always going to be a difficult one for the Welsh Conservative Party to fight. Nick Bourne conceded as much during an interview with Adrian Masters on ITV's *Wales Decides 2011* on 7 April. He stated that the steady increase in the number of Welsh Tories elected to the Assembly, from nine in 1999 to eleven in 2003 and up to twelve in 2007, with the Mohammad Asghar defection from Plaid Cymru in 2009 bringing the number up to thirteen, was 'bound to come to an end sometime'.

In an article in the Welsh-language current affairs magazine *Golwg* on 7 April I claimed that with the possible exception of Montgomeryshire, where the Liberal Democrats were in internal turmoil due to the Lambit Opik and Mick Bates 'fiascos', it was 'most unlikely' that the Welsh Conservative Party would be able to capture any constituency seats not won by them at the 2007 National Assembly election. However, I speculated that if support for Plaid Cymru declined significantly, partially as a consequence of their coalition with the Labour Party in the National Assembly, the Welsh Tories could emerge as the second largest party group in that institution, even if Conservative electoral support remained generally static.

The Welsh Conservative Party election manifesto – *A New Voice for Wales* – was launched in Llandudno on 15 April. Amongst the promises made were giving money directly to schools; scrapping business rates for small businesses; introducing an armed forces card with benefits such as free bus travel and priority NHS treatment for forces personnel. Whilst these policies were very commendable, the Welsh Conservative pledges to protect the NHS budget from cuts for four years, eliminate child poverty in Wales by

2020 and appoint a minister with special responsibilities for north Wales seemed to be largely 'populist sweeteners'.

Since spending on the NHS amounts to over 40 per cent of the total Assembly budget, a far greater percentage than in England, protecting this sometimes inefficient public sector monolith would make it very difficult to carry out the necessary reductions in Welsh Government expenditure in order to reduce the country's debt. The child poverty policy could at best be described as an aspiration, while the 'special treatment' for north Wales merited the question asked by one Welsh Conservative AM during the manifesto discussions, 'why not a specific minister for every other region of Wales?'

Overall, it is little wonder that several 'true Tories' informed me that the Welsh Conservative manifesto generally lacked any genuinely radical policies that offered a real alternative to the 'soggy centrist smug politically-correct consensus prevailing in Cardiff Bay'. I was also told by a former Tory AM that the Welsh Conservative Party leadership was 'love-bombing' Plaid Cymru' to try and form a non-Labour rainbow coalition with them and the Liberal Democrats in the event of no party gaining an overall majority in the sixty-strong National Assembly after polling day. This opinion was given further credibility in the *Western Mail* of 30 April, where David Melding was quoted as saying that 'the prospect of a "rainbow coalition" with Plaid Cymru and the Liberal Democrats must be kept alive'.

In spite of the general absence of a distinctively Tory boldness in the Welsh Conservative manifesto, I campaigned vigorously to try and secure the re-election of Paul Davies as the Tory AM for Preseli Pembrokeshire. After all, Paul had worked very conscientiously to champion the interests of his constituents since his election to the National Assembly in 2007 and is clearly on the pro-devolution 'progressive' wing of the Welsh Conservative Party, like myself, as far as constitutional affairs are concerned. His subsequent victory by 2,175 votes over his Labour opponent Terry Mills, brought great satisfaction to me.

Campaigning with Paul Davies in Crymych, April 2011

All things considered, I was delighted that the Welsh Conservative Party had performed extraordinary well at the polls when the final results of the National Assembly elections were announced on 6 May. Nick Bourne and his team deserve enormous credit for succeeding in their objectives of replacing Plaid Cymru for the first time as the official opposition party to Labour in terms of the number of AMs elected to the National Assembly and in decisively out-polling the Welsh Nationalists in the overall number of votes cast for each party throughout Wales in both the constituencies and on the regional lists.

On an all-Wales turnout of 42.2 per cent, the Welsh Conservative Party had gained 25 per cent of the votes cast in the constituencies and 22.5 per cent on the regional Lists – up more than 2 per cent on the 2007 figures and by far their best performance in any Assembly election. This had resulted in fourteen Welsh Tory AM's being elected to Cardiff Bay, an increase of two on the 2007 election results. Whilst I was overjoyed that Russell George had captured Montgomeryshire from the Liberal Democrats by a majority of 2,324 votes and Janet Finch-Saunders had ousted Plaid Cymru from Aberconwy by 1,567 votes, I was disappointed that the very able Jonathan Morgan was defeated in Cardiff North by Labour's Julie Morgan – the former MP for the seat and wife of ex-First Minister Rhodri Morgan.

Overall, the Welsh Conservatives increased the number of constituencies held by them from five to six – two gains in Montgomeryshire and Aberconwy against one loss in Cardiff North. Similarly, there was an increase from seven to eight Regional List Welsh Tory AMs elected. The election of three new women AMs – Suzy Davies (South Wales West), Antoinette Sandbach (North Wales) and Janet Finch-Saunders (Aberconwy) – greatly increased the female Welsh Conservative Party representation in the National Assembly from one to four.

I was, however, saddened to learn than Nick Bourne had lost his Regional List seat in Mid and West Wales as a result of the Welsh Conservatives gaining one additional constituency member in that electoral region and also because some die-hard Tory anti-devolutionists had given their second vote to UKIP. Although we have sometimes disagreed over the time-scale for the Welsh Tory leadership to publicly support strengthening the powers of the National Assembly and in my conviction that Welsh

Conservative AM's should generally be more robust in order to provide a 'genuine opposition' to the often 'soggy centrist mutual back-slapping consensus' prevailing in Cardiff Bay, Nick Bourne deserves enormous praise for making the Welsh Conservative Party far more distinctively 'Welsh' in its sentiments and aspirations during his leadership over the past decade. He has also presided over a period of consistent growth in popular support for the Welsh Conservative Party in every set of elections in Wales since 2003. Upon hearing the news of his defeat, Welsh Secretary Cheryl Gillan paid tribute to the role Nick Bourne played in 'transforming the image and fortunes of the Welsh Conservative Party for more than a decade', adding that 'the result is a great loss to the National Assembly and to me personally'.

Conversely, Nick Bourne's predecessor as Welsh Conservative Assembly Group leader Rod Richards, who has long regarded Nick with ill-disguised contempt, was quoted by Martin Shipton in the *Western Mail* of 7 May as saying: 'What a wonderful week: Bin Laden on Sunday, Bourne on Friday. Christmas has come early this year'. Wholly opposed to Nick Bourne's attempt to 'Welshify' the Tories, Rod – unlike Nick, a fluent Welsh-speaker – added: 'It's achieved nothing in terms of taking the party forward. All it's about is sucking up to Plaid Cymru'.

The Assembly elections were undoubtedly a success for the Welsh Labour Party and an endorsement of the strategy pursued by its astute leader Carwyn Jones. He saw his Labour team in Cardiff Bay increase from twenty-six AMs to thirty – thereby enabling Carwyn to form an exclusively Labour Welsh Government. Matt Withers, writing in *Wales on Sunday* on 1 May, correctly predicted: 'They'll be celebrating success for a campaign that has failed to inspire, focusing as it did entirely on "sending a message to David

Cameron and Nick Clegg" and the vague "standing up for Wales". In terms of strategy, it was broadly effective at doing the job in hand.'

For Plaid Cymru, their very poor Assembly election results were but a continuation of the severe disappointments the Welsh Nationalists had had to endure at the May 2010 general election. Being decisively defeated by the Welsh Conservative Party in terms of seats and votes in May 2011 was bad enough, but Plaid Cymru also saw its representation in Cardiff Bay decline from fifteen AM's in 2007 to just eleven. This was by far the worst performance by the Welsh Nationalists in any Assembly election. Amongst Plaid's most prominent incumbent casualties was the party's deputy leader, Helen Mary Jones, who lost to Labour in Llanelli. The Welsh Nationalists found themselves in third place after their failed attempt to capture their number one target seat of Carmarthen West and South Pembrokeshire. Here, Angela Burns succeeded in increasing the Welsh Conservative majority from a miniscule ninety-eight votes in 2007 to a much more comfortable 1,504 votes. By contrast, Plaid Cymru's director of policy Nerys Evans's gamble to relinquish her Regional List seat in a bid to gain election for her native constituency completely back-fired. Furthermore, from my experience in the Trelech and Meidrim areas, Nerys's derogatory anti-royalist and pro-republican remarks on *Pawb a'i Farn* on the eve of the royal wedding were responsible for her losing support amongst moderate Welsh-speaking voters. In the south Wales valleys, Ron Davies's attempt at a 'big time' political comeback came to nothing when he lost to Labour in Caerphilly by 4,924 votes.

Plaid Cymru's electoral failure was to a large extent the party's own fault. Whilst Welsh Labour turned their guns on

attacking the Conservative-led Westminster government's
cuts in public services in order to maximise their anti-Tory
vote, Plaid Cymru rather hypocritically concentrated on
attacking the record of the same Welsh Labour Party which
they had been junior partners with in a coalition
government in Cardiff Bay for four years until just weeks
before polling day. It is therefore hardly surprising that the
astute Lord Dafydd Elis-Thomas was extremely critical of
this 'very negative' failed Welsh Nationalist election strategy
during several television and radio interviews on 8 May.

I was also delighted that the Liberal Democrat inspired
proposal to replace the current tried and tested first-past-
the-post voting system of electing UK governments at
general elections by introducing the Alternative Vote, was
decisively rejected by nearly 70 per cent of those people
who voted across the United Kingdom in the referendum
on 5 May 2011. First-past-the-post is simple, it is
understood, it is fair, and, above all, it is effective. There
should be one simple democratic principle in British
elections – whoever gets the most votes always wins.
Conversely, the introduction of AV would have served to
turn many election losers into winners, and would also have
ended the cherished democratic British principle of 'one
person, one vote'.

As a consequence of Nick Bourne's failure to get re-elected
to the National Assembly due to the anomalies of the
complex electoral system, there now had to be a leadership
contest within the Welsh Conservative Party in order to find
a new Assembly group leader. Paul Davies was appointed
interim leader, and arrangements were made to send
nomination papers out on 11 May with the winner to be
declared on 14 July. Although I repeatedly urged Paul
Davies to stand, because I regarded his impeccable Welsh

cultural and linguistic background, together with his undoubted ability, as an enormous asset towards further advancing the Conservative cause in Wales, he eventually declined to do so.

The subsequent contest was to become a two-horse race between the clear early favourite Andrew R. T. Davies, regarded by the media as a more old-fashioned Tory Unionist, and the progressive pro-devolutionist modernizer Nick Ramsay. Although Nick's views on moving the devolution project forward were at least superficially more akin to mine, Andrew's far more boisterous personality appealed to me, as well as his combative debating manner. He has a desire to mould the Welsh Conservatives into a moderate and credible centre-right alternative with distinctive policies from the 'broadly left-wing soggy consensus' currently prevailing within the Labour, Plaid Cymru and Liberal Democrat parties. However, as someone who had already described Paul Davies as an 'ideal potential candidate' in several briefings to journalists, it would have been difficult for me to publicly endorse Andrew R. T. Davies via the media without it being interpreted that he was my second preference. Nonetheless, I was later to actively promote Andrew's candidature amongst members of the Welsh Conservative Party in west Wales.

Events were to show there would be considerable acrimony between the two protagonists. The *Western Mail* of 10 May quoted a 'senior Tory source' as saying, 'Nick Bourne is still trying to control things. He will do what he can to stop Andrew R. T. Davies winning the leadership. Nick doesn't like him'. Although he was careful not to specifically endorse any particular candidate, Nick Bourne stated in the same newspaper article that 'I think we need to avoid the extremes and to carry on as a Welsh party committed to the Welsh language and Welsh culture'. These remarks were widely interpreted as a criticism of Andrew Davies, as someone who would allegedly find it difficult to reach out to voters who were not Conservative by nature. Similar criticisms were also directed by Nick Ramsay towards his more Tory traditionalist opponent, when he told Matt Withers in the *Western Mail* of 17 May that 'we cannot go backwards. I think there's a very real danger that the Welsh Conservatives could go backwards under another candidate'.

Writing in *Golwg* on 19 May and 23 June, I stated that Nick Ramsay was generally perceived to be little more than the pro-Nick Bourne Welsh Conservative establishment's designated 'Stop Andrew R. T. Davies candidate' which feared a possible 'loose cannon' at the helm of the party. This appraisal was given further credibility when it was announced that Jonathan Morgan, generally regarded as Nick Bourne's 'natural successor' if he had not lost his Cardiff North seat in May 2011, had been appointed as Nick Ramsay's campaign manager. During the launch of his personal manifesto at Chepstow Racecourse on 6 June, Nick Ramsay did little to dispel the general perception of himself as 'Nick Bourne's apprentice'. Indeed, he stated, 'I see myself as a liberal, progressive Conservative' and he praised his former leader for turning the Welsh Conservatives into a 'progressive caring party'. His manifesto took a personal sideswipe at his rival Andrew Davies when it stated, 'it has never crossed my mind to abandon the responsibilities of the Shadow Cabinet for the luxury of a backbench life'.

By contrast, Andrew Davies largely based his leadership campaign on traditional Tory family values and the fact that he already had a successful career as a Vale of Glamorgan farmer prior to going into politics. This was surely intended to contrast sharply with Nick Ramsay being single and the fact that he had never really had a 'proper job' outside politics, having been a political researcher before becoming an AM. With political pundits predicting a narrowing of Andrew Davies's lead over Nick Ramsay in the closing stages of the leadership campaign, things became even more personal between the two Tory protagonists. This became most apparent when Andrew Davies was criticised by a pro-Nick Ramsay 'source' for 'wasting public cash', for taking an Assembly assistant to support him at hustings meetings in north Wales while also meeting local business people. This 'senior Tory source' stated in the *Western Mail* of 1 July that 'once again Andrew demonstrates poor judgement. The group needs a man with the skill to lead, not a man who keeps tripping himself up'.

On 14 July at Cardiff's Swalec Stadium, following a lengthy and tense count which ran several hours over schedule, Andrew R. T. Davies was declared the winner in the Welsh Conservative Assembly Group leadership ballot, with 53.1 per cent of the vote. Andrew's numerical margin of victory was actually only 153 votes. Matt Withers, writing in the *Western Mail* of 15 July, correctly observed that:

> His success will inevitably be seen as a narrow victory for the right of the party in Wales. He represents that strand which never fully signed up to Nick Bourne's mission to 'Welshify' the Conservative brand, being more of an old-fashioned 'One Nation' Tory.

Andrew R. T. Davies now appointed Paul Davies as Deputy Leader, rather than his defeated opponent Nick Ramsay, who had to be content with the post of Shadow Business Minister.

Andrew Davies deserves a great deal of credit for the way he has performed in his role as the leader of the Welsh Conservative Group in the National Assembly since his election in July 2011. During, for example, his first head-to-head confrontation with Carwyn Jones during First Minister's Question Time on 20 September, Andrew demonstrated that his style was certainly much more 'bellicose' than his somewhat 'bookish' predecessor Nick Bourne. Andrew Davies also made a very effective critique of the Labour Welsh Government's proposed legislative programme for the new Assembly. On 27 September, he stated:

> After 12 years of Labour, Wales is the poorest nation of the UK, our schools are blighted by systemic failure, and the Welsh NHS budget is facing the biggest budget cut in the UK. Since Carwyn Jones became First Minister, NHS waiting lists have risen by almost 70 per cent, while the number of patients waiting more than 36 weeks for treatment is 200 times greater.

Andrew Davies further developed this theme during his first speech at his party's UK conference as Assembly group leader in October 2011, when he claimed that Labour NHS pioneer Aneurin Bevan must be 'turning in his grave' at the state of the health service in Wales. He also pledged his commitment to devolution, stating that 'I want to see devolution work because I believe that in the right hands it empowers people and it empowers communities'.

I also welcomed the fact that in October 2011 Cheryl Gillan launched the £1million Silk Commission, which will examine devolution in Wales, with particular reference to the financial accountability of the National Assembly. Nick Bourne was appointed as the Welsh Conservative Party representative on this commission. It was decided on 8 March 2012 that the commission's final recommendations would be made public by the spring of 2014. In my opinion, more powers to the Assembly should be accompanied by more financial responsibility on the part of the Welsh Government.

Thankfully, this 'progressive' view was supported by the Welsh Conservative group in the National Assembly. The *Western Mail* of 16 February 2012 reported that in its submission to the Silk Commission, the Welsh Tory AM's called for the devolution of some aspects of income tax to be considered in Wales. Indeed, some control over the tax could make the Assembly 'more accountable to the people it represents for the money it spends', they said. The Welsh Conservative AM's also noted in their submission the potential benefits of devolving corporation tax to the Assembly. By contrast, David Davies, the 'devo-sceptic' Welsh Tory MP for Monmouth, rather ironically suggested in the press that it would save £1 million of taxpayer's money by just giving the National Assembly additional powers, because every previous government commission had recommended that course of action!

In practice Andrew R. T. Davies has broadly continued the general 'Welshifying' policies of Nick Bourne by now suggesting that the Welsh Conservatives must consider having their own leader fully in charge of the party in Wales, rather than just an Assembly group leader. Although a late convert to this idea since he opposed it during his Assembly group leadership campaign the previous year, I'm delighted that Andrew now supports the concept of a Welsh Conservative Party leader which people like David Melding and myself have espoused for over a decade.

Andrew's current position as Assembly group leader contrasts sharply with that of Ruth Davidson, who last year became the first full leader of the Scottish Conservatives, with control over the entire party in Scotland. A similar change would also bring the Welsh Conservatives into line with Welsh Labour, the Welsh Liberal Democrats and Plaid Cymru who all have their respective Welsh party leaders.

Andrew R. T. Davies's apparent view was that a situation which occurred in April 2011, when Nick Bourne's preamble to the Welsh Conservatives Assembly elections manifesto came third after David Cameron and Cheryl Gillan must not happen again. Moreover, Andrew stated in the *Western Mail* of 1 February 2012, 'I would very much welcome the opportunity for the Assembly group leader to emerge from a ballot of the membership to be the leader of the party here in Wales'. These comments provoked controversy since it was claimed in the *Western Mail* of 8 February that Cheryl Gillan had been 'irritated' by Andrew's remarks, and had allegedly told him so in a telephone call. If true this would be hardly surprising, since there will always be underlying tensions between any political party's Assembly and Westminster branches over who controls the 'levers of power'.

I attended the Preseli Pembrokeshire Conservative Association Annual General Meeting at Rudbaxton Hall, on the outskirts of Haverfordwest, on 18 February. Here Andrew R. T. Davies made a devastating critique of Carwyn Jones's Labour Welsh Government's 'total failure' to improve public services in Wales. According to Andrew, this 'failure' was best illustrated by the fact that up to February 2012 not one major piece of legislation had been brought forward by the Labour Welsh Government since the Assembly elections in May 2011.This excellent speech was greatly appreciated by everyone present which included the AM and MP for the constituency - Paul Davies and Stephen Crabb.

I was also delighted that Andrew R. T. Davies re-affirmed his enthusiastic support for the whole devolution project while addressing the National Assembly on 14 March. Here

With Stephen Crabb, MP, Andrew R. T. Davies and Paul Davies, AMs.
Preseli Pembrokeshire Conservative Association AGM, February 2012

he said there was a 'clear consensus that there is an appetite for devolution amongst the people of Wales, and we on these benches recognise that, and we will be playing our part to make sure that is supported'. Demonstrating that delivering a better quality of life for the people of Wales is the practical 'test' for the success of Welsh devolution, Andrew correctly added: 'What a lot of people also want is delivery, and they want to see success for the devolved model of government and improvement in their lives'.

In arguably the most important 'progressive' constitutional announcement ever made by a Welsh Conservative 'leader', Andrew R. T. Davies publicly declared, during the week the National Eisteddfod was held in the Vale of Glamorgan, that the National Assembly should be called the Welsh Parliament. The *Western Mail*'s Matt Withers reported on 10 August 2012 that Andrew Davies had said:

When we look at other countries like Australia, state parliaments operate alongside the national parliament. In the UK, we have the Scottish Parliament and the Westminster Parliament. So in this week of celebration of Welsh culture, I call on other leaders to consider this change. There is no reason why we couldn't have the Welsh Parliament too. There is no hurry to overnight changes, but in 2016 wouldn't it be a great thing for the Welsh people to vote in elections for a Welsh Parliament for the first time since the fifteenth century?

Andrew concluded his remarks by stressing that such a move would not be 'simply a rebrand for the sake of rebranding'. He said:

This is a statement about the institution that now legislates for our great nation. The Assembly deserves to be respected. It deserves the respect of the executive, and it deserves to be an institution that stands out. Some may question why there needs to be any change at all. There is a parliament in Scotland with primary law-making powers, so why not in Wales?

In my view, this is a truly historic moment in Welsh politics. It amounts to the victory of those patriotic and progressive Welsh Conservatives like me who have campaigned over the past fifteen years, in the face of considerable opposition from some die-hard Tory reactionaries, for the Welsh Conservative leadership to champion, officially, the establishment of a full Welsh Parliament.

'Welshifying' the Welsh Conservative Party continued on 4 September 2012 after David Cameron's cabinet re-shuffle, when Cheryl Gillan was replaced as Secretary of State for

Wales by her deputy David Jones. This Welsh-speaking MP for Clwyd West is the first Conservative Secretary of State for Wales to represent a Welsh constituency at Westminster since Nicholas Edwards (from 1979 to 1987).

The *Western Mail*'s Martin Shipton rightly appraised Cheryl Gillan's record on 5 September: 'During her time as Secretary of State, her relations with the Tory group at the Assembly have sometimes bordered on the fractious'. A Welsh political commentator told me some Conservative AMs privately called Cheryl Gillan the 'Colonial Governor-General' due to the imperious way she sometimes spoke to them. Moreover, David Jones's deputy Stephen Crabb, MP for Preseli Pembrokeshire, revealingly said he was 'really confident' the Wales Office will now establish a 'warmer relationship' with the Assembly.

David Jones's appointment was described by Andrew R. T. Davies as the 'right choice'. But several Welsh Conservative AMs and MPs stated privately they would have preferred Stephen Crabb, and some believe that while neither David nor Stephen is a 'greatly enthusiastic pro-devolutionist', Stephen is 'more personally approachable' and 'politically pragmatic'.

I believe Andrew R. T. Davies must establish even more 'clear blue water' between the Tory AMs and the Wales Office in London to further advance their distinctively Welsh Conservative political agenda. Truly, the job of Welsh Secretary is increasingly irrelevant in this age of devolved governments. It will surely be better long-term for the First Ministers of Wales, Scotland and Northern Ireland to negotiate directly with the Prime Minister of the UK Government. During an interview for Radio Cymru on 9 September, I said: 'Having representatives of the Westminster Government presiding over the respective administrations of the devolved nations amounts to little more than an obsolete relic from Britain's colonial past'.

12

Although I have not contested an election since 2001, largely because of my increasing media work commitments, I continue to be a loyal and active member of the Welsh Conservative Party. I have been asked on numerous occasions, why I am a Conservative in my political opinions. My simple answer is that I believe in helping people to help themselves in a Britain which is free, prosperous and strong. As a patriotic Welshman I also believe that Wales's overall interests are served by remaining an integral part of the United Kingdom, and that this is best safeguarded by the Welsh Conservative Party.

One of my most enjoyable activities on behalf of the Welsh Conservative Party was appearing on S4C's *Pawb a'i Farn* on 22 January 2009. The programme was broadcast live from the Sir Thomas Picton School Leisure Centre, Haverfordwest. On the panel with me were the broadcaster Brychan Llŷr, the business woman Catherine Rees and the Welsh Language Society activist, Ffred Ffransis. This proved to be a most enjoyable occasion, with an excellent response from the audience that had been amassed from all over Pembrokeshire.

I was convinced that the programme's presenter Dewi Llwyd, together with the production team, were hoping for a verbal 'punch up' between the militant Welsh Language Society activist, Ffred, and the Welsh Conservative firebrand now resident in Trelech, me. We both realised this and were simply not prepared to 'play the media script'. Dewi Llwyd was shocked when I described Ffred Ffransis as a man of principle who was prepared to practice what he preached. I was astonished when Ffred Ffransis stated that he admired me in many ways. He also claimed that I was 'too honest to be a MP'.

Nonetheless there was some lively debate, although good-natured and often quite humorous between us. This became apparent over the contentious issue of immigration into Wales and the banking crisis. What Dewi Llwyd and his team had failed to recognise is that both Ffred Ffransis and I are fervent Welsh Congregationalists, with the former an active member at Tabernacle Chapel, Pencader. The media must remember there are some things that transcend politics, and can have a significant effect on the tone of a public debate. Incidentally, Ffred Ffransis and I enjoyed a 'battle royal repeat performance' when we were panellists on Radio Cymru's *Hawl i Holi* current affairs programme, which was broadcast from Myddfai Community Hall, Carmarthenshire, on 14 May 2012.

Another very interesting political debate took place on Radio Cymru's *Dau o'r Bae*, presented by Vaughan Roderick and Bethan Lewis. The programme was broadcast live on 10 July 2009 and the panellists included the actress Sharon Morgan, Terry Davies, Labour, Mark Cole (Liberal Democrat) and me. Whilst everyone condemned the excessive expenses claimed by MPs and AMs to varying degrees, a clash occurred on whom the Welsh people should support in the Ashes Cricket Test between England and Australia held in Cardiff. When Sharon Morgan said that she endorsed Plaid Cymru MP Adam Price's suggestion that Wales should support Australia because there is no formal Welsh cricket team, the other three panellists criticised her. All three emphasised that what people wanted to enjoy was the cricket and not politics.

I stated that Adam Price's views represented that small-minded 'anyone but England' Welsh Nationalist mentality. I then referred to my teaching experiences in London, where English people would support a team from another part of the United Kingdom, if England was not involved in this sporting event. This rather pathetic anti-British mentality, personified by Adam Price, later reminded me of the Falklands War in 1982. During that time some Welsh Nationalists wore Argentine football shirts, while Welsh Guardsmen were sacrificing their lives in order to liberate the Falkland Islanders from the illegal invasion orchestrated by the Argentine military regime.

Incidentally, these very introspective and narrow-minded sentiments re-emerged in March 2012. Writing in the *Western Mail* of 10 March, Bethan Jenkins, the Plaid Cymru AM for South Wales West, vehemently opposed players from the Celtic nations participating in the Team GB football team during the forthcoming London Olympics. Thankfully, Andrew R. T. Davies spoke for the 'moderate majority' of people when he retorted, 'I always find it amusing to hear it suggested that supporters of Team GB are anti-Welsh. I have no problem in perceiving myself as both Welsh and British'.

Rather ironically, I appeared with Adam Price on a *Pawb a'i Farn* panel, held at the Carmarthen Leisure Centre, Johnstown, on 29 October, 2009. Whilst I had prepared myself for a 'real verbal punch-up' with this formidable gentleman, I was pleasantly surprised to discover that our first 'face to face meeting', just prior to the commencement of the debate, was a cordial one. The conversation flowed easily between us and it was obvious that we both shared some common aspirations regarding promoting Wales as a country and the Welsh people as a nation on the world stage. This obvious rapport between us was utilised very effectively during the actual debate because we both 'ganged up' on the Labour MP for Llanelli, Nia Griffith. I shall never forget Adam Price's stinging attack on Nia Griffith when he stated publicly that 'you should be ashamed of the fact that a Welsh Conservative in the person of Felix Aubel is much more favourably disposed towards establishing a proper Welsh Parliament than the Labour Party'. That was some compliment from Adam Price! For the well-being of Welsh politics, I hope that Adam Price succeeds in gaining election to the National Assembly in May 2016, because that institution badly needs someone who is prepared to speak their mind and to give those numerous complacent and self-righteous politicians residing in Cardiff Bay a real shaking.

This self-righteous attitude is symbolised by Siôn (really John) White, the character from S4C's popular Welsh-language soap *Pobol y Cwm*. Here we have a working-class Anglo-Welsh boy from the Rhondda whose father is a socialist. Siôn attends the University of Wales in Aberystwyth, where he seeks to portray himself as a Welsh patriot in order to gain popularity with the offspring of 'respectable' middle-class Welsh Nationalists. This means getting involved with the Welsh Language Society and supporting Plaid Cymru. Having established his 'good Welsh' credentials, he then moves to the *Fro Gymraeg* (Welsh-speaking area) – the mythical Cwm Deri in *Pobol y Cwm* – in order to live out his fantasies.

Some years later, Siôn White has the audacity to tell the native-born Welsh-speaking population what constitutes being a 'good Welshman'. This now economically middle-class gentleman, who is a self-employed Welsh translator, accuses some of his more working-class neighbours of having no concern for the preservation of the Welsh language and culture. However, these people have other priorities, namely the need to earn a living in order to provide for themselves and their families. They cannot afford to indulge in essentially middle-class Welsh Nationalist pursuits, such as condemning anything that is associated with 'Britishness'. Also, many of the native Welsh-speakers see no inconsistency in being proud to be British as well as

Welsh. They are comfortable with their dual national identity, and tend to regard Siôn White as an 'oddball'.

Siôn White and his fellow travellers earn a living largely at the expense of taxpayers by undertaking translation work on behalf of primarily public bodies. Many native Welsh speakers believe that translating every public document into Welsh and then circulating them to everyone, contributes virtually nothing towards preserving the Welsh language. Indeed, the very technical language used by Siôn White and his colleagues is so complicated that it is little wonder that over 90 per cent of Welsh speakers fill in bilingual forms in English.

The enormous amount of public money wasted on circulating fully bilingual material to everyone would be far better spent on providing more financial assistance to Welsh learners' classes. Nevertheless, Welsh-language versions of forms should be available on request. This would ensure equality for the Welsh language without the financial extravagance of sending out bilingual forms to the 80 per cent of people who do not speak Welsh and the overwhelming majority of Welsh speakers who prefer to fill them in English. This latter category will only show a greater willingness to use Welsh-medium forms if these are produced in the everyday language people use, rather than the often largely incomprehensible jargon utilised by Siôn White and co.

In a very perceptive article written in the *Western Mail* of 16 September 2009, David Rosser of the Wales CBI claimed that the best means to promote the Welsh language is not through 'the slavish approach we have been taking of, if it moves translate it'. He then cited practical innovations by some private companies to increase Welsh language facilities. They included the launches by Orange of a Welsh-language mobile handset, and by Google of the Welsh

Guest speaker at the St Clears Welsh learners'
St David's Day Luncheon, March 2012

language translator and search engine.

In a very significant letter in the *Western Mail* of 24 September 2009 the highly-respected Plaid Cymru member Dr Dafydd Huws of Caerphilly reflected the opinions of people like me regarding the futility of translating every public document into Welsh. Dafydd Huws asserted: 'If our dream is to secure a truly bilingual Wales, the over-riding priority must be to have more people speaking the Welsh language. Any language thrives if it is spoken and heard, and not through spending scarce financial resources on undertaking unnecessary bureaucratic translation work'.

The Welsh Language Board quango was given £13.3 million of taxpayer's money in 2010 to promote the use of Welsh and S4C received £100 million in public money during the same year. Despite S4C's budget being cut by nearly 25 per cent over the next four years and the arrangements for the channel to be partly-funded from the

BBC licence fee from 2013, S4C allegedly remains the most heavily-subsidised minority language TV channel in the whole of Europe. No one can therefore argue with any credibility that the Welsh language is not well-supported financially from taxpayer's money. The Welsh language press, for example, receives very large government grants to sustain it, due to the apparent indifference of Welsh-speakers towards reading material in their own language. It was revealed on S4C's politics programme *CF99* on 19 January 2011 that the current affairs magazine *Golwg*, with a weekly circulation of 2,900, now receives £73,000 a year in subsidy from the National Assembly. This is, however, dwarfed by *Barn*, a Welsh language periodical with a monthly circulation of only 1,000, which obtains an annual subsidy of £80,000. In practice, this means that each copy of *Barn* is subsidised to the tune of £8 by the taxpayer, while it is actually sold for £2.99. It is now up to the people of Wales to ensure that the Welsh language survives and expands as a living language – by speaking, reading, and writing it.

Considering all the financial support the Welsh language already receives, I was somewhat astonished to read in the *Western Mail* of 13 March 2012 that the Welsh Language Board believed that the Welsh Government 'must double its expenditure on the Welsh language to ensure its survival'. In practice, this meant that the Welsh Government needed to 'push its annual spending on the Welsh language towards the £20 million mark over the next five years'. When will these people realise that the survival of Welsh depends very significantly upon the goodwill of the 80 per cent of the population of Wales who do not speak the language? Unfortunately, this goodwill is in danger of being eroded by these over-zealous Welsh language activists.

This general assessment was given further credibility by Martin Shipton's devastating critique in the *Western Mail* of

22 and 23 May 2012 of the all-party recommendation that all proceedings of the National Assembly should be translated into Welsh. According to this very astute journalist, 'the total cost of translating all Assembly proceedings could rise to as much as £400,000 a year'. Surely, any reasonable person would agree with Martin Shipton that 'at a time of austerity ... it is inappropriate to increase the cost of translation by such a significant amount'. Furthermore, the same newspaper reported on 25 May that less than 5 per cent of people who access the National Assembly's Record of Proceedings do so via the Welsh-language version of the Assembly's website. It appears to me that the simplest solution to this problem of unnecessary expenditure on translation services would be to follow the procedure that exists in the Irish Republic. In that country proceedings are recorded only in the language in which they are spoken, and most Irish politicians appear to be satisfied with this arrangement.

Thankfully common sense has apparently prevailed, since the *Western Mail* of 16 June 2012 reported that this proposal to translate all National Assembly proceedings into Welsh 'appears to be dead in the water'. The newspaper claimed that this proposal had failed to gain enough support from AMs across the political spectrum to make it a reality.

I was a panellist on a *Pawb a'i Farn* programme held at Rhydywaun Welsh Medium Comprehensive School on 9 December 2010. In the programme the issues of a new Welsh Language Act and the future of S4C were discussed. Here I reiterated my view that no legislation will save the Welsh language, only the desire of people to continue speaking it as a 'living language'. Coincidentally, in a letter in the *Western Mail* on the same day, Barry's C. E. Lambert stated that 'Welsh doesn't need legislation to survive; it needs many more proficient speakers'.

Likewise, I criticised Plaid Cymru's behaviour of opposing David Cameron's offer to devolve the responsibility for Welsh-language broadcasting to the National Assembly on the grounds that Plaid still wanted to receive British taxpayer's money to finance a Welsh-language TV channel. I accused Plaid Cymru of hypocrisy on a grand scale here, because the Welsh Nationalists wanted to continue the Westminster government's financial subsidy to S4C, while at the same time wishing to have more powers for the National Assembly in other fields.

It was therefore most encouraging to read in the *Western Mail* of 16 December that Lord Dafydd Elis-Thomas called for the urgent transfer of the responsibility for maintaining Welsh-language television broadcasting from the UK Department for Culture, Media and Sport to the Welsh Assembly Government. Launching a possible broadside at his own party's somewhat hypocritical official position, the astute Presiding Officer said, 'People prefer to get money for nothing from the UK taxpayer, I suppose'. He also stated that he was happy to see S4C part-funded by the licence fee, as proposed by the UK Government.

With members of the Welsh-speaking elitist *crachach* at its helm, no wonder S4C has been in such a financial mess. No reasonable person can really criticise Jeremy Hunt, the Conservative Culture, Media and Sports Minister for pointing out that viewing figures for S4C have fallen while its financial subsidy, prior to the recent government financial cuts, has steadily increased. It was my contention that S4C should become a genuinely bilingual TV channel, as it was to some extent in practice prior to the advent of digital television, when its viewing figures were considerably higher.

A very sensible suggestion for improving the viewing figures for S4C was made by D. N. Norman, of Porthcawl, in the *Western Mail* of 26 March 2011. He suggested that English-language programmes relating to Wales currently broadcast on BBC2, and which are under threat if BBC2 ends regional opt-outs, should be broadcast on S4C. S4C would therefore get much more support from the people of Wales if it provided a service to non-Welsh-speakers as well as to Welsh-speakers.

I was appalled that the Welsh Language Society began a national campaign of 'direct action' to allegedly 'save' S4C. The *Western Mail* of 7 March 2011 reported that two Welsh Language Society members were arrested after breaking into the constituency office of the Welsh Conservative AM for Cardiff North, Jonathan Morgan. He rightly responded to this act of pre-meditated vandalism by saying, 'Anyone who undertakes this sort of criminal activity should be put in prison, regardless of the cause. I feel absolutely disgusted that they feel the need to break in and wreak havoc in an office there to serve the people of Cardiff North'.

It was brought to my attention as a Welsh Congregational minister in Trelech, that some pupils from at least two secondary schools in west Carmarthenshire and north Pembrokeshire were apparently being 'indoctrinated' or even 'brainwashed' by some over-zealous Welsh Nationalist teachers and prefects into actively supporting the Welsh Language Society's campaign. This sort of behaviour on school premises was wholly unacceptable to me and should be condemned in the strongest possible terms.

The *Western Mail* of 2 February 2012 reported that the well-travelled and very experienced Ian Jones had been appointed as the new chief executive of S4C. He is a genuinely forward-thinking pragmatist who wishes to utilise the many advantages of working closely with the BBC and of maximizing to the utmost the restructured S4C budget. I like his stipulated progressive aim to 'inform, educate and entertain any time, any place, anywhere'. I wish Ian Jones every success in, I hope, transforming S4C into a genuinely 'people-orientated' television channel which caters for all tastes.

My general critique of the Welsh-speaking *crachach* social elite was further developed by Penywaun-born Dr Kim Howells. In an excellent BBC Wales documentary called *Kim Howells – A Valleys View of the World*, broadcast on 28 November 2010, the former Labour MP for Pontypridd was devastating in his criticism of this *crachach* elite who masquerade as *gwerin* or common people. According to Kim Howells, 'I've never met such narrow-minded, introspective and bigoted people as the members of the Welsh *crachach*'. He proceeded by describing them as 'a kind of establishment, a *crachach*, a ruling class, which I think is incredibly insular, self-sustaining and self-serving in so many ways'. Furthermore, Kim Howells regarded this crachach ruling class as typifying one of the worst aspects of the 'whingeing Welsh mentality' which usually seeks to blame somebody else, almost invariably their English neighbours, for their own failures and deficiencies.

Similar sentiments were expressed by Rod Richards during a *Pawb a'i Farn* programme relating specifically to the future of the Welsh language. The programme was broadcast from the Brangwyn Hall, Swansea, on 16 February 2012. Rod claimed that the Welsh-speaking middle-class social elite had deliberately 'politicised' the issue of promoting the Welsh language in order to further their own 'separatist Welsh Nationalist and anti-English political agenda'. He even went as far as to claim that 'this narrow-minded clique were responsible for alienating many ordinary people from supporting the Welsh language'.

In contrast to the rather juvenile protests of the Welsh

Language Society, I very much welcome the establishment of the pressure group *Dyfodol i'r Iaith* (A Future for the Language). The *Western Mail* of 16 July quoted Dr Simon Brooks, a leading member of the new group, who said: 'In setting up *Dyfodol i'r Iaith* we have made the irrevocable decision that under no circumstances will we break the law'. For many years I have held Simon Brooks in the highest esteem as a genuine Welsh patriot, and I'm sure that he will continue to make a very significant contribution to promoting the Welsh language and culture. I was also delighted that *Dyfodol i'r Iaith* has declared itself to be an independent non-party political pressure group pledged to establishing a good working relationship with the Welsh government and other public bodies. I wish this organisation every success in the future.

Siôn White can frequently be a mass of contradictions. On the one hand, he sees himself as one of the people or mythical *gwerin*, frequently emphasising that he is the son of a miner in order to try and 'prove' his working-class pedigree. On the other hand, Siôn White enjoys the 'good life' associated with a comfortable middle-class lifestyle. He is really no better than the often very materialistic Essex man or woman as far as accumulating material possessions as status symbols are concerned. The real difference is that Essex man or woman is more honest than Siôn White. The former makes no attempt to disguise their material-possessions-equals-social-status ethos, while the latter hides this under the cloak of promoting Welsh community values.

Likewise, many members of the 'respectable' Welsh-speaking middle-class who are vocal in their opposition to English people buying holiday homes in *Y Fro Gymraeg* are guilty of hypocrisy on a grand scale. Indeed, several prominent Plaid Cymru members actually own holiday homes in Spain, Portugal and France. If anglicisation is meant to weaken the indigenous Welsh culture in places like Aberaeron and New Quay, what are Welsh part-time colonists doing to the indigenous cultures in continental Europe? This Welsh Nationalist hypocrisy is incomprehensible to me and is an example par excellence of the pot calling the kettle black.

Siôn White will also seek to delude himself that he is still a socialist who remains true to his working-class south Wales valleys roots. In reality, he is perceived by the general public as a capitalist entrepreneur. There is nothing wrong with this, but in Siôn White's mind capitalism is a dirty word. This is an incomprehensible attitude to me, since socialism and communism have been completely discredited as economic systems during the twentieth-century.

Siôn White and his fellow-travellers are not only obsessed with preserving the Welsh language and culture at home, but also in campaigning against 'selective injustice' abroad. For example, these Welsh Nationalists oppose wars involving the United Kingdom like those in Afghanistan and Iraq. Conversely, I have declared my own opposition to these wars, but for different reasons. It is my view that neither the Afghan or Iraq wars serve British interests. This theme was elaborated upon by me during a *Dau o'r Bae* panel discussion with Paul Flynn, the high-profile Labour MP for Newport West on 20 July 2012. Our broad agreement on this issue demonstrates how 'free-thinking' people from across the political spectrum can reach similar conclusions. If the United States wishes to get involved militarily in these countries, it is entirely a matter for them. But those wars have nothing to do with the specific strategic interests of Great Britain. However, if British interests are directly threatened anywhere in the world as was the case with the Falkland Islands in 1982, the UK has the right to do whatever is at its disposal to defend itself.

I can understand why so many of the 'respectable' Welsh-speaking middle-class symbolised by Siôn White opposed the now annual Armed Forces Day which was first celebrated on 27 June 2009. This event was intended as a display of public support for Great Britain's armed forces who have given immeasurable service by ensuring that the British Isles have remained free from foreign oppression over the centuries. Moreover, if it wasn't for their heroics during the Second World War, Britain, including Wales, would have been under Nazi tyranny and would have suffered the horrendous consequences. This would have included the genocide of so-called 'undesirables' such as Jews, Slavs, gypsies, gays, and almost certainly the Welsh language and culture. In other words, if everyone had been a pacifist, Hitler would have won the war.

Plaid Cymru still ought to feel ashamed of its official policy of neutrality towards Nazi Germany during the Second World War and public support for General Franco's fascists during the Spanish Civil War immediately preceding it. In a letter in the *Western Mail* on 22 September 2009, the Labour Party stalwart Eddie Legg of Blaina, Abertillery, spoke on behalf of many people when he said:

> When will Plaid say sorry for their behaviour during World War Two? Plaid wanted Wales to be neutral, hoping Welshmen would refuse conscription on the grounds that they were Welsh. While Plaid and her conscientious objectors slept safe and sound in their Welsh Nationalist beds at night, my father and thousands of Welshmen and women joined ranks with our neighbours in Britain, Europe and the rest of the world to keep us free from the madness of Adolph Hitler and his Nazi war machine. Lest we forget, that war

resulted in the deaths of 50,000,000 people and the destruction of thousands of cities and towns.

Armed Forces Day was really opposed by many 'respectable' middle-class Welsh Nationalists in the mould of Siôn White because they feared that it reinforced common British values in Wales. They have, however, to accept that these British values, which go back for centuries and link the respective nations of the British Isles together, are characteristics that are supported by the clear majority of the people of Wales. Other visual expressions of this British solidarity are that most Welsh people welcomed the 40th anniversary of the Investiture of Prince Charles in July 2009 and the wedding of Prince William and Kate Middleton on 29 April 2011. The great public displays of enthusiasm in Wales, as elsewhere, for Queen Elizabeth's Diamond Jubilee celebrations in June 2012, clearly demonstrate the loyalty of the overwhelming majority of the Welsh people to the Royal Family. As the *Western Mail*'s headline on 6 June read: 'Wales came together and showed its affection for the Queen'.

I would therefore place the promotion of shared 'British interests', such as the defence of the realm and the preservation of our democratic freedoms against 'common' external and internal threats, above any allegedly specific 'Welsh Nationalistic' considerations. On the other hand, those of a more Welsh Nationalist disposition believe in the old Irish separatist dictum of 'England's difficulty is Ireland's opportunity'. I just cannot understand this very parochial and introspective 'cut off your nose in order to spite your face' mentality. It is for this reason that I and many other Welsh patriots would find it difficult to be a member of Plaid Cymru, a party that wishes to establish an independent Welsh socialist republic that would withdraw from NATO and be politically neutral in any military international conflict. To me this is simply an abdication of our international responsibilities to champion the principles of freedom and democracy throughout the world via the United Nations and NATO.

It is for this reason that I supported the international military action to enforce the 17 March 2011 United Nations-approved 'no-fly zone' against the tyrannical dictator Colonel Muammar Gaddafi in Libya. One could not simply stand on the sidelines while this brutal despot, who had sponsored international terrorism, massacred his own people.

13

Although I am critical of the Siôn White 'respectable' Welsh-speaking middle-class stereotype, I do share some of the general characteristics. My south Wales valleys social background is essentially lower middle-class, with a primary school teacher as a mother and a shopkeeper as a father. I received an essentially middle-class education at Rhydfelen Welsh School and then attended two University of Wales institutions. My religious background is also Welsh-speaking, having been brought up at Ebeneser Welsh Congregational Church, Trecynon. I am also a Welsh Congregational minister, clearly a middle-class occupation in terms of social status if not necessary in economic terms.

However, I also possess characteristics that contrast sharply with the Welsh-speaking middle-class Siôn White stereotype. I have been heavily influenced by my father's Slovenian background, which was conservative, pro-monarchist and fervently anti-communist. The strong military tradition within the Aubel family has also led to my opposition to appeasement and pacifism. My father's experiences as a coal miner have created a suspicion in me of trade union leaders, some of whom have sought to turn industrial disputes into political confrontations.

My mother's liberal-conservative background was also right of centre in the political spectrum. Even her Nonconformist upbringing cannot be described as radical, since it was heavily-influenced by her mother's Anglican conservatism. These inherited characteristics have created in me a rather liberal-inclined Welsh Congregationalism, with strong support expressed for bilingual religious services. Indeed, I view the Welsh language as a means of communicating the Gospel message during Christian worship rather than as an essential cultural component of the service. This contrasts sharply with the opinions of the majority of Welsh Congregational ministers who see the use of the Welsh language as an integral part of worship.

This Welsh-Slovenian genetic mix can sometimes create tensions within me. On the one hand, I have almost certainly inherited several arguably 'Slovenian' characteristics from my father. These include a strict honour code, rigorous self-discipline and an independent spirit. My father may well have been significantly responsible for implanting in me a somewhat paradoxical 'anarchic conservatism', which combines libertarianism and authoritarianism.

My mother must surely have played a significant part in moulding those aspects of my character that can be described as 'Welsh'. These include a love of Welsh history and culture, without any political implications attached to them. My mother represented an older form of Welsh patriotism that could appreciate the virtues of 'all things best' in Welsh cultural life without being anti-British in any way. She believed that you could be a Welsh patriot without voting Plaid Cymru or supporting the law-breaking activities of the Welsh Language Society. This legacy has been crucial in moulding many of my views regarding Welsh Nationalism.

I have a pragmatic attitude to life that has been largely inherited from both my parents. My father was forced to be a pragmatist due to the very uncertain nature of his life, primarily as a consequence of the Second World War. Moreover, he had to be pragmatic in his approach to everything upon arriving as a displaced person in Great Britain in 1948. With personal success and social acceptance in his adopted country the norm, my father just did what he needed to do. Similarly, my mother was largely a pragmatist.

She learnt to make the best out of her life, having felt obligated to return to Aberdare in order to look after her increasingly infirm parents. My mother also implanted in me the necessity of trying to make the most out of opportunities coming my way.

It has been said that while I am quite an astute tactician, I am a generally mediocre long-term strategist. This short- and medium-term outlook has resulted in me being unwilling or unable to take several episodes in my life to their logical conclusion. Indeed, I have been criticised by several people over the years for allowing my life to be allegedly 'blown off course' by distractions. Yet I would have described these 'distractions' as opportunities.

Instead of me pursuing an academic career, possibly ending up as a university lecturer, it has been alleged that I have allowed myself to be distracted by political ambitions. Nevertheless, my political interests did not have an adverse affect on my academic studies, which were always given priority by me. With the benefit of hindsight, I have had three major career options. I could have earned a living from teaching or lecturing. Alternatively, I could have gone into the ministry at a younger age. There was also the political option. In the event, I have had the opportunity to pursue all three options with varying degrees of success. Such is my liking for variety in life. Nonetheless, I would almost certainly have achieved more material success by concentrating exclusively on any one of these options.

I sometimes talk excessively about my father, who died in 1987. In reality, I still live in the 'shadow' of my father. Whatever I achieve in life is often measured against what my father did during the war and post-war years. To make matters worse, I was born under the Virgo star sign that tends to make me a perfectionist. This has made me somewhat unfairly critical of other people, as well as being very harsh upon myself. As a consequence, things sometimes seem to fall just short of the mark for me in life. This has sometimes made it difficult for me to be content with my lot, which has occasionally led me to a feeing of boredom and stagnation. It is for this reason that the 'roaring lion' inside me makes me search for new challenges to overcome.

What the future has in store for me is a mystery. I hope to see a full law-making parliament with control over Wales's domestic affairs. This would bring Wales to a similar position politically to my beloved Jersey. Nevertheless, I believe that the UK government should remain responsible for defence and foreign policy. In other words, I believe in 'Home Rule' for Wales in domestic policy, but not in any concept of 'independence' outside Great Britain. I therefore view devolution as an end in itself rather than a forerunner to the separation of Wales from the United Kingdom. I remain convinced that Wales's interests are best served by remaining an integral part of Great Britain and actually believe that overall Wales has done rather well from being incorporated into the United Kingdom.

Those people who think that Wales could prosper as an 'independent' country within the European Union have a fundamentally erroneous belief. This is because a Wales separated from the rest of Britain would not legally be a member of the European Union in the first place. After all, Wales became a constituent part of the European Union when the United Kingdom formally joined that institution in January 1973. Therefore, an 'independent' Wales would have to re-apply to become a member of the European Union. It is probable that Wales's application would be vetoed by Spain and France. This is because accepting Wales's application to join the European Union as an 'independent' country would only encourage Basque,

Catalan, and Breton nationalists within these respective countries to seek to emulate this possible constitutional precedent. In other words, no 'sane' European state would plant the seeds of its own destruction by allowing Wales to join the European Union as a separate entity from the United Kingdom.

While I was a panellist on a *Pawb a'i Farn* programme from the Senedd in Cardiff on 9 February 2012, there was quite a heated debate between myself and Bethan Jenkins, the very left-wing Plaid Cymru AM for South Wales West. The debate related to the proposed referendum on Scottish independence and its possible implications for Wales. I pointed out that the results of an opinion poll by ITV Wales published in the *Western Mail* of 3 February showed that only 10 per cent of those people questioned supported an independent Wales, even if Scotland actually voted to leave the United Kingdom. Even with an independent Scotland, two out of three Plaid Cymru voters were opposed to the idea of separating Wales from the remainder of the United Kingdom.

The Plaid Cymru leadership has therefore, I argued, completely failed to convince even its own supporters of the wisdom of their flagship policy of an 'independent Wales within the European Union'. They are also unable to answer the all-important economic question of whether a so-called independent Wales would be part of the Euro currency, conveniently ignoring the fact that all 'new' countries joining the EU are now required to adopt the Euro as their main currency.

Although opposed to Scotland's First Minister Alex Salmond's demands for Scottish independence because of my strongly held British Federalist beliefs, I stated that I would enthusiastically support a 'devo-max' option if it were ever presented as an additional question on any referendum ballot paper in either Scotland or Wales. In reality, 'devo-max' would achieve my objective of 'Home Rule All Round' in domestic affairs for the respective nations of the British Isles.

The findings of an opinion poll carried out for BBC Wales to mark St David's Day strongly supported my view that while the process of Welsh devolution should be moved forward, 'independence' must be firmly rejected. Just 7 per cent of people wanted Wales to break away from the rest of the UK, a figure that grew to 12 per cent if Scotland were to vote yes in its independence referendum. The survey also showed that 64 per cent of those polled thought that the National Assembly should have the power to vary all or some taxes in Wales, 'within limits agreed by the UK Government at Westminster'.

Whilst debating the opinion poll's findings on Radio Cymru's *Taro'r Post* on 1 March 2012 with the prominent Plaid Cymru member Mabon ap Gwynfor, I just could not understand the logic of his wholly uncompromising advocacy of Welsh independence despite the overwhelming rejection of this view by the electorate at large. Mabon's words reminded me of Michael Foot's Labour Party's politically disastrous manifesto policies of one-sided nuclear disarmament and whole-scale nationalization at the 1983 general election, which was later described by its deputy-leader Dennis Healey as the 'longest suicide note in history'.

By 'going for broke', people like Mabon ap Gwynfor are unfortunately undermining attempts by 'progressive pragmatists' like Carwyn Jones, Dafydd Elis-Thomas, David Melding and me to advance a specifically Welsh political agenda in a piecemeal way. These 'die-hard' Welsh Nationalist utterances only serve to provide some credibility to the arguments of those 'devo-sceptics' within the three major political parties in Wales, that further devolution will only give impetus to those people favouring the complete separation of Wales from the United Kingdom.

The economic viability of a Wales separated from the rest of the UK was recently discredited. In an article for the Institute of Welsh Affairs, which was summarised in the Western Mail of 31 July 2012, Gerald Holtham, who had earlier chaired a commission on the financing of the Assembly, wrote: 'The brute facts of pounds and pence are what will limit Welsh devolution now, whatever the Scots do'. This highly respected academic demonstrated that the Welsh government receives an annual budget of just under £15bn from the Westminster Parliament. However, total government spending in Wales, including social security payments, is approximately £25bn. Moreover, Wales's share, on a population basis, of general UK expenditures like defence, overseas aid and debt servicing costs, would increase it by another £5bn or so. While total Welsh spending amounts to appromiately £30bn a year, the amount of tax raised in Wales is only around £18-19bn. This economic deficit of some £12bn amounts to no less than 25 per cent of Welsh GDP, which is proportionally more than double the UK deficit. Gerald Holtham concluded his appraisal by stating: 'While England and Scotland had a deficit of over £2,000 for every resident in 2010, in Wales and Northern Ireland the deficit per head is over £6,000'. In other words, an independent Wales is simply not an economically viable proposition at present.

The result of the Plaid Cymru leadership contest to succeed Ieuan Wyn Jones was declared in Cardiff on 15 March. It was announced that nearly three-quarters of Plaid Cymru's membership had actually cast their votes in the election, which demonstrated that there was considerable grassroots interest in this fascinating leadership contest.

In the first round of voting the Rhondda left-wing socialist and nationalist republican firebrand Leanne Wood, AM for South Wales Central, had polled 2,879 votes against her economically more pragmatic although strongly nationalistic opponent Elin Jones, AM for Ceredigion, who received 1,884 votes. With Leanne Wood just falling short of a first round victory with nearly 48 per cent of the votes cast, the second preference votes of former National Assembly Presiding Officer Lord Dafydd Elis-Thomas, the 'achieve more powers for Wales by working within the British establishment candidate', who polled 1,278 votes, were redistributed between the first two candidates. This resulted in a wholly unexpected decisive win for Leanne Wood over the bookies consistent favourite Elin Jones by 3,326 votes against 2,494, with the former winning by the very comfortable margin of 832 votes. In percentage terms, Leanne Wood achieved 55.1 per cent of the votes cast against 41.3 per cent for Elin Jones. These percentage figures fell slightly short of 100 per cent because some 'die-hard' supporters of Lord Elis-Thomas did not indicate a second preference on their ballot paper.

Plaid Cymru has made a huge tactical gamble in electing Leanne Wood the new leader of the party. She is the first ever female leader since the party's foundation in 1925 and its first leader who is not a fluent Welsh speaker. Moreover, her roots are strongly working-class south Wales's valleys, which contrast sharply with the comfortable middle-class professional backgrounds of previous Welsh Nationalist leaders. There were therefore clearly enough Plaid Cymru members who wanted to see genuine radical change within the party. Leanne Wood was also undoubtedly the candidate least like the capable but nonetheless over-cautious and uncharismatic 'technocrat' Ieuan Wyn Jones who had presided over a consistent decline in the party's electoral fortunes for more than a decade. Matt Withers correctly stated in the *Western Mail* of 17 March that 'Ms Wood – radical, republican, feminist, pro-independence – is about as far removed from Ieuan Wyn Jones, the "good country solicitor", as Adam Price once damned him with faint praise, as she could be'. Lord Dafydd Elis-Thomas also appreciated the momentous significance of Leanne Wood's victory when he asserted that Plaid Cymru had 'taken a hugely radical step to elect a feminist woman of the left'.

During her very effective leadership campaign, championed by leading Plaid Cymru figures such as Adam Price and Dafydd Iwan, Leanne Wood was wholly uncompromising in declaring her strongly held left-wing political beliefs. She unashamedly stated on several occasions, 'I am a socialist republican and a supporter of real Welsh independence'. A staunch republican, in 2004 Leanne was ordered to leave the National Assembly chamber by Lord Elis-Thomas when she rather mockingly referred to the Queen as 'Mrs Windsor' and refused to withdraw the remark. She was also arrested in 2007 during a protest against Britain's Trident nuclear deterrent, and is implacably opposed to all nuclear power. It is therefore hardly surprising that the veteran political commentator Michael Crick described Leanne Wood as 'the most left-wing leader of any mainstream political party in Britain'.

On a personal level, I really admire the affable Leanne Wood for her straight-talking approach to politics. She is obviously a 'conviction politician' and is one of the very few 'what you see is what you get' politicians present in the National Assembly. I genuinely hope that as the new leader of the National Assembly's third largest political party, Leanne will bring a 'much needed breath of fresh air' to political debates within that institution. She will undoubtedly be far more assertive than Ieuan Wyn Jones in expressing her sincerely-held political beliefs, and her serious effort to learn the Welsh language is also most commendable.

As a Welsh Conservative, however, I have political reasons to be delighted with the election of Leanne Wood as the new leader of Plaid Cymru. I very much hope that her 'undiluted' socialist beliefs will be able to attract some traditional Labour voters to Plaid Cymru, and away from the 'technocratic' party of Ed Miliband and Carwyn Jones, thereby increasingly dividing the left-wing vote in two-way marginal constituencies where the contest is really between the Conservative and Labour parties.

However, the results of the Welsh county council election held on 3 May 2012 demonstrate that Leanne Wood's policy of seeking to 'out-left' Welsh Labour on the political spectrum had been a complete electoral failure. Plaid Cymru made an overall loss of forty-one seats compared with 2008. By contrast, Welsh Labour, under Carwyn Jones's very astute leadership, made an overall gain of 231 seats. Phil Bevan, a former Plaid Cymru cabinet member on Caerphilly Council, claimed that Leanne Wood's refusal to attend a special ceremony held in Llandaff Cathedral in April, to commemorate the Queen's sixty-year reign, where her Majesty was present, had been an important factor behind Plaid's loss of Caerphilly. He said, 'The majority of people support the royal family, and we had a poor response on the doorstep over this. Leanne has been naive'. The *Western Mail* of 2 June reported that Lord Dafydd Elis-Thomas had later expressed his support for Phil Bevan's comments during a private dinner, and as a consequence he was severely criticised by several of his fellow Plaid AMs.

Things only worsened when Lord Elis-Thomas called on his party's leadership to 'grow up' in its relationship with the monarchy, after Sinn Fein's Martin McGuinness made the truly historic gesture of reconciliation by shaking hands with the Queen during her Diamond Jubilee visit to Belfast on 27 June. Dafydd Elis-Thomas was quoted in the *Western Mail* of 30 June as saying, 'It's a very strange situation when Sinn Fein's policy on the unity of Ireland, and how that may happen, and their policy on the monarchy, appears more reasonable than the attitude of some people in the nationalist movement in Wales'.

With Lord Elis-Thomas subsequently refusing to rule out unequivocally the possibility of him leaving the Plaid group of AMs in Cardiff Bay, the *Western Mail*'s Matt Withers made the very astute observation on 20 July that 'Leanne Wood's Plaid Cymru is not Lord Elis-Thomas's Plaid Cymru. From rural Gwynedd, sceptical on independence and with a reverence for the Royal Family, he now sits in an Assembly group led by a radical Valleys socialist'.

Leanne Wood's attempts to build a left-wing 'alliance of progressives' against UK government cuts also appears doomed to failure, as the Unite union described them as 'an opportunistic publicity stunt' ahead of the Wales TUC Conference in Llandudno at the end of May. In a statement to the *Western Mail* on 19 May, the Union's secretary, Andy Richards, demonstrated the exclusively pro-Labour tribal loyalty of the trade union movement by stating: 'There is only one party for the working people of Wales, the party that the trade unions founded to give voice to working people – the Labour Party'.

Leanne Wood's abilities to unite Plaid Cymru under her leadership will also be tested in the traditionally Welsh-speaking rural areas of south-west and north-west Wales. There will undoubtedly be some Welsh-speaking broadly 'conservative' or centre-right traditional Plaid Cymru voters who will be 'disturbed' by Leanne Wood's remarks in the

Western Mail of 16 March, that she would 'not budge from her strong left-wing views and support for independence'. On 9 April, I was speaking to a man who was a Plaid Cymru county council election candidate in upland west Carmarthenshire in 2008. He told me that both he and his wife had immediately left the party upon hearing the news of Leanne Wood's election victory.

The challenge now facing the Welsh Conservative Party is to try and gain the support of even more of these 'conservative' elements amongst Plaid Cymru voters. These 'Welsh patriots' have hitherto supported Plaid Cymru as a sign of being 'proud to be Welsh', although most of them are anti-socialist, non-republican, pro-Welsh language and culture, pro-devolution but anti-independence, and moderately pro-nuclear power. It is likely that some of these people were Plaid Cymru members who voted for the pragmatic Lord Dafydd Elis-Thomas in the leadership election.

Lord Dafydd Elis-Thomas admitted during a television debate on 8 February between the three candidates for the Plaid Cymru leadership that between 1,000 and 1,500 'natural Conservative voters' in his Dwyfor Meirionnydd constituency actually voted for him at the May 2011 Assembly elections. He also said that an 'out of the mainstream far left' Plaid Cymru leader, in the person of Leanne Wood, could well drive these people into the arms of the Welsh Conservative Party. Lord Elis-Thomas also claimed that 'total opposition' to nuclear power, as vociferously advocated by Leanne Wood, would result in Plaid Cymru losing its Ynys Môn constituency at the 2016 Assembly elections.

I was delighted that during the one-day Welsh Conservative Party rally held in St Asaph, Denbighshire, on 25 March, Andrew R. T. Davies used his speech to appeal directly to Plaid Cymru voters to examine the policies of the Conservatives to see if they actually chimed with them more than the hard left-wing republican socialism and independence isolationism of Leanne Wood. He asserted: 'If you're a patriot, if you're proud of your community, if you're proud of your heritage and your culture and your language, then your beliefs are our beliefs in the Welsh Conservative Party'. This theme was echoed by Cheryl Gillan who said, 'I hope that Plaid voters will see in Welsh Conservatives a great alternative. It is interdependence, not independence that we want'. I was fascinated to read in the *Western Mail* of 28 March that Plaid Cymru peer Lord Dafydd Wigley stated that Gwynfor Evans, Plaid's iconic leader from 1945 to 1981, 'always argued against independence on the basis that it precluded interdependence, that it was an isolationist position and precluded any form of confederation'. I hope to play an active part in helping to achieve this possible re-alignment on the moderate centre-right of Welsh politics.

I favour the return of powers from the European Union back to the Westminster Parliament or indeed transferred to the National Assembly in Cardiff. I am opposed to a United States of Europe, because I believe that sovereignty and law-making powers should be in the hands of the peoples of the United Kingdom, rather than controlled by unelected Brussels bureaucrats. I also favour keeping the British pound, since trying to establish a 'one size fits all' uniform interest rate across those EU member states that have adopted the Euro currency has proved to be a complete economic failure. The resulting severe economic crises affecting euro zone countries such as Portugal, Ireland, Italy and especially Spain and Greece in September 2012, clearly demonstrate the disastrous consequences of all attempts towards European economic union.

It is for these reasons that I was delighted that Eurosceptic political parties did so well in the European Parliamentary elections on 4 June 2009. The Conservative Party, which I voted for, and UKIP won twenty-five and thirteen seats respectively, with the pro-EU Labour and Liberal Democrat parties relegated to third and fourth place. These election results demonstrate that the people of the UK oppose the further transfer of powers from the Westminster Parliament to the European Union and wish to be largely responsible for their own governance.

Many English people move to live in Wales because they feel that their Anglo-Saxon culture is being eroded by immigration from the Third World. They seek to recreate in Wales the kind of life-style they were familiar with in the England of the 1950s and early 1960s when the indigenous culture was dominant. Whilst opposed to any form of racism, I believe in my father's dictum 'When in Rome, do what the Romans do'. Whilst every culture needs to be respected, the indigenous tradition should always be given priority. This is just common sense and the practice in most countries of the world, particularly Muslim ones.

I therefore supported the contents of David Cameron's speech to the Munich Security Conference on 5 February 2011, when the Prime Minister criticised 'state multiculturalism' where successive British governments had encouraged different cultures to live separate lives rather than actively promoting a stronger national identity to unify the ethnically diverse population of modern Britain. He therefore called for the UK to have a stronger shared national identity and also emphasised the necessity to take a tougher stance against indigenous Islamic extremism, which is in part a consequence of the failed multicultural experiment.

In a speech to Conservative party activists in

Southampton on 14 April 2011 David Cameron correctly (in my view) stated that for too long immigration has been too high. He informed his audience that between 1997 and 2009, 2.2 million more people came to live in Britain than left, 'the largest influx of people Britain has ever had'. The Prime Minister also astutely observed that 'when there have been significant numbers of new people arriving in neighbourhoods, perhaps not able to speak the same language as those living there, on occasions not really wanting or even being willing to integrate, that has created a kind of discomfort and disjointedness in some areas'.

I believe that everyone, irrespective of their ethnic origin, should be treated equally under the traditional British laws of the land. It is for this reason that I believe that any moves towards granting special legal rights to imported religious practices are incompatible with the concept of equality for everyone. Again it is the duty of everyone who decides to settle within the UK not only to accept the established laws and customs, but to integrate fully with the historical traditions of this land. This is precisely what my father did upon coming to live here in 1948. Just as the cultural traditions and laws of Saudi Arabia are Islamic in origin, and therefore should to be adhered to within that country, the culture and laws of the UK are Christian inspired and deserve to be treated similarly. I would also favour the UK withdrawing its membership from the European Court of Human Rights, since no 'overseas institution' should have the authority to over-turn decisions made by democratically elected UK governments.

One of the great questions in life is 'What if?' Politically, I might have been elected as a Labour MP had I been prepared to sacrifice principles for the sake of political expediency. After the 1983 general election my father was told by Ben Shellard, who had been a very prominent Labour Party member in Aberdare since 1929, that if his 'very able son' changed sides, he would 'eventually be well rewarded'. After all, Dr Kim Howells, who had been a prominent member of the Communist Party, was later elected as the Labour MP for Pontypridd in 1989. There is also the case of Peter Hain, who had been a former chairman of the Young Liberals before becoming the Labour MP for Neath in 1991. On the other hand, I would have found it difficult to assimilate with the class-based ethos of the south Wales valleys Labour Party. On balance, I have no regrets for not pursuing this possible political direction.

Career-wise, my life would have taken a different direction had I not attended university after successfully completing my A levels at Rhydfelen School. I would have taken over the family greengrocery business. Although still quite profitable at the time, the expansion in the number of supermarkets meant that the 'writing was on the wall' for small corner shops in Aberdare. It is therefore most unlikely that I would have been able to earn a comfortable living for my whole working life from being a shopkeeper. Furthermore, I would have felt 'almost a prisoner' behind the shop counter, just as my father eventually did. The Ronnie Barker *Open All Hours* lifestyle would not have been suitable for my 'action man' temperament. Also, I could have become like some of my contemporaries, part of the south Wales valleys 'pub culture', and would have sought to drown my boredom with the bottle. I certainly have no regrets for having attended university, and for having escaped from a life behind the shop counter.

I could well have ended up as a father at eighteen years of age, had my father's 'extreme action' not put an end to that possibility. This was the right policy to pursue, because I had no interest in marrying Julie. Indeed, had I been forced to do so for the sake of 'respectability', as was the case with several of my contemporaries, the consequences would have been disastrous. My independent spirit would have led to me eventually just walking away from my responsibilities in pursuit of greener pastures.

My experience has led to my liberal pro-abortion moral stance. I have also been influenced there by my mother, who is known to have had an abortion prior to meeting her husband. Suffice to say that the father was the brother of a Welsh actor whom she met during the 1940s. My very independently-minded mother was also very critical of the anti-abortion moral position of the Roman Catholic Church. It was her opinion that it was the woman who should have the right to decide if she wishes to terminate a pregnancy. After all, it is her body and her future that is under discussion.

These liberal views on abortion can be interpreted as an example of that rather 'secular' Christian influence that I inherited from my mother. Whilst holding mostly conservative views in politics, I have quite liberal or progressive opinions regarding religion and morality. Again, here is yet another instance of how authoritarianism and libertarianism rest comfortably within my personality.

A subject where I have changed my opinion is that of homosexuality. Both my parents had inherited the rather homophobic opinions of their generation. My father had beaten a gentleman called Bertie senseless after he had 'touched' him in an inappropriate place while working at Aberaman Colliery in 1949. Meanwhile, my mother described such practices as 'simply unnatural'. I recall a boy called Ian at Rhydfelen School propositioning another boy by the name of Gary in the children's toilets. This appalled me and I would have responded just like my father did to Bertie, had I been in the same position. Nevertheless, what I encountered while teaching in London resulted in my U-turn on the subject of homosexuality. Here I socialised with teaching colleagues who were openly gay and my inherited homophobic prejudices gradually disappeared. I therefore applauded Nigel Evans's honesty in publicly declaring his homosexuality in an interview with the *Mail on Sunday* on 19 December 2010. The one-time Conservative Shadow Welsh Secretary, and one of the current Deputy Speakers in the House of Commons, became the twenty-second MP to 'come out'.

I have sometimes been described as a 'virtual workaholic', but this is a misunderstanding of how my mind works. I concede that the dividing line between work and pleasure can often be a very narrow one for me. For instance, broadcasting on antiques for *Wedi 3*, *Wedi 7*, and the new *Prynhawn Da* is technically employment-related, but I nonetheless get a great deal of pleasure from doing this. It is therefore an ideal combination of helping to earn a living while at the same time bringing much enjoyment. The same is also true of my antique evenings and computer studies.

There are, however, other hobbies in my life that are not directly employment-related. For example, I enjoy continuing to search for Victorian Staffordshire pottery flat-back figures. There is also my first real hobby as a child, that of coin-collecting. Likewise, I remain a passionate collector of Welsh antiquarian books and I am becoming increasingly interested in Welsh poetry. Hearing Archbishop Rowan Williams giving a very moving lecture on the eminent Welsh poet Waldo Williams at Pisgah Chapel, Llandysilio, Pembrokeshire, on 23 March 2012, was indeed a great privilege.

Professional boxing remains a key element of my interest in sport, something that again goes back to my childhood. I am a big fan of Bolton's Amir Khan who has taken over the role of British ambassador for the sport on the world stage vacated by the retirement in 2009 of the brilliant and undefeated Super-Middleweight 'King' Joe Calzaghe. There is also rugby and football. I was delighted that Wales successfully completed the Six Nations Rugby Grand Slam by defeating France by 16 points to 9 at Cardiff's Millennium Stadium on 17 March 2012. The Llanelli Scarlets are my favourite rugby team and I am a Manchester United football fan. Support for the former goes back to the time when Delme Thomas's Llanelli team famously beat the New Zealand All Blacks by 9 points to 3 in October 1972, while Bobby Charlton and George Best were my earliest football heroes.

I was also delighted that Team GB did so brilliantly at the Olympic and Paralympic Games, held in London in August and September 2012, winning so many gold, silver and bronze medals. It was wonderful to see people of such diverse ethnic origins, such as Somalia-born Mo Farah, not only proudly competing, but also winning glory for Great Britain.

I am also a big film fan and visits to the cinema bring me much enjoyment, particularly seeing historical, paranormal and detective films. By way of television comedy, *High Hopes*, in my opinion, stands head and shoulders above any other, with its devastatingly accurate portrayal of the rather 'sado-masochistic' south Wales valleys humour that I grew up with.

Occasional visits to the theatre also bring me much pleasure, particularly going to see *Abba Mania* in the Princess Theatre Torquay, on 21 July 2009. This brought back fond memories of my favourite pop group *Abba* during the 1970s and 1980s. Indeed, the lyrics and tune of their famous winning song 'Waterloo' during the 1974

Eurovision song contest, still pleasantly echo through my mind. Furthermore, such is my enthusiasm for Abba music that I again saw *Abba Mania*, this time at the Winter Gardens, Blackpool, on 29 July 2010.

On holiday in Lanzarote, January 2007

A hobby that has taken an increasing amount of my time and energy over the past decade or so is that of photography. During this period I have taken nearly 12,000 photographs and have filled several dozen photo albums and computer files that chronicle my travels. These include, for example, trips to Ireland, Jersey, Guernsey, France, Spain, Portugal, Croatia, Slovenia, Lanzarote, Ibiza, Madeira and Tenerife, and I have taken hundreds of photos across the British Isles, particularly in Wales.

I also enjoy undertaking many public speaking engagements for miscellaneous organisations such as Rotary, Round Table, Probus, Women's Institute, Merched y Wawr and the University of the Third Age. My speaking topics range from antiques, coins, militaria, and antiquarian books, together with aspects of Welsh history and literature.

Over the past fifty-two years I have had a colourful and eventful life. Whilst aware that I ought to have gained more materially from my alleged 'miscellaneous talents', I have never wanted material objects for the sake of keeping up with or indeed overtaking the proverbial Joneses.

Guest speaker with the University of the Third Age in Carmarthen, February 2012

Guest speaker at the Aberystwyth Merched y Wawr Branch, March 2012

Becoming Vice-Chairman of the West Carmarthenshire Association of Welsh Congregational Churches, Henllan Amgoed, March 2012

Officiating at the Wedding of TV and Radio personality Eleri Siôn at Neuaddlwyd Chapel, June 2012

Furthermore, I have never used a credit card, and pay in cash for almost everything that I purchase, although I do internet banking. My father used to say, 'If you can't afford it, save up for it. Pay in cash for it in order to be able to request a discount'. Unfortunately, today's companies prefer people to buy things on hire purchase in order to obtain more money for their products. No wonder the country is in such a mess, with what is a 'Buy now, pay later' credit card economy.

Furthermore, many people bring personal debt upon themselves because of their 'must have now' greedy attitude to material objects. My parents planted in me the idea that what lies between our ears is of the greatest importance. After all, no one can take academic achievement away from us, while monetary fortunes can be made and lost without anything to show for it at the end of the day.

With Mary at the Cefn Sidan Rotary Club dinner, Pembrey, August 2012

Although my nearly fifteen-year relationship with Mary Davies ended in November 2011, we were thankfully reunited in late June 2012. Mary deserves a gold medal for taking me back after my 'no excuses' relationship with another woman.

I seek to maintain a positive attitude towards the future, because nobody knows what awaits us around the corner in life.

I hope that my commitment to the Welsh Congregational ministry will prove sufficient for me to remain associated with that vocation for the immediate future. Nonetheless I have to accept that the available statistical data indicates that well over half the chapels in Wales will be closed by the end of this decade, and that the pattern of religious worship will have to change radically if Christianity is to survive in this post-Christian age.

In my view, the 'orthodox' or 'conventional' Christianity associated with the major religious denominations in Wales appears to be becoming increasingly irrelevant to cater for people's spiritual needs. This 'religious' vacuum may eventually be filled by some form of 'natural spirituality,' which extends way beyond narrow 'denominationalism' or indeed 'Christianity' in its most 'exclusive' sense, to encompass discovering 'universal religious truths'.

It is doubtful that my present Trelech and District pastorate will be able to maintain a full-time minister by 2016, in the unlikely event that I decide to stay there for that long. This pastorate of five churches will either have to be expanded or I may need to go and minister in another part of Wales. I may well have to make a career change, and all possible options will have to be considered. Whatever potential opportunities come along, I will approach them with the same pragmatism that I have sought to cultivate over the years.

Whatever the world may think of my successes and failures, I can say that I, the 'rebel', have, like Frank Sinatra, done everything 'my way'.